THE BE
ST PAR

The Bells of St Paradis

A love affair with the Limousin

by Anne Loader

Illustrated by Patricia Kelsall

An imprint of
ANNE LOADER
PUBLICATIONS

Dedicated with love to

Joan Ward, Julien Pauly and Bep Lippens

ISBN
1 901253 26 0
First published December 2001

Published by:
Léonie Press
an imprint of
Anne Loader Publications
13 Vale Road, Hartford,
Northwich, Cheshire CW8 1PL
Gt Britain
Tel: 01606 75660 Fax: 01606 77609
e-mail: anne@aloaderpubs.u-net.com
Website: www.anneloaderpublications.co.uk
www.leoniepress.com

Printed by:
Anne Loader Publications

About the author and illustrator

Anne Loader is a writer and publisher. She was born in Lincolnshire in 1948 and trained as a journalist with East Midland Allied Press. In 1969 she married Jack Loader who was doing a PhD at Southampton University. She worked at the *Southern Evening Echo* until the couple moved to Cheshire in 1970 when Jack started work as a research scientist in the chemical industry. They had two sons and for the next ten years Anne worked from home as a writer and printer. She edited and contributed to *Pregnancy and Parenthood* on behalf of The National Childbirth Trust, which was published by OUP in 1980. The same year she returned to journalism as a feature writer on *Northwich World* and in 1984 she helped to start the *Crewe and Nantwich Guardian,* becoming editor in 1985. She was made redundant as editor in 1995 and in 1996 she set up as a freelance writer and page designer. Shortly afterwards, she started the Léonie Press as an imprint of Anne Loader Publications, specialising in producing books on local history and autobiography. Her first book about France, *A Bull by the Back Door,* originally written for her mother, was published in October 1997, and was widely acclaimed. It was followed by *The Duck with a Dirty Laugh,* which was equally well received. Extracts from both were serialised in *Living France* magazine. Anne has also written for *FRANCE Magazine.*

Patricia Kelsall is a part-time lecturer in Art & Design at Mid-Cheshire College teaching drawing and painting to full-time and part-time students. She has exhibited her work mainly in the North East of England and in Cheshire as well as the Royal Academy in London, the Manchester Academy of Fine Art and at the Annual Salon in Mornant, France. Patricia's illustrations and paintings have appeared in numerous publications including Newcastle 900 by Frank Graham, greetings card designs for Bucentaur Gallery and many limited edition publications including publicity brochures, letterheads, menus and local authority town trail leaflets. Her paintings have been reviewed in *The Observer Magazine* and *The Guardian* newspaper. She has done all the illustrations for books published by Anne Loader, including *A Bull by the Back Door* and *The Duck with a Dirty Laugh,* and undertakes many private commissions. Patricia loves visiting France and she and her artist husband Richard have spent many Summer holidays in France where they enjoy walking combined with outdoor sketching and painting.

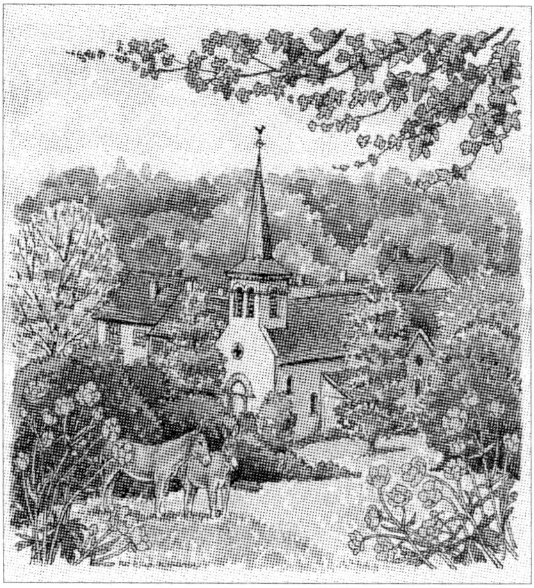

The Bells of St Paradis

Everything described in this book is true, to the best of my knowledge, and based on our diaries. However to protect the privacy of our friends and relations in France I have changed their names and the names of the towns and villages mentioned. They are very special to us because they are marvellous people — not because they think that they will be the subjects of a book. We thank them from the bottom of our hearts. Our dear English friends keep their real names.

I have mentioned my beloved mother's sad affliction with Alzheimer's Disease because this book is about real life. What was happening to her dominated almost every waking moment for us during the early part of the timespan described. Perhaps what I have written may help others in the same situation to know that they are not alone in their pain.

Anne Loader

Illustrations

Contents

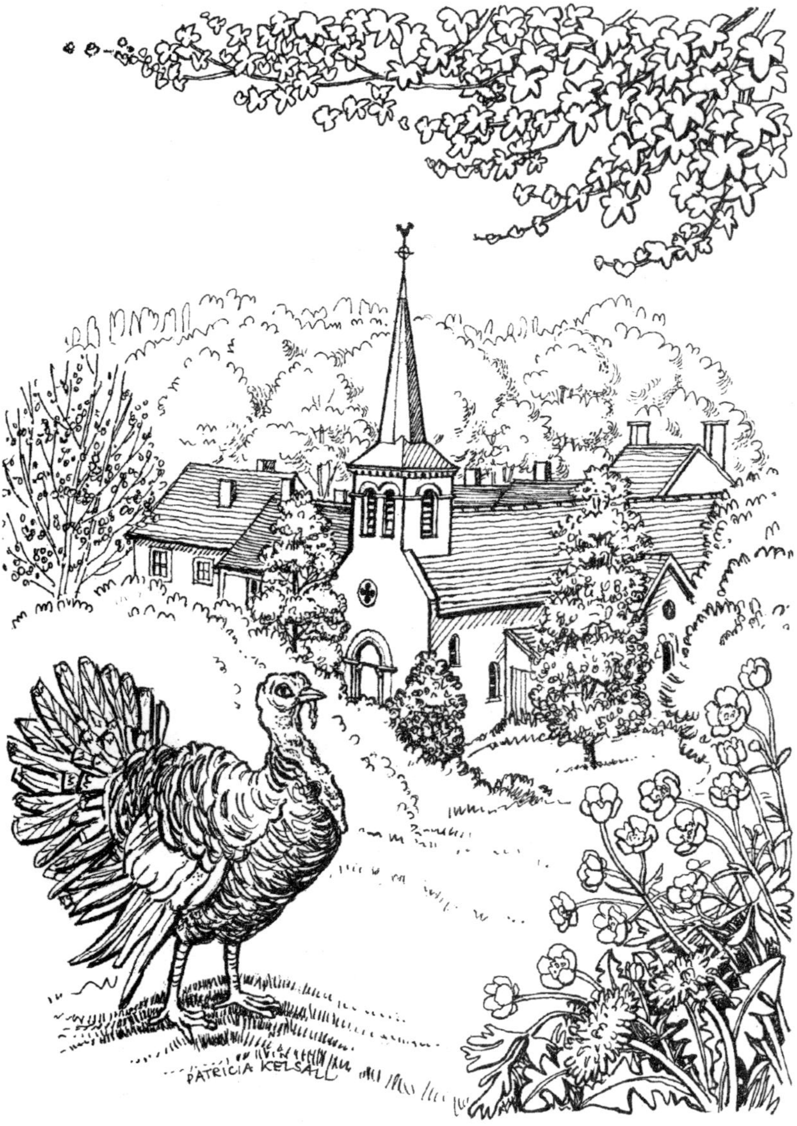

Cédric could rely on the bells for a staccato conversation twice an hour, and when the Angelus clanged merrily for two full minutes he could sing along too.

Introduction

The Turkey who sang the Angelus

He was destined to be Mme Echelle's Christmas Dinner, 1999. But the saint who cares for the human souls of St Paradis also smiles upon some of its lesser creatures. At the last minute Mme Echelle was let off her gory chores of killing, plucking and eviscerating, and was invited to enjoy a seasonal meal with other members of her large family. Cédric the turkey was spared. He celebrated his good fortune by telling everyone about it and by being so vocal, and making such a mark on the hamlet's *ambience,* that he hoped to put off the day of judgment until his flesh was too tough to tackle with a carving knife. Mme Echelle, secretly pleased, acquired a wife for him. But her son harboured dark thoughts of the family gathering to mark *le quatorze juillet* 2000.

Cédric lived opposite the church on a narrow stretch of land which until a few years before had housed goats, rabbits, geese and chickens galore. The Duck with a Dirty Laugh had told jokes to his harem from a pond on the other side of the fence – until the fox got him.

The church dated back hundreds of years and the carved stone image installed beside it was well over a thousand years old. The neat tower with its elegant spire had three bells, one from the 15th century and two from the 19th, when the church was modernised and extended. As part of a nationwide Millennium project in the 21st century, the two newer bells now automatically tolled the hours and the half-hours from 7am to 7pm, prompted by signals from a national computer. They sounded the monastic Angelus with frantic relish at 7am, noon and 7pm, theoretically calling the Catholic faithful to prayer but in reality announcing lunchtime and suppertime to hungry farmers in the fields. The secular council of the tiny commune and its inhabitants agreed that the tuneless chiming bells had brought life back into the slumbering community.

Cédric loved them. A convivial bird, he answered every sound in the vicinity with a series of loud gobbles, responding equally to chugging tractors, moaning strimmers, bellowing bulls, yapping dogs and the occasional human shout. But the bells were the best. He could rely on them for a staccato conversation twice an hour, and when the Angelus clanged merrily for two full minutes he and his wife could sing along too.

The bells were happy to be of use again, for recently they had only been rung for funerals and at Pentecost. They had seen many changes in St Paradis. Installed by a fiercely proud congregation during the brief time when the impoverished rural *département* of the Creuse was prospering, they had seen the self-sufficient village bustling with big families – going to Mass, arranging marriages, supporting one another, squabbling, improving their beautiful stone houses and prizing every square centimetre of soil that they could acquire by purchase, exchange or inheritance.

Then the decline had set in. The drift from the land was accelerated when all able-bodied men were conscripted at the beginning of the First World War, leaving the farms in the hands of women, children and old men. Some conscripts, whose names now adorned the war memorial, were slaughtered on the battlefield. Others discovered that a whole new world existed outside their tight-knit, hard-working, closed-in community, and never came back to stay.

By the Second World War, when Italian planes strafed columns of refugees on the roads nearby and the Resistance later carried out its sabotage, the population of St Paradis was dwindling. In the 1950s the use of tractors instead of horses and oxen meant that the farms could be run by fewer people. Land which was difficult to manage was left to revert to wilderness. With poor employment prospects, the young went away and once-thriving businesses closed down. There were not enough customers to support the inn, dairy and craftsmen. Houses began to fall into decay. Far more deaths were recorded than births. By the 1980s many homes in St Paradis were empty, with Nature trying to claim back the solid shuttered buildings by filling them with mice and cobwebs, smothering them with ivy and covering their gardens with prickly shoulder-high brambles.

Then a gentle invasion started. It was one which would have been bitterly resented in parts of England and Wales, but the pragmatic Creusois accepted it. Families who had moved away to better themselves in other parts of France inherited their parents' and grandparents' homes and renovated them as *maisons secondaires* for holiday and weekend use. Even Parisians were tolerated. In the mid-1980s Elisabeth, a Dutch woman, came to live in St Paradis, renting her little house from the local landowner, in order to be near her daughter and son-in-law in a nearby hamlet. Other Dutch families influenced by their compatriots' presence, purchased holiday homes, and then permanent homes in the commune. In 1994, we bought a 200-year-old house in the centre of the village which had been empty for years, and by the year 2000 other buildings had been acquired by French purchasers for all sorts of reasons from storing vintage cars to investing in property. There was talk of a Belgian family viewing a house which was for sale.

The rot had stopped, but St Paradis had changed. The clock could not be put back.

Someone who had lived here 100 years ago would find in the 21st century a familiar granite-grey environment, populated by some of the old families but also by unfamiliar, occasionally foreign people with different accents and unimaginable backgrounds in science, the French Army, journalism, technology, mathematics, classical music, teaching and computing, to name but a few, living in harmony and with a shared love of the hamlet.

And, as a common backdrop, was the optimistic sound of Cédric's bold karaoke with the ageless Angelus, while he enjoyed the first months of the new Millennium (on borrowed time).

St Paradis
July 2000

Chapter One – August 1998
Sophie's Wedding

My mother always looked very elegant but she had a complex about clothes. She could never decide what to buy or what to wear for any given occasion. She would go to Lincoln on the train, agonise over her purchases, try them on when she returned and either consign them for ever to the depths of her wardrobe or take them back to the shop to exchange for another dilemma-inducing purchase. When cruel Alzheimer's Disease destroyed her personality, only this trait remained. Until her dying day she would stand in front of the mirror and repeat in despair every morning: "I haven't got a thing to put on!"

I empathised with her totally when I came to do the packing for a short trip to France at the end of August 1998. We were going to the wedding of my French 'honorary' cousin Annette's youngest daughter Sophie in a town not far from Le Mans, and then planned to spend a day or two at St Paradis, having taken another trailer-load of essential junk with us. The weather at home was chilly but we knew from news bulletins that there was a heatwave in the Mediterranean. Neither of these meteorological conditions had the slightest bearing on what it would be like for the marriage in Normandy.

I always choose the wrong clothes when we go to St Paradis, mainly because I haven't got a clue what the weather will be in France. If it's baking hot in England when I'm doing the packing, we go to St Paradis equipped with shorts and tee-shirts only to find ourselves shivering in unseasonal cold. Conversely, if it's wet and miserable in England, then I pack long-sleeved shirts, thick trousers and fleecy sweatshirts, which are totally inappropriate when global warming has kicked in unexpectedly in the Limousin and everyone else is facing the ensuing drought in skimpy attire. Fortunately, I always chuck in one or two alternative garments just for luck, which I am sure we will never use, and we end up living in them for three weeks.

Like my dear old mum, I agonised over what to wear for the wedding. We had been to one in France when I was overdressed by the other guests' standards and a second one where I had erred on the side of being too casual. To Jack's amusement, I finally packed three full outfits which took up an unreasonable amount of space in the car: a pale peach chiffon suit and navy hat which I'd worn for our son Chris's wedding, a shocking pink and blue spotted suit and matching hat I'd had at our elder son Alex's nuptials a month later, and a red jacket and multicoloured skirt which I'd bought months in advance for Chris's marriage and rejected in panic three days before. (My mother had done exactly the same with a smart blue costume just before our own wedding, so I knew I was a chip off the old block.) For good measure I added in a pretty ankle-length cotton dress patterned with mauve, blue and red flowers that I thought might come in for anything formal at St Paradis.

Jack had had similar packing problems on a grander scale when he was filling the trailer. We were stopping off at the wedding en route to St Paradis and the bride had promised that we could put the trailer in her parents-in-law's property while we parked the car at the hotel where she had booked us a room for the night. Among our goodies this time were a scaffold tower to facilitate roof repairs, my mother's old twin-tub washing machine, an IKEA bookcase and some clematis plants grown from our own cuttings. They had to find space among all the tools that we transported backwards and forwards across the Channel every time we went to the Limousin.

After an adverse weather forecast we had packed the trailer the previous weekend, covered it with three blue plastic tarpaulins and crossed our fingers. It then rained for days.

I drove over to Lincolnshire to collect my aunt who was going to look after the dogs while we were away, and pay regular visits with Alex to my mother in the special home for Alzheimer's patients where she now lived. The two women, close friends as well as sisters-in-law, had shared a house in Spalding for 22 years after my father died. When dementia struck my mother in her late 80s, my aunt had cared for her devotedly, continuing to share the burden with me for weeks on end after Mother had eventually moved to live with us in Cheshire.

A few weeks after we had returned from our previous visit to France in June, Mother had suffered a stroke which had aggravated her condition to the point where I could no longer look after her myself. I was faced with the heart-rending decision of preserving my own sanity at the expense of her quality of life. We managed to find a place for her in a home associated with the psycho-geriatric day unit she had attended for more than a year.

She had spent her 90th birthday in the home in a state of polite exasperation, not understanding why she was receiving presents, being fussed over by everyone, eating a specially decorated cake and sipping champagne.

We left Cheshire just after 2pm on Friday, August 28, cross with ourselves because we were late. We were travelling via Cherbourg because it was the bank holiday weekend and we couldn't get tickets for the crossing to Le Havre. This ferry departed much earlier than our usual late evening boat from Portsmouth. We'd tried to set off earlier but discovered that our Peugeot 405 estate wouldn't start because the battery was flat. Perhaps we had flattened it by leaving the doors and tailgate open while we packed the car. As we were driving down the Northwich by-pass I selected a CD only to find that the flat battery had knocked out the radio and we didn't know the anti-theft code for it. The third and decisive Test Match against Sri Lanka at the Oval would have been broadcast all through our journey to France, but we couldn't listen to it now. Every trip to France seemed to be carried out against a background of ball-by-ball commentaries from Blowers and Co, and while this latest technical hitch was an enormous deliverance for me, it was a great disappointment for cricket-loving Jack.

We had a frustrating six and a quarter hour journey to Portsmouth, doing 48 miles in the first hour and 15 at snail's pace during the second. We improved to 41 miles in the third hour then slowed right down again when we hit the Oxford by-pass at the rush-hour. The ring road was solid in the other direction for miles on end, and there were massive jams on the Newbury by-pass caused by the building of the controversial new road. We saw lots of abandoned vehicles and Newbury itself was solid.

Churned up inside, we arrived at the port at 8.24pm, only to spot an ominous sign. Cars were going very slowly through the check-in booths and each one was being handed an A4 sheet of paper together with the normal documents. This usually meant that the ferry company's customer care department was apologising for a delay. When it was our turn, we were told that a child had gone down with appendicitis on the boat out from Cherbourg, which had then turned round and gone back to France. It now wasn't due in until 11pm and was not expected to sail until 12.15am.

We knew it was no-one's fault, and were sorry for the child, but it was a pain. Time stands still when you're marooned in a queue on a quay without a car radio and only some plastic-packed Sainsbury's sandwiches and a litre of peach springwater by way of a diversion. However, this time Fate was kind to us. We started to hear tremendous explosions reverberating round the port, and wondered what on earth they could be. Had a war started? Jack wandered along the lines of cars to look at a dumper truck being taken to France on a trailer and came back to tell me that the sky was ablaze with fireworks. We found a place along the security fence where we could see across to the naval dockyard, which seemed to be the launch site for the magnificent display. We suddenly remembered that the Festival of the Sea was being held that weekend at Portsmouth. We could make out the towering masts of the famous Tall Ships and there were many extra naval vessels at anchor in the channel.

The spectacle was impressive. Close-up I'm frightened of fireworks, but these weren't errant domestic Catherine Wheels, they represented thousands of pounds worth of pyrotechnic splendour. Rockets shot hundreds of feet into the sky and burst like multi-coloured crystal puffballs, each more beautiful than the last. We were captivated and really disappointed when the tremendous boom from the last orgasmic blast had settled in the air. People on the quay watching with us burst into spontaneous applause, which the far-away organisers would never have heard.

We called Alex on the mobile phone and asked if he would go round to our house, find the Peugeot information in the filing cabinet and let us know the code number for the radio. He did, and it was a great relief to face the prospect of some in-car entertainment for the rest of the long trip.

Many scores of vehicles now filled the numbered lanes on the quayside, and all their occupants were bored. Dads took toddlers for rides on their shoulders, children bickered in the backs of people-carriers and families heading for France in convoy got together to chat beside their cars.

We idly watched the massive articulated trucks being sorted into order on an adjacent lorry park. As always, I tried and failed to pronounce my favourite onomatopoeic freight company: "Olloquiegui". I hoped I would never be called upon to spell it from memory. We pottered about a bit to stretch our legs and were engaged in conversation by a woman with a heavy Hampshire accent whom we snobbily thought was on a bank holiday coach trip. We mentioned our farmhouse in France and she told us she had a house and big boat at St Tropez. Whatever subject we raised, she could cap our humble stories. In the end, we didn't believe a word she said. If she was so rich, why was she waiting on her own for the night ferry to Cherbourg?

When we eventually got on board we found the boat was old-fashioned with tiny wood-panelled cabins and minimal facilities like those we remembered from years gone by when our sons were young. We had to use a communal loo and there was hardly room to turn round in the cabin. I requested extra pillows and chatting to the cabin staff it was clear that the crew were exhausted. Tired and grumpy, we asked ourselves why the sick child had not been air-lifted off by helicopter and decided that helicopters cost money while it didn't matter if the passengers were held up at the next point of departure. The captain would just make up the lost time with a faster Channel crossing and arrive at Cherbourg at the usual hour.

We eventually got to bed at 1am and spent the next four hours buffeted by noise and vibration as the ship forged along at 'full speed ahead'. When we got up at the equivalent of 5am we were feeling very delicate – not in the best physical state for facing a French wedding which was likely to go on until the small hours of the following day.

We left the ship at 6.56am French time and failed to recognise the landmarks in Cherbourg, which we had last visited in the early 1980s when Alex and Chris were small enough to climb all over the guns in the old fort. Eventually we found the Route de la Liberation with its special monumental kilometre markers, and sped on our way. When we pulled up for breakfast at an Esso station my brain was not working at all. It wouldn't go into French mode and I nearly bought myself an *Equipe* sports newspaper instead of *Le Figaro*.

We drove past the World War II beaches and many military cemeteries, which we had visited reverentially in the past. Now time was what mattered. The weather was glorious and we admired the roundabouts near Caen which are festooned with sculptures of 'Norman' soldiers complete with visors and shields in red metal. We wasted time at a big *bricolage* (DIY store) buying bellows and an oxygen cylinder for the welding set and saw some good quality railway sleepers for sale at a merchants on the main road near La Chapelle près Sées. Our hearts beat a bit faster as we realised that we were massively behind the schedule we had set ourselves. We have been travelling in France for 20 years but we never leave enough time. The wedding was due to start at 2pm.

We had a quick lunch at a McDonalds in the middle of the country near Alençon, kidding ourselves that it wasn't far to our destination at Tuffé and that we would have time to get changed into our finery at the bridegroom's parents' house. We were in the same (now grubby) casual clothes that we'd worn for the journey from Cheshire the previous day. Then we got lost going cross country. Normally I'm a good map-reader but this time I couldn't get the diagram on the map to correspond with the maze of tiny roads on the ground. Eventually we drove into Tuffé at 1.30pm – almost in time, we reasoned. The house we were looking for was in the Rue des Acacias. Translating that as the equivalent of 'Acacia Avenue' I thought it must be a residential estate. We drove round every *lotissement* in the town, following each flowery name in case it led to the precious acacias. None did.

At 1.50pm, with me nearly in tears of embarrassment and shame, we turned yet another corner and almost ran over the bride and groom. They were resplendent passengers in a trap drawn by a bay pony, followed by the rest of the family on foot in their best clothes. They had just been married officially at the *Mairie* and were on their way to the church for the religious ceremony. No-one had told us about the civil wedding. We jumped out of the car, hugging and kissing all our elegant long-lost relations – feeling very, very stupid in our tee-shirts and denims.

Annette's son Marcel (whose own wedding we'd enjoyed some years before) left the entourage and directed us quickly to the hotel where we were booked in as part of a family package. There was to be no leisurely changing, preening and choosing of knick-knacks. I looked at my outfits flung haphazardly on the hotel bed, and hyperventilated. The marriage was in the church a few yards from the hotel in the town square and most guests were in there already. Jack hopped about in his underpants and flapping shirt, putting on his suit trousers. It was too hot for my formal finery. I grabbed the nearest hanger with the mauve, blue and red cotton dress, chose the blue hat and fumbled to fix a pearl necklace. Then I dragged on some tights, forced my hot feet into high-heeled shoes, smeared on some foundation, powder and blusher, applied a clashing scarlet lipstick at random, and we ran.

We tumbled into a pew towards the middle of the church where all the villagers were sitting, many rows from our relations in the posh seats at the front. Then we were immensely relieved to be joined by Annette's sister, Vivienne, and her husband, Jacques. They said they were staying at the local campsite and had just arrived too. We needn't have worried about being late, as the congregation chatted and wielded cameras for several minutes before everything started.

The bridal procession was led by the youngest members of the family, looking angelic and carrying lighted candles which lit their faces from below with an orange glow. They were followed by the bridegroom, Denis, and his mother, then Sophie, her mother and her future father-in-law.

As is the French custom, Sophie and Denis had written most of the wedding ceremony themselves and it was romantic and moving. Everyone was handed a pink A5 booklet containing the order of service with a picture of the church on the front cover together with the following quote: "Nothing in the world is more beautiful than a couple and when I hear it said that to love is to lose one's liberty and one's integrity, I ask myself if we are talking about the same emotion." The first reading was a favourite of ours from Khalil Gibran, about the importance of loving togetherness tempered with personal space, which is certainly our motto and seems to have struck an almost universal chord. I've recited it myself at a Quaker wedding and heard it at many other weddings and marriage blessings. It was interesting to see that the words had the same ponderous rhythms in French as they do in English:

...Vous êtes nés ensemble et ensemble vous resterez pour toujours.
Vous resterez ensemble quand les blanches ailes de la mort disperseront vos jours.
Oui, vous serez ensemble jusque dans la silencieuse mémoire de Dieu.
Mais qu'il y ait des espaces dans votre communion
et que les vents du ciel dansent entre vous...

"...You were born together, and together you shall be for evermore.
You shall be together when the white wings of death scatter your days.
Aye, you shall be together even in the silent memory of God.
But let there be spaces in your togetherness.
And let the winds of the heavens dance between you..."

Denis was a local fireman and some of the music was provided by his fellow players in the town *sapeurs pompiers* bugle band. It was such a revelation to hear "Air on a G String" played on French bugles that it wasn't until days later when we heard it on a CD that we recognised what it had been.

A radiant Sophie and Denis left the church to a snowstorm of large round pieces of confetti. The bride was magnificent in a white dress with a lace bodice and a matching brimmed hat with an attached veil. The couple were walking under an arch of honour formed by their friends at the church porch. I couldn't quite see what was being held aloft. A cousin standing beside me said that Sophie and Denis were renowned for their love of the mountains. They were walking through an unusual arch of *sapeurs'* bugles and mountaineers' climbing-axes.

All the guests milled around the town square, chatting, while photographs were taken of the happy couple outside the church and in their gladioli-decorated pony-trap which was being driven by a man in a voluminous black peasant smock and black felt hat. Some spectators stood on our trailer, which we'd left outside the hotel, to get a better view – not something Jack had anticipated when packing it, but fortunately the table top which happened to be on top of everything else took the weight. Annette fell over the tow-bar and bruised her leg. I was beginning to feel as if the Loaders might be a liability at this wedding.

We were introduced to some English cousins of our own age, called David and Ann, whom we'd often heard mentioned but had never met before. David was doing a family tree and wanted all the French to fill in their places on the chart. We were grateful for this would help us, too, to sort out the names of some of the children whose parentage we tended to muddle up. The various parents seemed to choose the same names across the generations and without knowing the children as individuals it was hard for us to sort them all out.

At this point I should explain that Jack and I aren't exactly blood relations of our French 'cousins', but they are the family of my mother's best friend, Helen. The two girls had been sent to France for a year to be 'finished' in the 1920s and Helen had married the son of the house. She spent the rest of her life in France. My mum had become like a second mother to her friend's children – especially when Helen had died tragically young not long after the end of the war, and her husband had died shortly afterwards from what was generally agreed to have been a broken heart. The two families are so close that we all feel related, even if we aren't.

After the bridal couple had clip-clopped away in their carriage, waving happily and serenaded on the accordion by a man in shirt-sleeves and a white cap, the guests followed them to the reception by car. It was held in the town *salle des fêtes* which was attractively situated by a large lake and campsite. But before we could enjoy the *vin d'honneur* we all had to pose for the souvenir group photographs in the car park. Jack and I had often driven past churches and seen people tottering on vertiginous metal stands for the classical French wedding photographs, but we'd never taken part in the ritual before. Behind a row of large flower arrangements and gift bouquets which had been brought from the church, there were eight 'strata' of people, starting with tinies sitting at the front, then a row of seated guests, a row of people standing and five rows balanced higher and higher on the purpose-built metal frame. As someone suffering from vertigo on any sort of raised structure without a handrail, I was quite terrified enough on the second row up, looking down on Sophie, Denis and their attendants. My plank on the frame was only about 2ft 6ins high, but I daren't move. Mercifully, I was with Ann and David, so I had them for moral support. Jack, an old campaigner on ladders, who wouldn't have minded being several rows above with the more athletic younger members of the family, was actually below me, too. The photographer was very bossy, as indeed he had to be. Anyone who can control a hugging, kissing, chattering huddle of a hundred French people who haven't seen one another since the last wedding, needs the charms of Attila the Hun.

Eventually everyone had been still long enough, all facing in approximately the same direction, for the photographer to get his mass portrait. We climbed stiffly down from our perches and tottered off thirstily for the *vin*.

From long tables outside in the summer sun, we helped ourselves to champagne and the delicious sugary fingers of *petits gâteaux secs* known in our local Sainsbury's as 'trifle sponges'. Through no fault of their own, they are a family joke. Jack's nonagenarian mother has them every lunchtime with fruit and ice cream for her pudding. Since she suffered a slight stroke some years ago, her spelling has gone awry and she always describes them on her shopping list as "triffle spongs". Bubbly and triffle spongs was a nice new taste experience for us.

A jazz band was playing in the shade of one of the walls of the *salle des fêtes* and the accordionist joined them. Occasionally couples danced to the music on the paved terrace outside the hall. Half the village seemed to be there to celebrate with Sophie and Denis. Then we were all asked to gather round while the bridegroom joined the *sapeurs pompiers* to play a rousing brass fanfare accompanied by cymbals and big drum.

We teamed up with David and Ann, standing on the grassy bank facing the lake, or sitting on the stone wall round the *salle*. We got on famously and discovered we had much in common, including much hoped-for but as yet unconfirmed early retirement on the part of David and Jack. Ann's mother (Helen's sister) had died recently in her nineties and they had brought along many of her old photographs showing the French connection over several generations, which gave a lot of pleasure to the various cousins who joined us for a gossip.

Eventually after a couple of hours' non-stop chatting in English, French and Franglais, everyone dispersed to get ready for the evening reception.

We took our trailer round to Denis's parents' home in the Rue des Acacias, which was an old house adjoining their *graineterie* (feedstore) shop exactly opposite the hotel on the other side of the square. It had never occurred to us to look there. We must have driven past it numerous times earlier in the day.

My feet, having spent the summer in sloppy sandals, were killing me after being squashed into tight leather court shoes and tights on a baking hot day. Back at the hotel I decided to soak them in the bidet. This was a very ingenious mobile arrangement with a flexible hose which could be wheeled out from under the hand-basin in the tiny en-suite bathroom which had been created in a corner of the room. Afterwards we lay down on the double bed for a rest.

In spite of bringing three separate 'wedding' outfits, I had made my perennial mistake. None of them was really suitable and I was so relieved that I'd packed the cotton dress at the last minute. Elegant as they were, my smart suits were all too heavy for the glorious Continental weather we were experiencing. The light silk and cotton clothes worn by the French women guests were ideal, and no-one looked under-dressed. Their legs were tanned a lovely shade of brown and they hadn't dreamed of wearing tights. And my saucer-brimmed blue hat was too formally English. Annette, as a major figure in the nuptials, had a simple straw hat and her immensely chic sister-in-law sported a glamorous droopy one,

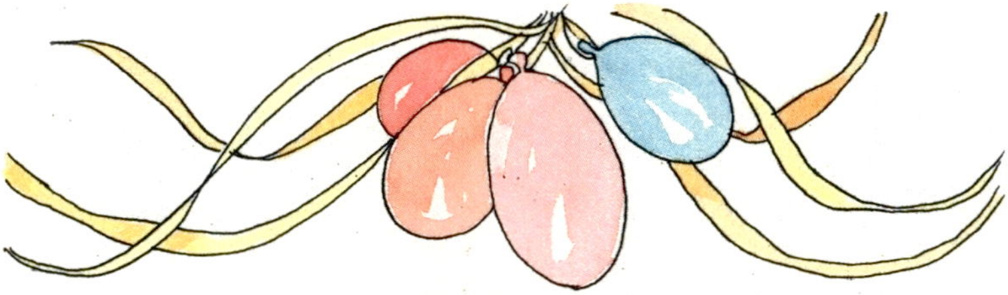

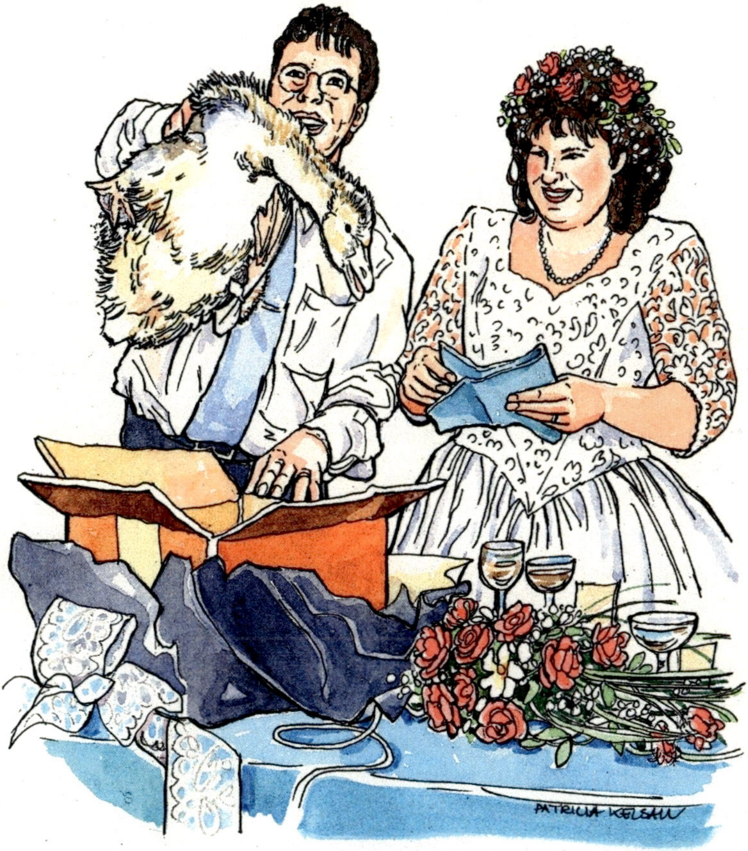

When they pulled off the last piece of wrapping paper, out popped a very frightened gosling, to the bridal couple's shock and amazement, and the ribaldry of their guests.

but that was about all. Wearing it, I looked more 'mother of the bride' than 'auntie by proxy of the bride'. I was sure my dear old mum would have sympathised if she had understood what was happening to her sartorially challenged daughter.

I changed into some different smart shoes, so that the leather rubbed on new parts of my suffering feet, and packed a pair of comfortable sandals into our video camera bag as a last resort.

Back at the *salle des fêtes* we met up with Ann and David and discovered that we were placed opposite one another on one of the long tables which filled the function room. We were delighted also to be with Vivienne and Jacques, who'd visited our house at St Paradis a year or two before, and her brother Hubert and his wife Martine, whom I hadn't met since I was a child. He had worked as a senior manager for a major airline in airports all over the world and had only fairly recently returned to France to retire. Nearby too were Vivienne's daughter and her husband, and Annette's other married children and their spouses. It was great to be together. I'm slightly deaf and can't hear a word at large gatherings if people are outside a radius of about five feet, so it was a marvellous bonus to be able to make real conversation with people whose company I treasured.

Each place setting had a menu, a little basket of sugared almonds decorated with an ear of *blé*, and a duplicated book of songs. We'd been to lots of French functions where there was impromptu singing but we'd never seen such forward planning before. The menu was wonderful:

Eau Bleue et ses Gourmandises
(I'm not sure what the 'blue water' was but it tasted alcoholic and looked beautiful)
Assiette de la Mer
(Jack is allergic to shellfish but a fellow guest in the table behind us was only too happy to eat his portion for him, together with his own companions' whelks – which he adored and they didn't – and to pass back enough shells to leave on the plates of the ungrateful diners to satisfy the caterers)
Filet de Saint-Pierre Sauce Poulette
(Yum)

Trou Normand
(The classic Normandy mid-meal shot of Calvados to kick-start a sluggish digestive system)
Pièce de Boeuf et ses Garnitures
(Yum, again)
Delices des Escargots
(A pleasantry which fooled the English. We expected snails but actually received tossed lettuce!)
Plateau de Berger
(Cheese)
Montagne des Mariés
(Wedding cake – more about that later)

Washing it all down was an inexhaustible supply of red and white Orléanais wines, champagne and a further liqueur. The meal took about four hours to eat and was a feast.

Between courses there was community singing from the song-book with the younger guests occasionally standing on their chairs performing the appropriate actions such as *"Si tu as d'la joie au coeur, frappe du pied!"* ("If you're happy and you know it, stamp your feet!"), a special chorale, comedy acts by the children and a song about Denis and Sophie – in colloquial French that was too hard for me to translate literally – composed and performed by their friends. They also opened their wedding presents between the courses and were puzzled by one large box wrapped in shiny black paper which was prompting a bit of giggling among the cognoscenti. First out was a bag of grain which increased the puzzlement. When they pulled off the last piece of wrapping paper, out popped a very frightened gosling, to the bridal couple's shock and amazement, and the ribaldry of their guests. We didn't understand the connotation and being truly English animal-lovers, Jack, David, Ann and I spent the rest of the evening vaguely worrying about the poor thing, which remained in its card-board box on the wedding present table, complete with a handful of grain.

This wasn't the only source of hilarity. There were games too and practical jokes – two memorable ones involving string. In one, each member of a couple had their hands tied together with a long piece of string, such that they were also linked together. They then had to work out how to separate themselves. This involved contortions worthy of the Kama Sutra and we never did see how the winners managed it. A lot of fun was had in the trying, though...

The other game involved threading a hundred metres or so of nylon cord through all the guests seated at table, starting with the groom, going up and down every table in turn and finishing back with the bride. The cord had to pass through something you were wearing, such as your clothing or jewellery. The English were spared the worst of the consequences when it was whispered to us that the point of the game was that at the end you had to take off whatever was on the string which was deemed to be a 'gift' for the happy couple! We prudently attached watches or rings, but some of the more adventurous (or exhibitionist) guests had threaded the string through their dresses or shirts and were faced with stripping off! Fortunately for them, the 'gifts' were soon returned.

We were incredibly impressed when, part way through the evening, it was announced that the photographer had already produced proofs of his pictures for us to see and would be taking orders in a side room. We joined the queue and ordered a group photograph, which we thought would show more members of the family in one place than we had ever seen before. His composition was excellent. There was no trace of the metal frame, just rows upon rows of colourful smiling figures, with only Martine's face partly obscured behind Sophie.

The climax of the meal was the grand entrance of the wedding cake, which was wheeled into the darkened room on a trolley, illuminated by fireworks. We had admired gorgeous cakes at other weddings, made from intricate concoctions of *profiteroles*, but when the lights were turned on we could see that this was a masterpiece of the *patissier*'s art. There was a mountain chalet and a guitar, all in iced cake, standing against green mountains and decorated with flowers. It was far too beautiful to eat!

After the singing and games, there was dancing to the jazz band in the space near the stage. It was lovely to see grown-ups 'dancing' with toddlers in their arms. Indeed, as always, we remarked on how well all the French children were behaving. Long after midnight, most were still on the go, but one little girl lay curled up fast asleep on the floor, covered by a travelling rug, with a long white balloon in one hand and her thumb in her mouth.

At 2am we were all called outside to enjoy a firework display on the banks of the lake. It was spectacular and noisy and we wondered what the neighbours and campers would think! We hoped they would enter into the spirit of the happy wedding.

After the fireworks we made our excuses and left. We didn't want to be party poopers and were having a marvellous time, but we were also shattered from lack of sleep the previous night. We could hardly keep our eyes open. But nearly everyone else carried on partying.

As we crept back along the dimly lit corridors of the small-town hotel, we discovered that it was entirely occupied by members of our French family. The weekend block booking must have been a bonanza for the owners!

Chapter Two – August-Sept 1998
Cleaning the *cantou*

We slept until about 9am and then got up, tired but not at all hung over. Although we'd had a pretty good consumption of alcohol, it hadn't had any adverse effect because it had been mixed with food and stretched over a long time.

We went down to breakfast in the small dining area and found David and Ann already there. We were joined by Vivienne's daughter and two of Annette's daughters and we were able to chat in a more relaxed manner without the background noise of the wedding reception. They said the 'do' had finished very late indeed.

We packed our belongings and went across the road about 11am to get the trailer from Denis's drive, which was reached through a locked gate. We gathered that many of the bride and groom's friends were staying at the house. The slowness of the inhabitants to respond bore witness to their dawn gallivanting and we felt guilty about waking them.

The family said they were all going to get together again for lunch a bit later on and were disappointed that we couldn't stay – but we needed to get to St Paradis. Many of them lived not too far away from Tuffé and they had the time to make another leisurely day of it.

We eventually left at 11.30am, having exchanged addresses with David and Ann and promised to meet again in England. We felt really pleased to have made such congenial new friends. More honorary 'cousins' to add to our list!

The area around Le Mans was new to us and we were in the mood to enjoy a magical drive through fields of sunflowers and maize, once again in brilliant sunshine. The Test Match was forgotten. Now that we could use the car radio we were able to link in our CD player and our journey was carried out to the glorious strains of Baroque music, including Pachelbel's "Canon". We love this particular piece, which has very sentimental personal connotations, and we have collected at least half a dozen versions of it.

The land was very dry and we felt sorry for the animals trying to graze on it. As we got to the Creuse, everything became greener.

It was 5pm by the time we arrived at St Paradis and immediately we saw nearly all our neighbours, as they pottered about outside in the late afternoon sun. It was great to be home. Paul, our dear octogenarian neighbour who looked after the house in our absence, helped us to unload the trailer and cut his hand on a sharp piece of scaffold tower. I offered him a plaster but he waved away all such effete suggestions. He said he had just come back from his annual holiday with a fellow *garagiste* friend near Nantes.

We went over to see his Dutch wife Elisabeth and give her a belated birthday card and little gift. They had two homes, Paul's big former hotel/bistro/garage in a village about five kilometres away, and the cosy little cottage opposite us, where they now lived, which Elisabeth had rented since before she met the widowed Paul. Her daughter Anne-Marie arrived a few minutes later accompanied by three dogs, her own Golden Labrador and Alsatian, and Daisy, a brave little local sheepdog who had lost a leg in a gruesome accident with some farm machinery. She managed incredibly well with only three legs and loved accompanying Anne-Marie on walks.

We told Anne-Marie that the reason for our flying visit was to bring a trailer-load of stuff and also to sand-blast our traditional *cantou* inglenook fireplace before installing a magnificent new woodburning stove in it on our next stay in October. We were short of a piece of stainless steel flue and asked her advice where we could get some. Her husband, Martin, was a builder and she knew about these things. She recommended a builders' merchants which we hadn't come across before, in a nearby small town.

We told Paul we had been to a wedding in Normandy, so he immediately sought out a bottle of Calvados to give us an appropriate little drink.

Eventually we made our way home across the road, unpacked the essentials, had a quick supper and dropped into bed before

10pm. Everywhere was very dusty and spidery after the house had been shut up during August but we were too tired to do anything about it.

When we woke and turned on the radio for our daily early-morning 'fix' of the *Today* programme, we discovered that it was the first anniversary of the death of Diana, Princess of Wales. We'd been in France when it had happened the year before and had been bemused by the reaction at home in Britain. We were pleased not to be there and subject to a tide of sentimentality all over again.

We had a big, messy task ahead of us with the *cantou* but first we had to drive a couple of miles into the nearest town to get some vegetables and meat. We bumped into our Dutch friends Jan and Beatrice and told them how much we'd enjoyed Sophie's wedding. They lived nearby, with their two show *épagneuls français* gundogs, Grisette and Gamine, in a modern house in an idyllic hilltop setting with views over to the mountains.

Back home we changed into our oldest and dirtiest work clothes. The *cantou* in the kitchen was massive – nearly six feet high and about eight feet across. You could stand in it easily and see all the way up the wide chimney to the sky above. We had found that the heat from any fire burning in the hearth went straight up this chimney and only raised the temperature of the room by a couple of degrees, which was the main reason behind the purchase of the woodburning stove. We'd found out by experimenting with a little second-hand Godin *poêle* that it would make the kitchen toasting hot in a short time and preclude the need for the extra portable gas fires we'd always used in the past when it was cold.

The fireplace was built from granite blocks and there was a blackened part-round stone set in behind the place where the fire had burned for nearly 200 years, to protect the wall. In one side a stone had been left out so that there was a little hidey-hole to keep salt dry. To the left was the arched opening to the semi-circular bread oven which spread out a good two metres behind, into its own building, beneath a domed roof of fireproof bricks. Under the entrance to the bread oven, which was closed off with a black metal cover, was a deep hollow cavity filled with wood ash which had originally been kept for use as a crude potash detergent for doing the washing. The faces of all the granite blocks were blackened by centuries of smoky deposits and the stone itself was discoloured from the heat. Several people we knew who had modernised their old houses had asked their builders to sandblast this blackened surface away completely to reveal the original grey/cream stone, but we didn't want to destroy the character of the fireplace. We knew that an ever-present log fire had been the focal point of the house throughout its history, and felt we didn't have the right to 'sanitise' it to fit in with our generation's ideas of picturesque rusticity. We could imagine the family that had owned the house sitting around the fire in the evenings telling stories or watching the flames as they mulled over their problems, and generations of farmers' wives doing their cooking over it in a cauldron. Indeed, the notched black irons to hold the cauldron were still hanging there. Later I read somewhere that it was very bad luck to remove them.

We did, however, want to clean the *cantou* up a bit, so that its darkness stopped being a brooding black presence dominating the kitchen. We had bought a beautiful new Godin stove in what would be described in England as a 'Victorian' style, which we were going to fit in the fireplace. It had a decorated door with a glass front, curved legs, an almost black-leaded appearance, and fitted the *ambience* of the old kitchen exactly. But we needed the background to be a little less murky in order to make it look its best.

We owned a pressure washer which we had used to great effect to clean the granite steps and the back outside wall of the house when we had first purchased it in 1994. Since then we had bought some special grit which could be used with the apparatus to make it act as a sandblasting tool. We moved all the furniture, then took up the brown carpet tiles which covered the stark concrete of the kitchen floor and stacked them in the *arrière cuisine*. We got out our wet/dry vacuum cleaner ready to suck up the water and gunge produced as a result of the sandblasting process. Never having used this version of the tool before, we didn't know what to expect or how effective it would be. We had previously tried scrubbing the blackened stones with Flash, and brushing them with a wire brush, without making a great deal of difference.

Jack connected the pressure washer to the cold tap in the old porcelain kitchen sink and switched it on. Water charged with sand surged out of the nozzle as he started to spray the black stones. It was hard to see if there was any effect on the stones themselves but the water which ran off them was filthy. I applied myself sucking it up with the vacuum cleaner. There would have been a very symbiotic relationship between the two appliances but for the fact that the pressure washer pumped out seven litres per minute and the vacuum cleaner sucked up one litre per minute. I began to feel like the Sorcerer's Apprentice.

We worked hard, 'blasting', sucking and then emptying the vacuum cleaner's waterproof container on to the flower bed outside. The floor became covered in deep puddles and we had to resort to mopping up the excess. Unfortunately our best squeegee mop, an expensive model to which we had treated ourselves a couple of years before, had been left hanging wet and had seized up with rust. We had to use a sponge, which was not really designed for such a big job.

Eventually – worn out, wet and with our hair full of sand – we decided to call it a day. We had no idea if we had been successful. The water had soaked into the stones making them darker than ever, but we reckoned that so much filth had been washed off (and deposited on us) that by the laws of Nature the *cantou* must be a bit cleaner.

As we were standing admiring the chaos we'd created, we heard a noise from the *arrière cuisine*. Jack went to investigate and traced the sound to the cardboard box of dog biscuits we kept for our canine friends at St Paradis. Inside was a tiny field mouse with sweet little ears which jumped out and sped up the curtains which were draped just by the box. For a few seconds it hung, whiskers twitching, looking at us over the top of the curtains where they were suspended from the oak rail by wooden rings. Then it disappeared. Later we saw it under the hi-fi trolley. It appeared frequently throughout the day as a little brown blur on the horizon. We didn't mind – in fact, we were happy to offer it some temporary shelter so long as it didn't make a mess or do any

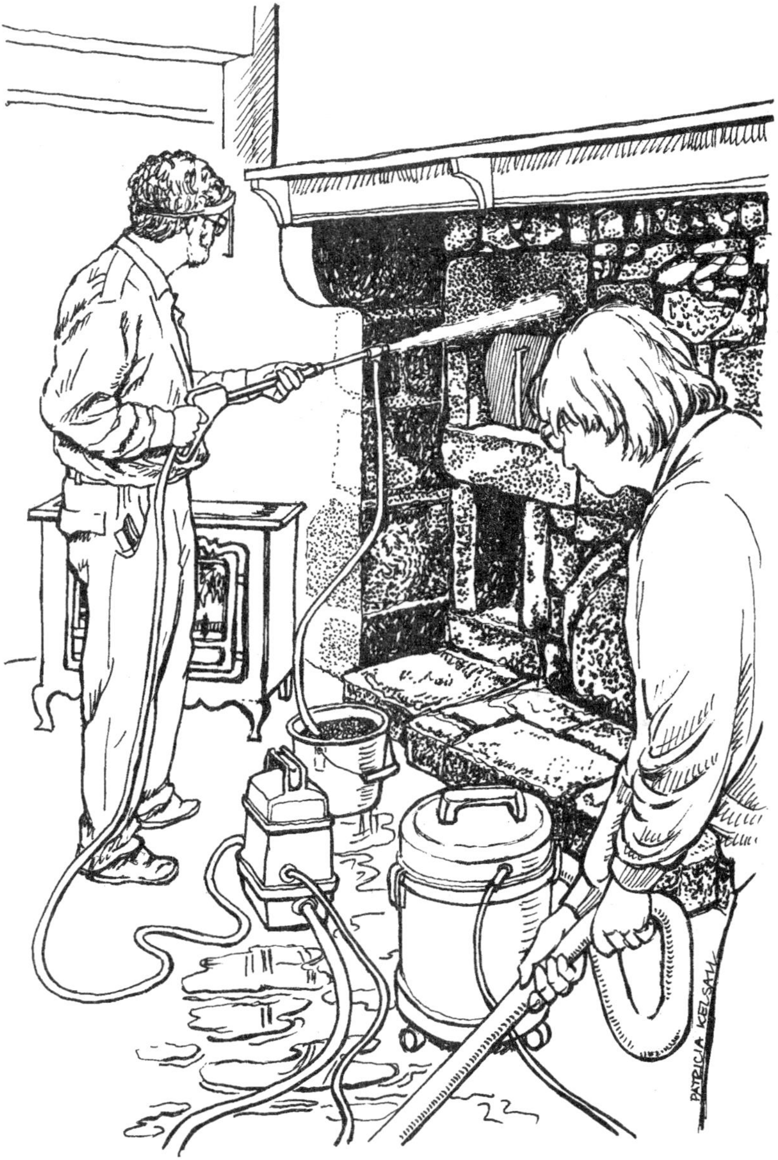

Water charged with sand surged out of the pressure washer nozzle and Jack started to blast the black stones. I felt like the Sorcerer's Apprentice as I tried to vacuum up the water and gunge.

damage.

We were still tired from the ferry, the wedding and our exertions with the pressure washer, so we went to sleep upstairs for a few hours in the afternoon. I was 51 and Jack was 54. Old age was obviously catching up with us.

When we woke up, refreshed, we walked down to the wood which the house's previous owners had given us permission to use in perpetuity. We wanted – and soon found – a long thin tree trunk that would take the place of one forming a cow barrier by the pig-sties, which we noticed had been broken. We stripped the branches and sawed it to the right length. When we were putting it in place, our neighbour Michel Vallet stopped by and mentioned in passing that what we had always thought of as pig-sties had actually been a stable for the original Xavier family's donkey, which had been used to pull a little cart. We were enchanted by the change of species in our minds' eye. Donkeys were much more interesting than mere *cochons*.

Perhaps this is the point to give a little background information for readers who aren't familiar with the story of how we originally bought our house at St Paradis. From the very first moment in June 1994 that we saw the beautiful old house, which we viewed by what appeared to be pure chance, we were welcomed in the community. The first thing that was said to us, by a couple who later turned out to be Michel and his wife, was: "We hope you buy the house and repopulate the village." Other residents, who 'just happened to be walking past' and later became good friends, told us a little about the history of the property, saying it had belonged to Marguerite Xavier, a woman whose only son had been in the Resistance and who had disappeared during the war. After her marriage to a farmer in the next *département* she had lived in a village about 25 kilometres away, but had come back to her beloved family home every summer for a couple of months until she was too old and infirm to do so. It had clearly been loved because the remains of the decor inside showed that it had once been very attractive. We found out later that Marguerite's mother had died comparatively young and that the house had subsequently been lived in by her father and uncle, who had been too busy farming to bother with the feminine niceties of interior decoration. After her death in 1985, the furniture had been removed and the house had stood shuttered and empty for nine years, while the land and barn were rented out to a local farmer. Eventually Jean-Luc Martin, the cousin who had inherited the property from Marguerite along with a lot of other land in the village, decided to sell our portion to give it a new life. Because the house and its other outbuildings had effectively not been touched for years, it was in a timewarp when we bought it. Apart from three-phase electricity (which provided antiquated lighting in the rooms and one power socket), piped water (to a cold tap above the porcelain sink in the kitchen), and a new downstairs lavatory (draining into a septic tank in the back garden), there were no 'mod cons' – but from our point of view we had the basics we required. The house was so superbly built and had such a strong personality that all the rest was cosmetic. As DIY enthusiasts we relished the challenge of revitalising the dirty but dignified old building. It had clasped us to its bosom from the beginning – and we gradually formulated a ten-year plan to make everything beautiful again without changing its character.

The first day we were in the house after we'd bought it, in September 1994, I had a very strong sense of Marguerite's presence as I worked alone in the dusty rooms. While Jack and Chris were outside attacking the jungle which surrounded the building and completely covered the outhouses, my mind was constantly preoccupied with thoughts of Marguerite and her family who had lived there for generations, and I grieved with her that she had been unable to pass it on to her son. Everywhere I looked, I found evidence of the Xaviers and their past life – letters, documents, books, newspapers, things written on the walls and objects which became our 'treasures'. There and then I promised solemnly: "We will look after your house, we will cherish it and we won't make any major changes to it."

From then on, for the next three years, I was quite convinced that Marguerite was communicating with me telepathically and that she had somehow 'chosen' us to be custodians of her house. I was the same age as she had been when her pharmacy student son Alain had died outside a Czech concentration camp, two days before it was liberated. He had been captured by the Gestapo, and deported as a slave labourer. Her life had never been the same again. I was the mother of sons, too, one of whom bore a marked resemblance to Alain at the time. She had always wanted to write, and I was a writer. Somehow she was living on in her precious house through me. It sounds silly to say it, but we have a close relationship. Her photograph is looking down on me as I type this. I have never seen her ghost but Jack may have done, one morning when he was getting washed in the porcelain sink by the front door. He thought he heard me coming downstairs, looked round and saw a figure in a long dress walk down the stairs which lead into the kitchen, turn at the bottom and walk straight through the *arrière cuisine* wall.

We became good friends with Jean-Luc and his wife Geneviève who had sold us the house and they said that it was extraordinary – we had done everything to it that Marguerite had ever wished. They were sure we had been 'chosen' too, and when Marguerite eventually ceased to be a regular familiar presence, they explained that she was happy and had handed over the house to us with her blessing. They teased us and said that to love the Limousin so much we must have had long-lost relatives who maybe were there in the Hundred Years War when this part of the country was fought over by the English and French.

Over the years, we learned a lot about Marguerite and many things happened to us which are beyond coincidence, but I can't write them down here because it would be a breach of trust. Suffice it to say that our emotional involvement with St Paradis goes far beyond it simply being a happy *maison secondaire*. Owning the house has been a life-changing experience.

After our chat with Michel we went inside and put up a small IKEA bookcase in the room which we had chosen to be a study. The house originally had four bedrooms. The smallest was ear-marked as a bathroom and we had bought a bath, hand-basin, loo and bidet in a rush of enthusiasm in 1995. They had only recently emerged from their cardboard boxes in the barn and been carried upstairs, but were not yet connected to anything. During our last trip we had put self-levelling compound on the floor prior to tiling it when we came next time in October. Two of the other rooms were large and we had decorated and furnished them as bedrooms, choosing a square old-fashioned one with golden oak beams as our own. The fourth was a nice room, 12ft x 9ft, with a glorious view over the fields to the hills beyond, but it connected with the spare bedroom and there would have been no privacy for anyone using it. We had decided at the beginning to make it into a study cum sitting-room where we could install a spare computer and sit in the evenings enjoying our rural panorama. To date, I'd spent many hours at the computer but we'd never had the time to pass more than five minutes sitting on the adjoining chairs and sofa. The view was appreciated only when we stood by the window in the dark, watching the many spectacular thunderstorms which occurred in the region and rolled towards us from the distant hills.

Back down in the kitchen we heard a scratch at the door and when we opened it we found a seething mass of five dogs outside belonging to our neighbour, Mme Echelle, who was with them. Our favourite, Gitane, had the big teats of a newly-delivered mother and it was clear she'd just had yet another litter of puppies. She and her daughter Soupette were the targets of all the randy dogs in the neighourhood and got pregnant every time they came into season. Mme Echelle said that one pup had been born dead and that she had killed the others. It was very sad but we supposed that she could not afford to have the bitches spayed.

The weather had turned very hot and close. Michel joined us all on the road outside the house, on the way back from his vegetable garden opposite, and warned that there would soon be a thunderstorm. There hadn't been any rain in St Paradis recently, he said, but they'd had a hailstorm. Other hailstorms across the country had threatened the *vignerons'* grape crops. We examined our own vine which grows over the front of the house and discovered that it was diseased. Michel put this down to a combination of mildew and late frosts – all the local dessert vines were the same. Our poor little grapes were the size of garden peas. The vine was very old, indeed Michel could remember 'scrumping' grapes off it when he was a boy, but we didn't want to remove it because it was such an integral part of the appearance of the house.

After supper we examined the *cantou*. It was not as clean as we had hoped but the stones no longer had soot encrusted on them. While I wrote the daily diary, Jack fixed up a halogen lamp to illuminate the fireplace so that he could start to fit an angle-iron frame out of sight up inside it. It was to hold insulated galvanised steel sheets across the chimney to close it off, keep the heat in the kitchen and prevent rain falling down onto the new stove. He'd measured it all previously and had prefabricated the frame at home in England. The bright light transformed the fireplace and brought out a glow in the brown-stained granite. The *cantou* looked wonderful and we decided to install some hidden spotlights to make the effect permanent.

In the night we were woken up by the mouse, which we tracked down to the plinth of our Victorian bedside cabinet. We couldn't see it, but we could hear it scuffling. We thought it might be sampling the odd sticky cough sweet or indigestion tablet that had fallen down the back of the cabinet over the years.

When Mme Echelle's dogs arrived for their breakfast biscuit, there was a new one with them, a little black and white fox terrier bitch puppy with a sharp nose, who looked just like Milord. We were sorry that Gitane's puppies had been regarded as expendable, while the little newcomer was obviously much-wanted. Milord was a good example of a French '*fox*' and it looked as if some intentional breeding would be on the cards when the pup grew up.

After our own breakfast of cereals and coffee, we set off to look for the builders' merchant recommended by Anne-Marie. It was a little hard to find because although we knew the village from passing through it frequently, we had never stopped to explore it before. There was an ironmonger's shop on the street facing the square which at first sight didn't have anything to do with the nearby side-road in which all the buildings had been converted from little homes and outhouses into dusty store-rooms for every kind of building material imaginable. Except the small piece of stainless steel flue we wanted, of course. We needed it to connect with ten metres of flexible flue which we were going to insert in the chimney as part of the installation of the new stove. We'd bought this in a town some distance away but the very helpful proprietor of the store had failed to order all the right bits and pieces. We were a frustratingly small length short.

After consulting the boss in the yard, we went into the shop to order the flue from his wife, who noted our request down in a ledger in an old-fashioned glassed-in booth which formed the *quincaillerie* office. I love the universal distinctive smell of traditional ironmongers' shops and the Aladdin's Cave promise of their shelves, stacked with everything from tin-tacks and patent brass polish to oil lamps and aluminium saucepans. This was a prime example.

We asked if the flue could be delivered so that we could collect it next time we came to St Paradis at the end of the month, and she agreed there would be no problems with that time-scale. We chatted and the conversation got on to rural depopulation. She told us sadly that she and a friend were the only remaining women in the village from her class at school, and complained about young people leaving the area and not wanting to work.

"Unemployment is now a profession!" she declared bitterly.

We drove on to the *départemental* capital to pay some money into the bank and look for some books about the Limousin and Dordogne/Perigord for a writing project I was doing. I'm addicted to books, but French ones are so expensive that I usually only treat myself to one per holiday. In an orgy of spending I bought four, including a fascinating illustrated guide to the *département* and a book of old photographs depicting the town where Jean-Luc and Geneviève live. Jean-Luc's family have been there for generations and they own several old houses which I hoped would be pictured in the book.

Then we went to one of our favourite *bricolages* and bought a pot of artificial flowers for Marguerite's grave. We try to keep one from us always on the family tomb, alongside more opulent arrangements from the Martins, but when we had been to pay our respects most recently we had spotted that the latest pot had gone – perhaps damaged by the wind. When we stopped at the village cemetery on the way home to put the new flowers in place, we were intrigued by a new family vault which was being constructed in concrete. It wasn't very deep or wide and would perhaps hold four or six coffins stacked side by side and on top of one another. We thought that opening it up for subsequent interments would not be a job for the squeamish if the original coffins were beginning to fall apart.

Back home we enjoyed a late lunch of goats' cheese with salad and a fresh *pain*, then Jack got on with the frame for the fireplace again. He discovered that his measurements were slightly wrong and that the chimney was actually too large for the pieces of metal he had cut in advance. He broke the bit for his drill too, making holes in the stubborn granite, so to cheer ourselves up we went for a little trip to the local agricultural merchant, Espace Emeraude, to buy another bit. While we were there we saw a humane mousetrap (and lots of inhumane ones) and bought that too. We didn't really want to leave our mousy visitor in the house for a month when we left for England the following day.

That night I put some nice Creusoise cheese in the trap and placed it beside our bed.

Quite sensibly, the mouse ignored it.

We didn't put the trap out again the next day because we did not want the mouse to get stuck in it and then starve to death slowly over the next few weeks. Our French neighbours would have thought we were mad if they'd known about our vermin-loving sensibilities.

Chapter Three – October 1998
Thank God for the Godin!

It hardly seemed five minutes since we had been at St Paradis before we were setting off again. In the meantime I'd been busy with freelance writing and had completed the last piece at noon on September 30. The client collected it as we were putting the finishing touches to packing the car and I tried to appear nonchalant whilst feeling internally panic-stricken as I watched the minutes tick by…

Once again, our plans were different from our normal Hartford-Portsmouth-Le Havre-St Paradis routine. The parents of Chris's wife, Linda, had a holiday flat at Broadstairs which they were doing up and they had offered us their old Bosch dishwasher for St Paradis. We are unashamed scavengers and the house in France is filled with furniture and items which we have been given by kind friends. After I had unexpectedly been made redundant as a newspaper editor in 1995 and had set up as a freelance writer and book publisher, we only had Jack's salary coming in regularly and that did not allow for buying brand-new equipment for St Paradis. So a free posh dishwasher of any age was a great bonus. I hate washing up.

Collecting it meant going to Broadstairs to meet Chris and Linda who were travelling over after work from West Sussex (and 'flexing' back in again the next morning), staying the night with them at the flat and catching a ferry from Dover to Calais at about 8.30am. Chris had said that the longest the journey could possibly be was seven hours, and consequently we had planned to leave at 1pm. However, things dragged on and we left at 2pm. The trailer contained Virginia creepers, wisteria and hydrangeas that we had bought at a local wholesale nursery and a plastic compost bin courtesy of a special offer by the borough council. We had left a hole for the dishwasher.

The traffic was diabolical, especially for a Wednesday. We did

50 miles in the first hour and 18 in the second. During part of the second hour we covered eight miles in 38 minutes. We weren't very familiar with the route and everywhere was very busy with traffic jams and road works. With me almost tearing my hair out in despair, we were held up on the far side of the Dartford Bridge. It was 8pm and it seemed like the last straw when we rang Chris and he estimated that the journey would take us another two hours from that point. I wasn't upset for ourselves but because we were messing the kids about so much. Fortunately we arrived safely at 9.15pm to discover that they had been going through their own drama. They had broken the key to the flat and needed to borrow one from the people who looked after the spare key for Linda's parents. The problem was that the keyholders lived in another block and while Linda knew whereabouts to find them she didn't know their name or the combination of the lock to open the main door to their building. She had to telephone her parents for the information. This would have been simple except that they were celebrating their wedding anniversary in Majorca...

Everything worked out in the end. We loaded up the dishwasher and sheeted down the trailer. Linda did us all proud with a supper of soup and stir-fried pork with haricots and new potatoes. We had a nice pudding and got through two bottles of Rioja before collapsing into bed.

Next day we got up early, had breakfast, changed the bed linen and set off for Dover at about 7.40am. There was yet another traffic jam on the Dover road which turned out to have been caused by a taxi with a handicapped child in the back travelling at 20mph. Having met this before in Cheshire, where we'd followed a taxi with its child passenger all the way to a special school at 20mph down twisting lanes, we wondered if it was some sort of crazy Social Services safety regulation. We arrived at the ferry terminal in good time and were loaded near the front of the roll-on roll-off car deck. We sat outside on the aft deck for most of the voyage. It was extremely windy and hard to stand up, but there was only a slight swell and the Channel wasn't rough. We love the sea and it was an exhilarating experience – a nice change from being cooped up overnight in a cabin.

Once in France we used the new autoroute from Calais to Amiens and then on to Beauvais. We stopped for a meal at an *aire* and the mobile phone made us jump when it rang just as Jack was about to put a plate of food on his tray. It was Alex calling from work. The fitter who was putting a new carpet in the bedroom of their bungalow had nailed through a water pipe and created a fountain. He'd turned off the water at the mains and disappeared. Michelle didn't know what to do and Alex wanted to know what his rights were when he rang up to tear a strip off the carpet suppliers. Jack advised. It was nice to be needed by your grown-up children!

The journey took forever. We couldn't go fast because of the trailer and the extra mileage seemed crippling. We stopped off at our favourite hypermarket in Orléans and bought two small strip lights to illuminate the *cantou* as well as some of our favourite wine in the *foire des vins*.

We drove into St Paradis at 11.08pm, exhausted, and left the car and trailer outside, still packed, to fend for themselves. In the kitchen, Jack thought he could hear the mouse again and there were mouse droppings in the *arrière cuisine*. As we carried our overnight bag up to bed, we saw an enormous black spider on the wall at the top of the stairs, obviously fed up that we were back in *his* house again. It rained all night and the trailer got wet inside. We didn't know or care – we were relaxed at last and fast asleep.

After a late breakfast the next day we went over to see Paul and Elisabeth and were very sorry to hear that they had waited up for us until 10.30pm. Elisabeth had made us some soup for supper. We were humbled to think we had such caring friends and distressed that we had inconvenienced them. They were usually tucked up in bed before 10pm unless it was a special social occasion.

Paul said that he had arranged for a local roofer to come and mend the roof for us the following week. It was suffering from wear and tear down the edges and the zinc flashing needed to be replaced. It was too high for Jack to do. We also wanted to ask the roofer to help us fix a 'hat' over the chimney to stop the rain going down it. This would be the first task we had delegated to someone else since we had bought the house.

We went out to undo the trailer and chatted with another neighbour, Charles, who spent a lot of time away from his home in Paris staying with his elderly mother-in-law in the village. He, Paul and Michel formed a "Last of the Summer Wine" trio, although there was probably nearly 20 years' age difference between Charles and Paul, with Michel in the middle.

We unpacked the hydrangeas, wisteria and the Virginia creeper and left them in their plastic pots by the stone seat under the kitchen window. Paul had kindly planted flowers in the bed in front of the kitchen and they were looking splendid, especially some purple Michaelmas daisies. He gave us an enormous bright orange pumpkin which he'd grown in his vegetable garden. We gave it pride of place in the kitchen as a talking-point rather than a meal ingredient.

Jack put the strip lights up inside the *cantou* temporarily and turned them on. It looked gorgeous and we were thrilled. The granite had now dried out completely but was still brown. The lights brought the ancient stone structure to life.

We walked gingerly over the bathroom floor and found that our weight on the self-levelling compound produced hairline cracks. It had been laid over a soundly-based and sealed foundation of exterior-grade chipboard, on top of hand-sawn oak floorboards supported by oak beams. This was a great disappointment, but since we had nerved ourselves up to lay the tiles, we decided to carry on with the plan.

After lunch we went to collect the stainless steel flue section that the builders' merchant's wife had assured us would have arrived by now. It hadn't.

We carried on to the *départemental* capital to buy some tile cement and to pay in some Travellers Cheques. Then we went on to our usual giant supermarket to get some food and investigate their *foires des vin*. We decided we didn't want any of the French wines but were amazed on consulting their brochure to find that our favourite Bulgarian Reserve wine was on sale and had been given a rare four-star rating of excellence. Normally the French don't bother with 'foreign' wine. We purchased the whole stock on the shelf for about £1.75 a bottle! Thinking that at least in this respect it must be our retailing lucky day, we also bought a little cherry tree to replace one in the garden which had died. It was in a batch from a Dutch market garden and had only just been delivered, so we reckoned it should be in good condition.

At home, I made the supper while Jack lit a fire in a little experimental Godin *poêle* that we'd bought second-hand the year before to see if a big one would be worth having. The temperature in the kitchen soon rose to a cosy 20°C. Now that it was the beginning of October, the house was cooling down and losing the warmth it had stored in its massive walls during the summer. Jack then tried out some amended bits of angle iron in the *cantou* which fitted much better. We sampled some of the Bulgarian wine and found it was the same as we bought regularly at home in Northwich – but less than half the price! We listened to records on our old hi-fi system while it poured with rain again outside, feeling very content to be 'at home' for a reasonable length of time and distanced from our usual daily worries about my mother and her increasingly serious dementia. In England, I lived my life with a permanently sick feeling in the pit of my stomach.

The next day was spent pottering about, cleaning the house and tinkering with the computer. In the evening we had a surprise visit from Georges, our friend and agricultural contractor who looks after the land for us. He had come along with his partner Angelique and their baby Eric, bringing us a bottle of champagne and some sugared almonds from the child's christening the weekend before. We chatted for a time and wearing his local councillor's 'hat' he said that the commune was going to improve the village church during the next year. We were delighted to hear that, as we loved the old church and it was beginning to deteriorate badly. They invited us round to their home for a drink the following evening.

We woke up in the early hours and couldn't get back to sleep for ages. This caused us to oversleep and made us late. Paul appeared at the front door with some potatoes and tomatoes from his garden. He was dressed in his best clothes and was going out. As a betting man, he told us that it was the *Prix de l'Arc de Triomphe* today, and we heard the French radio going on about it endlessly during the day.

Even though we didn't yet have the small piece of stainless steel flue which was the last piece in the *poêle* jigsaw puzzle, we decided to insert the ten metres of flexible stainless flue up the chimney from the bottom. Michel had already warned us that this manoeuvre would not work. He was right. Although the chimney was two metres wide at the bottom and a metre wide at the very top, the 155mm-diameter flexible flue would not go up. It had been delivered in a coil and whenever possible it reverted to a coiled shape, its sharp edges getting stuck on protruding stones and mortar. We tried three times with the shiny metal 'snake' squirming all over the kitchen floor and then gave up, agreeing we would have to ask the roofer to drop it down from above, attached to a guide-rope that we could pull on.

We had Paul's tomatoes for lunch, which he said had suffered during the recent heat and drought. As we ate, it was pouring with rain. We sometimes wondered if we carried around our own personal French raincloud.

Looking out of the back door across the field, we saw that we were playing host to three Limousin *vaches* and a *veau*. We had 'cows by the back door', which was nice. We wondered if they had escaped from someone else's field, like the original "Bull by the Back Door" and his family.

We mentioned them later to Georges and Angelique while we were enjoying an *apéritif* in their kitchen, and he said he'd put them there himself for a day or two. I told them that I was just finishing off "The Duck with a Dirty Laugh" and Georges suggested we should sell the St Paradis books in the village itself. I was a bit worried in case some people featured in them thought I hadn't done them justice, although I'd never knowingly misrepresented anyone and had changed all the names. I was very flattered when he said I ought to write a book on the history of the commune. I'd love to, but I don't know if I could understand the material in the archives.

We spent a delightful hour and a half with the couple. Georges is a generous host and we consumed two bottles of *kir* between the four of us, with Angelique being very restrained. The only other time I've known Jack to be drunk was after a previous visit to Georges, when he'd been on the Ricard and couldn't walk straight afterwards. This time the effect was less noticeable and he just zonked off to sleep on the sofa immediately after supper. At bedtime I was congratulating myself on a cast-iron journalist's constitution when I discovered that I had taken the last of my blood pressure pills the night before and had forgotten to bring the next fortnight's supply. I was furious – I always omit to pack something vital when we go away. Often it's Jack's pyjamas or my facial-cleansing milk, which is unobtainable in France.

I rang Alex at 7.30am to ask if he could find the pills and send them on. Michelle was starting a new job at ICI that morning and we wished her 'good luck'. It was a job she'd done before and she had been welcomed back after spending about 18 months as an air hostess. In spite of doing extremely well, she had found the unsocial hours and the long journeys to the airport too disruptive. Alex reported that the problem with the burst pipe had been sorted out.

It was a lovely sunny day at last, and although we had intended to make a start on the bathroom floor we spent most of it outside or gardening, bumping into our friends all the time.

Mme Vallet said that Michel's mother, who was 98, had not eaten for days and they thought she might pass away at any time. She, too, had Alzheimer's and no longer recognised them. It seemed strange to think that someone old enough to be my father should have their own parent still alive.

The little Godin burned small pieces of wood and our logs were delivered cut into half-metre lengths. Jack had to cut up a daily supply each morning using the circular saw in his workshop. He was just bending over the sawbench when his back suddenly started to hurt, and he decided it wouldn't be sensible to kneel down for hours cementing tiles in place. We knew from experience that if his back locked up we were in for trouble, unless we could find an osteopath quickly. He strimmed the grass instead, and everywhere outside began to look quite civilised.

I weeded the front flowerbed, taking out the dandelions and nettles which were growing alongside Paul's pretty flowers. We planted daffodil bulbs along the front of the house and barn, by the clematis which grew up the side of the donkey stable, and also all round the base of our big chestnut tree at the entrance to the field.

Next day we set off at 8am to visit Beryl and Geoff, some friends from Hartford who have a home in a little Deux-Sèvres village. They'd been to see us at St Paradis earlier in the year but we'd never seen their house. It turned out to be a typical Charentais cottage with the ground floor used for living and a first-floor *grenier* which had not been converted and was home to several noisy little animals that scampered about at night. The traditional beamed living room had an attractive fireplace and they were waiting to have a Godin-type stove of their own installed the following day before they went back to England for the winter. Blessed with green fingers, they had a pretty enclosed garden in front of the cottage and a large piece of land, which they used as a kitchen garden, about 200 yards away. Here, set in a grassy area with views over the rolling countryside, they had planted enough vegetables to be almost self-sufficient and a collection of different varieties of trees - 'living' presents from friends who had stayed with them. It was all lovely and we envied them being able to live there for six months at a time.

They had been adopted by lots of feral cats and one had just had four kittens which looked charming playing among the brightly-coloured flowers. Beryl was very worried that the kittens would die after they left, because they were only eight weeks old and wouldn't be able to stand the winter cold. Our friends had deliberately not tamed the baby cats so that they would not become reliant on human beings, but they still felt very emotionally attached to them.

We had a delicious lunch of *pintade* (guineafowl) and a supper of cheese, *terrine* and *pâté* cut into large slices and bought at a delicatessen. These were much nicer than the pre-wrapped portions I usually purchased in the supermarket and I resolved to be more adventurous in my food shopping.

We arrived home at 10pm after a very interesting day out. We enjoyed swopping experiences with other 'foreigners' who owned homes in France.

In the morning we had to go to our local Stoc supermarket to top up with provisions and I braved the deli counter to buy big wedges of some 'real' St Chabrais and Bleu d'Ambert cheeses. We began to tile the bathroom floor with the large light-brown tiles we had bought three years earlier, hoping that the floor underneath would not continue to flex. The roofer telephoned and I made a fool of myself by jumping to the conclusion that he was a 'wrong number'. I hate speaking on the telephone in French. Eventually we established that he was coming the next afternoon.

When we were relaxing in the evening, sitting on the sofa in front of the cheerful glowing stove, there was a scratch at the door. It was Soupette, who had always been too frightened to venture inside the house on her own before. We sat down again and she jumped on the sofa, going to sleep stretched across our laps. We missed our four English dogs, and it was very comforting to have a canine companion again.

Next day we moved the little Godin and all the furniture in the kitchen to give ourselves a clear run at the chimney. There was fine drizzle in the morning and rain in the afternoon. As we waited for the roofer we knew in our hearts that it was too dangerous for him to go up on the slates in those wet conditions. He didn't come. Eventually we cut our losses and drove to collect the piece of stainless steel flue. It hadn't come either. The *quincaillerie* promised it would be there the following day. We were getting wise after the event. We asked them to phone us when it appeared.

There was no sign of any pills in the post and we were freezing because we'd had to let the little *poêle* go out in order to move it. It wasn't a good day to have raised blood pressure!

The roofer turned up at exactly 8.30am, full of apologies. He was very nice. It was a bright and sunny day, with the thermometer reading 23°C. The omens felt much better. During the course of the day, he dropped the flexible flue down the chimney with the minimum of fuss and we guided it into place with a thin rope, then he put the 'hat' on the chimney and added his own covering

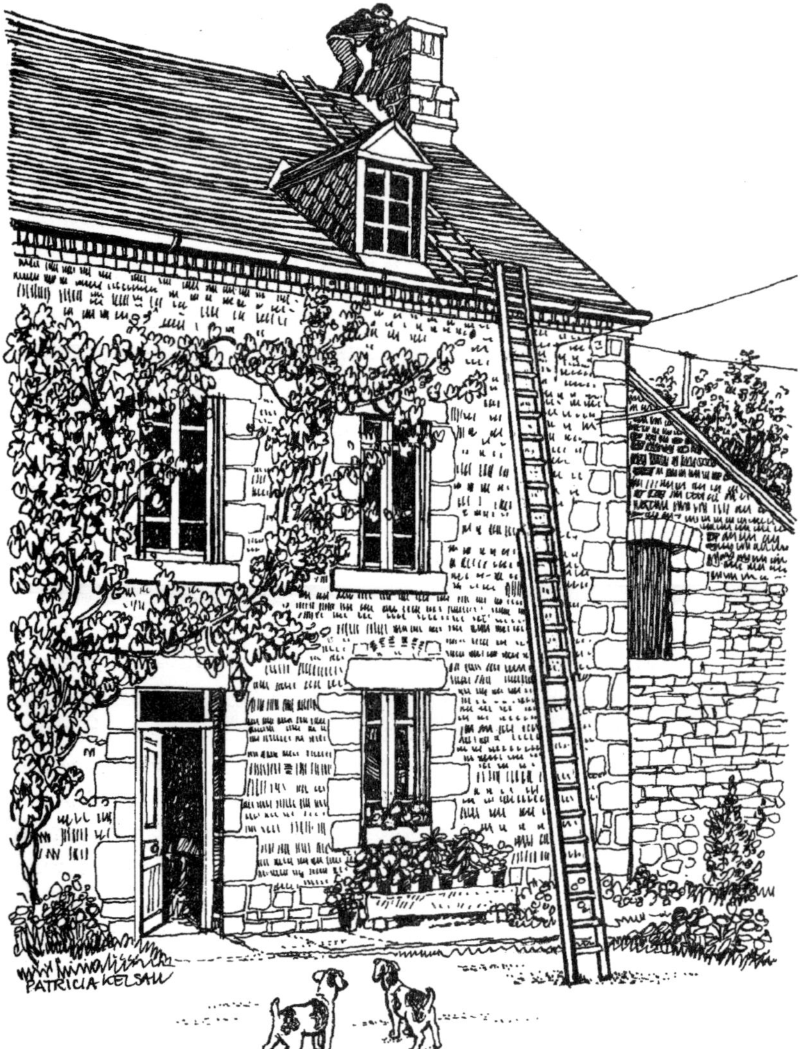

The roofer dropped the flue down the chimney and fitted the 'hat'. It was a pleasure to watch his ability to operate safely and skilfully at dizzying heights. There was something to be said for delegation after all!

of zinc which he cut to fit. He replaced the wood down the sides of the roof and put on shiny new zinc flashing, then he replaced some fallen tiles on the barn roof which we couldn't reach. He drew our attention to a bulge in the house roof which we had been trying to ignore for years and said he would come back the next day to deal with it. We thought he was wonderful. It was a pleasure to watch the skilful way he worked and his ability to operate safely at dizzying heights. There was something to be said for delegation after all!

An *artisan* working on our house was bound to attract an audience and various neighbours wandered by. Michel asked us for an *apéritif* that evening, which we were pleased to accept. We liked the quiet shy man and his lively wife very much and they were a fascinating source of information about St Paradis in times past.

I did the washing with my mother's modern twin-tub which we had brought over when we went to Sophie's wedding. It was so much better than the 1950s washing machine and mangle that I'd used before. Everything was quite straightforward but I had forgotten how time-consuming it was to do the washing this way, messing about with filling, rinsing and emptying via the kitchen sink. I'd had a twin-tub when the boys were small and just washing the nappies every few days used to take more than an hour. We couldn't yet install an automatic washer at St Paradis, because it would have taken too much power and water. For the same reason, we'd had to leave the Bosch dishwasher in the barn. One day soon, we intended to have the power allocation increased and dig a new soakaway so that the waste water from these appliances didn't drain into the septic tank and swamp it.

Studying the *cantou* and the flexible flue which was protruding from the chimney, Jack decided that there was enough for us to not to need the extra piece we'd ordered. The other supplier had actually given us a longer 'snake' than we had specified. The smart piece on top of the Godin would reach the end of the flexible bit without it showing in the kitchen. Jack joined them up.

The phone rang.

It was the *quincaillerie*. Our stainless steel tube was ready for us to collect.

We fetched it and put it in the workshop. It would be bound to come in useful for another task, we reasoned.

When we got back we met Jan and Beatrice, who had come to visit their compatriot Elisabeth. They asked us round for drinks the next week, to meet a Dutch fan of "A Bull by the Back Door", and his friend who lived not far from them. I was flattered to think that someone had bothered to read the book in what was to them a foreign language.

We then saw our immediate neighbours, the Lebruns and invited them for an *apéritif* the next week, too.

The contrast between today's convivial progress and the dreariness of yesterday was quite extraordinary.

We had just finished fitting the Godin by the time we needed to go to the Vallets'. They wanted to show us their middle son's wedding and christening photos. Both ceremonies had taken place recently on the same day in the village church followed by a reception at the *salle des fêtes*. We'd heard of other couples who had been living together, become parents and then decided to combine the two occasions. It seemed very sensible. We spent a happy hour together, then we came home to sample the Godin.

We lit the fire and the blazing logs looked magical through the big glass door. Then the smell hit us. It was revolting. We consulted the instructions, which said that the protective coating on the stove must be cleaned off with white spirit before a fire was started. It was too late to do anything now, so we tried to ignore the stench.

We closed the shutters and pulled down the blind over the kitchen window.

Then we sat in front of the fire hand-in-hand and went to sleep. What a picture of domestic bliss we made!

Chapter Four – October 1998
Learner drivers!

We were taking the car out of the barn the following morning when the roofer arrived. We said we'd just discovered that the bulge in the roof had been caused by the former owners hanging some iron barrel hoops on a wooden batten which had in turn deformed the line of the slates. The hand-forged hoops must have been there nearly 100 years. We had removed them ourselves before breakfast but we asked if he could adjust the slates so that they lay flat and were weatherproof.

As we wanted to go off to the nearest city to do some shopping we also asked if he would like us to pay him before we left. We knew we wouldn't be back before he had finished. He declined, saying that he would have to work out the bill and he would bring it round next time he was passing. In the city we stopped first at Auchan, which had just taken over the former Mammouth hypermarket. I was looking for some special lace or crocheted curtain material to hang along the edge of the mantelpiece so that it looked traditionally French and added a pretty focal point to the *cantou*. It would also stop anyone seeing the black steel plates which were closing off the chimney. In addition, we wanted an imitation oil-lamp to hang from our bedroom ceiling to improve the illumination in there. At present the room, which was nearly 6m x 6m, was only lit by one central hanging 'oil lamp' with an output of about 100 watts.

A shop in the foyer at Auchan specialises in expensive curtain material and Jack nearly passed out when I showed him a design which was exactly what I wanted. I needed a piece two and a half metres wide and about 30cm deep. It was 145FF per linear metre. We didn't buy it! Next we tried the *bricolage* opposite which had an ideal lamp but the assistant was so busy chatting to someone else that she didn't offer to serve me. By the time she had finished, the witching hour of 12 noon was approaching and we had another call to make. We knew we'd have to come back after lunch. We went into the city's commercial centre to the other *bricolage* and found some even prettier crocheted material for 59FF a metre. In comparison with the original it seemed quite cheap so I bought my length with a clear conscience. We were evicted at noon and went to the Continent hypermarket which stayed open at lunchtimes and did a roaring trade. We always wondered why none of the other big shops realised what business they were missing by closing for two hours in the middle of the day. We did the food shopping for the week, bought some dowelling to hold up the new curtain and treated ourselves to an enamelled cast-iron casserole for 99FF because it was too good to miss. We'd already got a similar one which had been considerably dearer. Eventually we whiled away two hours, dashed back for the lamp at 2pm exactly and went home. It always irked us that we couldn't go shopping quickly in France with this great chunk of available time missing from 12-2pm.

While we were having 'lunch' at 4pm, Paul brought over the post, which was always delivered to Elisabeth's house whether or not we were at home. The pills had arrived and I swallowed one quickly in case my blood pressure was soaring. The condition had been identified when I was 45. I had gone innocently to a routine Well Woman clinic at our GP's surgery and came out a decidedly 'unwell woman' with my blood pressure reading off the scale. I'd never had any symptoms so I had no way of telling if I wasn't in good shape, but I thought the strain of coping with my mother's dementia must have made me worse and I was pleased to be able to take the medicine again.

Paul admired the impressive new Godin and after he had gone we put the chimney plates in place and lit the fire. After the success of the previous night we were disappointed. We couldn't get it to make the room hotter than 19°C. There didn't seem to be a draught. Jack decided that all the heat was going up through the gaps in the chimney plates. He plugged the gaps between the stones and the angle iron with incongruous balls of pink rockwool, and asked me to make rockwool 'sandwiches' with elephant tape to go above the plates themselves. He finished by plastering up any remaining small gaps with Polyfilla and wrapping rockwool round the bottom part of the stainless steel flue. I was sceptical. I just wanted him to get on with fixing up my curtain rail but I knew he wouldn't while his mind was full of more interesting technical problems. His remedy worked straightaway and the temperature soared to 24°C in no time.

When we came downstairs in the morning we found that the fire had stayed in. Jack put some more wood on it and the thermometer soon registered 24°C again. It was actually too hot for comfort and we had to open the door to the stairs to let some of the heat out of the kitchen. This was a first-time experience.

We spent the next two or three hours at the local horse fair which was held in the nearby town every May and October. It was an unmissable social occasion for everyone in the neighbourhood. When we returned we fixed the curtain over the mantelpiece. It looked even better than I had hoped, adding a traditional homely touch and finishing off the transformation of the *cantou*. We switched off the main lights, turned on the temporary ones to spotlight the fireplace and sat down for a while to watch the fire like a television. It was hypnotic.

As it was Sunday I made a special lunch of *pintade* with an impromptu sauce concocted from some soup, wine, honey and blackcurrant jam which happened to be in the larder. It was delicious but I've no idea how to make it again.

We'd laid all the easy tiles on the bathroom floor and it was now time for Jack to cut the complicated shapes to fit round pipes and cupboards. We had a professional-type tile-cutting machine that made easy work of fiddly jobs. While he did that I thought I would wash out some of the old bottles we had found stored in the *grenier* years before. I wished to display them as *objets trouvés* in a traditional Limousin basket woven from willow and horsechestnut that also belonged to the house. We had some friends coming to visit us the next day and I wanted the old place to look as attractive as possible.

When we'd bought the house we had been intrigued by a strange brick structure under the kitchen window which we were later told was a *potager* or slow cooker which had been fuelled by charcoal embers – a very useful gadget when the alternative was cooking in a cauldron suspended over an open fire. These had been a common feature of ancient kitchens but most had been taken out years ago. Ours was a rare surviving example. It had a top covered with dark red patterned hand-made tiles which distinguished it from the other cruder ones I'd seen in museums. As I've said, the house had once been very fashionable and I could imagine that generations ago a Xavier farmer's wife had used her female wiles to get the 'state-of-the-art' version installed and had been inordinately proud of it.

In the days when we had to do all our washing-up in the adjacent porcelain sink, I'd used it as a sort of draining board. Now that we had a double sink and proper modern units in the *arrière cuisine*, I had filled the two deep grilles in the top of the *potager* with pots of trailing plants, but the space below where the containers of glowing embers would have been was just packed with random scrubbing brushes, bits of tatty soap and dodgy discoloured floorcloths. I thought I'd arrange some small logs in there, artistically, and then put my basket of *objets trouvés* in the arched bottom section.

First I scrubbed the basket, which was filthy. It had lost its handle but this was actually an advantage as it wouldn't have fitted in the *potager* otherwise. When it eventually looked as clean as it was ever likely to be, I put it where the warmth of the fire would dry it out gently.

The bottles were equally dirty, inside and out. There were hundreds in the *grenier* and I had selected ones with interesting shapes or whose labels were still intact. It seemed to me that the Xaviers had been hoarders after our own heart. They had obviously rarely thrown anything away, on the grounds that it might come in handy. Little did they know that a hundred years later an Englishwoman would be washing their patent medicine bottles very carefully and putting them on display as ornaments.

It was a strangely haunting experience. As I swilled out the bottles, the long-dormant scents of their contents wafted in the air for a few final moments. The last person to have smelled them had been dead for years.

Most of the labels were printed but quite a lot also carried

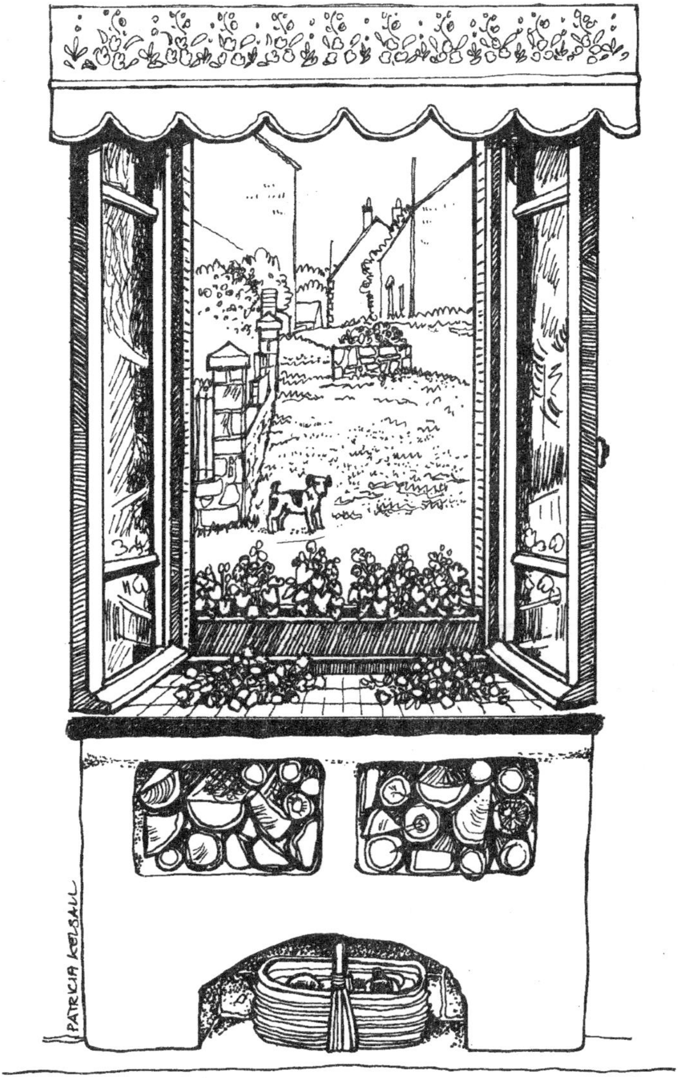

The two deep grilles in the top of the ***potager*** *were filled with pots of trailing plants. I arranged some small logs in the space below, where the containers of glowing embers would have been, and then put my basket of* ***objets trouvés*** *in the arched bottom section.*

additional instructions written in Indian ink. I found that if I was very quick and gentle with my dunking, the writing did not suffer but I was able to clean the glass and wash out the dirt that had collected inside those bottles which were uncorked. The potions would have treated all sorts of illnesses – indeed the same medication was often prescribed for completely unrelated conditions. From Rouen, Abbé Soury's *'Jouvence'* cured *"les maladies des Nerfs et de l'Estomac, les troubles de la Circulation du Sang, les Maladies de la Femme, les Accidents du Retour d'Age, la Faiblesse et la Neurasthénie..."* A large spoonful was to be taken in two spoonsful of water before meals. The engraving of the Abbé on the label made him look very wise and reliable.

Another elixir from A Mouneyrat of Villeneuve la Garenne, called *Histogénol Naline,* was a not-very-specific *specifique* for *"des Maladies de la Nutrition et des Affections Pulmonaires"* said to be used in the best Parisian sanatoria and hospitals for a mind-boggling collection of ailments: anaemia, neurasthenia, tuberculosis, malaria and diabetes. A label on the back of the bottle promised a long list of what would happen "under the influence" of two to four weeks' dosage of this marvellous stuff, including weight gains of 1-5 kilos, the disappearance of insomnia, the diminution of coughs and spitting, and the complete cessation of night sweats and fevers.

I looked up the ubiquitous 'neurasthenia' in our medical dictionary, which defined it as "a vague term denoting an irritable, hypersensitive weakness and depression ... originating in a disturbance of the mind" now dealt with by tranquillisers or psychological treatment. I hoped that the Xaviers' potions had also been good placebos.

When our English friends, Richard and Christine, came the following day, they were enchanted by the kitchen and I was thrilled that it looked so nice. The *cantou* no longer brooded – it was resplendent with its soft spotlights, crocheted hanging and traditional black-leaded stove with dancing flames. The *potager* suddenly had some character instead of being a nondescript and puzzling feature. I was sure Marguerite was delighted, too. Our friends, who had been weekend guests at a lavish wedding not far away, stayed for lunch and we showed them the house and the village. In the late afternoon, after they'd gone, I went over to see Elisabeth, who wasn't well. Her sister Hannah and brother-in-law Hugo were there and I asked if we could take our trailer round the next day to collect some stone they had promised us for the terrace we planned to build at the back of our house. They had knocked down a derelict bread oven building beside their own home in a nearby hamlet and were keen to get rid of the stone, which was cluttering up their garden. Anne-Marie arrived while we were sitting around having a *coup de rouge* and she asked if I would mind helping her with some translations. She worked at a big lakeside campsite and had been asked to translate the French brochures into Dutch. Her employers also wanted English versions. She could speak English but didn't feel competent to translate the brochures into it. I said I would be pleased to help – it would be nice to go a little way towards repaying years of her own kindnesses to us.

Jack hitched the trailer on to the Peugeot and we took it the six kilometres round to Hugo and Hannah's at 10.30am next morning. We backed up to the pile of stones and put them in, one by one – our hands protected by thick leather gloves. Because they were very heavy, we couldn't fill the trailer, but it took quite a time just to line the bottom of it with a layer of stone. When we'd finished, we were invited in for a rest and a cup of coffee.

Back home, we spread out a big black plastic sheet which had appeared as if by magic in the barn between holidays. We thought it must be a rick sheet from someone's haystack that had somehow become involved in the delivery of some logs. It made a good base at the back of the house on which to put the stones, which we also unloaded one by one. It was not the most exciting of occupations, and rather hard on the back.

After three loads we called it a day for the time being, although we didn't seem to have made much impression on the pile in Hugo's garden. At one point we had got the car stuck on chestnuts which had fallen from the big tree by the gate into our field. The weight of the car and trailer had squashed them into the earth and they sat there like greasy brown ball-bearings, making the car's tyres spin uselessly. When we'd pushed and pulled the vehicle over them, I then had the equally stimulating job of prising them up – one by one – to clear the track.

The roofer dropped by with his bill. It was very reasonable and we were delighted with his workmanship. We paid him by cheque on the spot and sealed the transaction with a glass of beer.

In the evening Hugo and Hannah came round for a 'thank you' meal. We hadn't seen much of them on the past couple of visits and wanted to remedy that. We enjoyed their company and it was interesting to hear about the bureaucratic obstacles which were facing them as they strove to become permanent residents in France.

Shopping beckoned again the following day. We'd promised to get some aluminium flue pipe for Elisabeth's woodburning *cuisinière*, a pan for roasting chestnuts (we thought they might as well earn their keep), a new interior container for my pressure cooker, a basket for serving bread, a *vide cendres* (a container which you attach to your vacuum cleaner to suck the ashes out of a stove) and various other goodies. It was one of those days. We could hardly find a single thing we wanted. I ended up getting a Taiwanese basketware plate just for the sake of buying something, and the low energy bulb that Jack bought died within seconds of being plugged in.

We were feeling guilty that we had neglected our gardening, so in the afternoon we planted the hydrangeas in the front, and the wisteria and Virginia creepers round the back. The rear of the house had been covered with ivy when we'd bought the property and it had been necessary to pull it all off. This left the naked grey stone looking very stark. The old burnt house next door which we had inadvertently bought at the same time as the farmhouse (and subsequently given to the Lebruns) had been ablaze each autumn with fiery-red Virginia creeper and we hoped to reproduce the effect on the back of the farmhouse. We also put in the little cherry tree from the hypermarket. It looked a bit dead now and we hoped it would recover.

In the evening we went to Jan and Beatrice's to meet their two friends, Dirk and Pieter. They were about our age and we took to them immediately. They lived in a fairytale setting: a beautifully renovated house with a barn, overlooking a lake, next to a little watermill and with a stream running round one side of their land. They had two little dogs, two cats, two doves in an aviary and two donkeys in the field.

Beatrice had described this idyll to us in advance but had confused us slightly by mixing up her words. She speaks beautiful English but it gets a bit rusty sometimes through lack of use and what she had told us was that Dirk and Pieter had "two monkeys". This conjured up a completely different scenario and Pieter was quite taken aback when I asked him to tell me all about his monkeys.

It was an easy mistake to make. I often tell French people that I'm off to the *coiffeuse* to have my horses *(chevaux)* cut instead of my *cheveux* (hair).

We talked about how Dirk had read my book, and he said he'd enjoyed it because so many of our early experiences with St Paradis mirrored theirs, including the thought that they had been 'fated' to have the house. They didn't have any ghostly help, but it certainly seemed that the house had picked them out and waited for them. It had been in an awful state and they had created a home of great charm and beauty out of quite unpromising material.

The evening was the start of a another happy and enduring friendship. We feel so grateful that St Paradis has brought us so many really good friends over the years.

We left at 11.30pm and arrived home in a state of wellbeing, fuelled in my case by a reasonable amount of wine and liqueurs. Jack banked up the fire with logs to keep the house warm all night and turned the damper right down. I sat on the sofa to watch it idly for a minute or two before going to bed.

Within a short time I was terrified. The fire had gone berserk, becoming a roaring inferno even when the draught was turned off completely. It was booming and vibrating, with fierce orange flames shooting up the chimney. I thought it was going to blow up.

While I was cowering, ready for instant annihilation, Jack went into research scientist mode.

"I think the fire is burning in the flue itself," he said calmly, and went to get his multimeter and a thermocouple to measure the temperature of the flue. We watched it climb up to 280°C while the Godin did everything but leap out of the *cantou* into the kitchen. The damper control was dancing up and down in its slot, creating a fearsome noise. I was convinced that the *poêle* itself would start to glow red and melt down, or the stove door would burst open and shower us with blazing logs. The house would catch fire and we would be incinerated...

"Don't be daft," said Jack. "The melting point for stainless steel is well over 1000°C."

After about half an hour the temperature in the flue had dropped to what Jack described as "an acceptable level" and the vibration had degenerated into the odd tremble. We deemed it safe to go to bed but we had no idea what had gone wrong. It was worrying.

Early the next afternoon Jack dropped me off at Anne-Marie's house and we worked on translating the brochures, each armed with a dictionary. Her husband's computer was newer than mine and set up slightly differently. Naturally, everything was in French, which threw me a bit. Although I've used computers confidently for years, I was scared in case I did something silly and lost all his building business accounts instead of setting up a folder called "lake". However, all was well and we had great fun together. It was the first time we had been on our own for any length of time because although we had been friends for four years, we had always been in a crowd. Anne-Marie asked if I'd like to go out with her socially for the day another time, and I was very pleased to accept. We were exactly the same age, almost to the day.

When we'd finished working, we had a long talk, sitting out in the garden with an iced drink, enjoying her beautiful panoramic view over the countryside – the reason she'd chosen the house in the first place. We spoke mostly French, which might have seemed incongruous to an onlooker, but Anne-Marie had lived in France for many years so her French was better than her English, and I didn't know any Dutch. Hugo was always offering to teach me but I thought my brain cells might pack up entirely if I tried to load them with a second foreign language. One was bad enough!

I told her how much we loved Elisabeth and Paul, and how grateful we were for all the things they had done to help us. She sympathised when I talked about the pain I felt over my mother's Alzheimer's Disease. Since going into the nursing home she had become occasionally violent, attacking the nurses when she felt threatened or frustrated, refusing to undress and sleeping in a chair because she felt claustrophobic lying down in a bed. Her legs had become ulcerated and were weeping pus. If anyone managed to bandage them, she pulled off the dressings. She couldn't remember having a daughter and thought I was her sister. She couldn't understand why her own mother didn't visit or rescue her from what she thought was a hellish boarding school in a Scouse/French foreign country. She didn't know that Alex and I screwed up our courage and visited her every other night. She thought there were months between our visits.

Getting it all off my chest to Anne-Marie was a great relief.

That night, Jack and I banked up the fire again, turned the damper almost off, waited to see if it would misbehave and went to bed when it didn't. Our bedroom is over the kitchen, and the bed is placed above the *cantou*. Shortly after our heads hit the pillows there was an almighty bang, followed by a crash and a smell of smoke.

"I told you it would blow up!" I said to Jack. "Go and see what's happened."

I was much too frightened to investigate myself.

The crash proved to be due to the cleaning plug on the bottom of the flue being blown off and hitting the hearth which, of course, had left a large hole for smoke to get out and air to get in, so that everything had sorted itself out.

I came downstairs in my dressing gown and looked up the little book of instructions that had come with the stove.

"It says you should let the logs burn for some time before you turn down the damper," I reported.

We did, in future, not knowing why. The inferno did not come back.

When we returned to England a few days later, we talked to our next-door neighbour, Glenn, who is an expert on kilns. He explained when the stove was very hot and the damper was suddenly closed the sudden shortage of air caused incomplete combustion and a build-up of carbon monoxide in the stove and the flue. This could have led to the gases burning in the flue as we had experienced originally. In the second case, the amount of unburnt carbon monoxide in the flue had taken the composition of the gases into the explosive region and the flames in the stove had subsequently ignited the mixture – with the resultant big bang. Fortunately, this sort of bang was classed as a 'slow' explosion and didn't do any damage (other than to our nerves!). Glenn added if it occurred in a kiln when you happened to be looking down it, the explosion was slow enough for you to see it coming, step aside and let it go past.

He pointed out that we had made matters worse by putting some dry rotten wood on the fire which had a very high internal surface area and burned very much more rapidly than the good solid six-year seasoned oak we normally used.

Too late, we even found a helpful English leaflet about using wood as fuel, which said: "After stoking, set to *fast burn* ensuring all gases are fully burned. Only set to *slow burn* when all wood has been reduced to charcoal and ash. Newly added wood set to burn slowly will create smoke and tarry deposits in the chimney. The stove should not be banked up with logs overnight. A bright fire which has turned the wood into charcoal should be left with the day's ash, no secondary air and normal primary air. Charcoal briquettes could be added."

We related this afterwards to our St Paradis friends who shook their heads and said everyone *knew* that you didn't put lots of wood in a stove and then cut off the draught. No self-respecting French *poêle* owner would have done it.

I was a bit miffed to discover that we'd been driving our lovely Godin on 'L' plates.

Chapter Five – March 1999
Trials and tribulations

When we returned to France five months later, on March 24, 1999, it was with a sense of trepidation. My mother was an in awful state, mentally and physically. She had reverted to her childhood and didn't know who we were, although she usually identified us as allies. Her legs were so bad that the doctors had considered amputating one of them. She was angry all the time and utterly miserable. All she wanted to do was die, and she begged God to take her quickly. That was her only topic of conversation. Every time Alex and I visited her, she would suggest ways of killing herself. There was hardly any trace now of her real sweet and considerate personality. Alzheimer's had engulfed her. It was so upsetting that Alex wouldn't let me go to see her on my own.

I was sure that I could detect an obvious deterioration in her physical condition and suggested to the nursing home staff that she might die while we planned to be in France. They disagreed, saying she wasn't suffering from anything which would cause her to die and there was no medical reason why we should not go as planned. I decided to make all the necessary provisional arrangements with a local undertaker, just in case. I wasn't being hard-hearted. I loved my mother dearly, but she wanted to die more than anything in the world. She longed to go to sleep and never wake up. If she did die, it would be the answer to her prayers and a merciful release. We would dash back from St Paradis without having to panic about making the sad practical decisions associated with a death – and we wouldn't leave other people with unpleasant responsibilities, either. If my hunch was wrong, then it didn't matter. I didn't want to cancel the holiday because Jack and I desperately needed it. I couldn't have carried on for a single day longer without breaking down myself. Both the nurses and the undertaker said my unusual preparations were very sensible.

Alex and Auntie assured us that they could cope while we were away, though I felt very guilty leaving them and knew how upsetting their visits to the nursing home would be.

The last visit before we left was heart-breaking. Mother worked herself up into such a state that we had to go after ten minutes. She hadn't a clue who we were. I kissed her forehead and hoped she would soon find the eternal peace that she craved.

We dealt with the trailer in advance as usual and packing the car on the day of our journey was easy for a change. We thought things were going too well until Jack took the tyre pressures on the trailer and discovered the tread on one tyre was much less than he'd thought when he'd checked it before. When he took it off he found that the surface was starting to split. He rang round the tyre dealers in the town and only one had the right size in stock. I was dispatched with the wheel to get it replaced.

When he'd refitted the wheel, Jack hitched the trailer up to the car to check the lights. After five months standing out in the rain these too were playing up and it looked as if the earth in the plug connecting the lights cable to the car was inadequate. I was dispatched to a motor parts shop to buy a new one. Jack fitted it and the problems continued. He eventually tracked the fault down to one of the light bulbs. I began to feel that fate was prolonging the agony.

However, things were plain sailing after that. We had a good run to Portsmouth and after a short wait on the quay drove straight on to the boat, which was going a quarter of an hour earlier this year than before. It left on time at 10.15pm – a rare event. We went to the duty-free shop to buy cigarettes and whisky for Elisabeth and Paul and returned to the cabin to sleep.

We had our mobile telephone switched on all the time, throughout the holiday, just in case someone needed to contact us urgently about Mother.

The ferry arrived a quarter of an hour earlier, thanks to the new timetable, and we were off by 7am French time. We had an uninterrupted passage through the docks and Customs. There was a *gendarme* there with his dog but he wasn't exactly threatening. The dog had just got its blanket out of the back of its boss's car and was pestering him to play with it.

We stopped for a breakfast of English sandwiches in the car park of a restaurant by the *autoroute* which we have used as a 'rest stop' for years. After we'd eaten we walked in for a cup of coffee and a visit to their loos. I went upstairs to the Ladies just as a coachload of school children was milling about. I was settling down with some of the establishment's tourist brochures as reading matter when there was a loud banging on my lavatory door and a command of *"dépêche-toi!"* (hurry up!) from one of the girls – which put me off no end. I declined to reply and stayed put. Jack told me afterwards that a waitress had come along and shoo-ed all the kids away to the nearby motorway service station café.

We arrived at Orléans nicely early and after our ritual visit to the vast Carrefour hypermarket went to Castorama where we found a *vide cendre* which would enable us to clean all the ashes out of the big Godin very easily. It was hopeless trying to use a dustpan and brush.

Driving up the little hill into St Paradis at 5.15pm, and seeing the property suddenly come into view, we were thrilled that the daffodils we had planted the previous autumn were in flower right across the front of the house, barn and donkey stables, somehow bringing the whole place to life.

When we opened the front door we found that Paul had already lit the stove for us, to bring some warmth back into a building that had been empty for five months and busy storing lots of 'coolth' in its walls. The temperature in the kitchen rose rapidly as soon as we put on some more wood and opened the damper.

Hugo and Hannah chatted with us while we emptied the trailer, teasing us about the smallness of the pile of stones on the plastic sheet at the back, over which we had expended so much effort in October. They reminded us that there were a lot more left.

After we'd made the bed and turned on the electric blanket, we went over to visit Paul and Elisabeth. It was lovely to see them again after so long, though we were sad to note that Paul didn't seem very well.

Next morning, it was so marvellous to be at St Paradis again that we went all weak at the knees with sheer relief from quitting the stress at home in England. As well as worrying about my poor mother, we were also concerned about Alex and Chris who were both taking up new jobs. Alex – who knows all about plastics and robotic machinery – had been head-hunted to go to an electronics components factory down in Kent, and Chris and Linda had got electronic engineering jobs together with Alcatel, which involved moving from West Sussex to the Banbury area. It was amazing – they had been together since their first day at university, working for Michelin on their 'year out', and then as graduates for Ericsson, until they decided it was time for a move when their department was out-sourced. Alex and Michelle were in the throes of renovating a beautifully-designed 1960s bungalow, which had to be finished before they could sell it, so Alex was going to live in company rented accommodation in Orpington for a time and commute home at the weekends. Chris and Linda were planning to put their own little bungalow in Haywards Heath up for sale and had their fingers firmly crossed for a quick sale.

Life for all the Loaders was extremely complicated just at the moment. For Jack and me, suddenly being in a position to do absolutely nothing about any of it was the coward's way out, but it was nice. In fact, I felt so lethargic that for the first time since 1994, I couldn't bring myself to write up our nightly St Paradis diary. We'd launched "The Duck with a Dirty Laugh" before Christmas and the part of my brain that took a delight in writing had gone into hibernation. Jack was cross with me and took over the task himself, logging things from his point of view. So, since our books are based on the diary, if this chapter is a bit DIY-centred, you'll know why!

Driving in to the *départemental* capital we realised that the roads had changed since our last visit. There were even signs of a new river crossing well to the south of the existing bridge. As yet it had no road attached to it. Ever since we had bought the house there had been roadworks on the main route to the town as part of a scheme to make it dual-carriageway along the whole of its path across France. The work seemed to go in fits and starts. Nothing would happen for months except that the condemned buildings along the route would become more decrepit, and then suddenly we would come back from England and find heavy plant crawling everywhere and a new section of road or a bridge appearing as if by magic. We were always impressed by the way that the civil engineers seemed to bring their own depot with them. Instead of lorries carrying tarmac or rubble from a distant source, a piece of land at one end of the latest improvements would be cleared ready for massive stockpiles of materials to be stored there. It seemed a very sensible idea.

Proof that I was going round the bend was furnished when we parked by the fountain in the imposing town square and went to get some money. In our absence, the interior of our bank had been reorganised and the position of the front door changed from one side of the glass-walled foyer to the other. I tried without success and increasing irritation to step through what had become a floor-to-ceiling plate glass window. Jack was highly amused as I searched for the non-existent door handle.

We walked to the warehouse of the big builders' merchants that specialised in large items like plywood and enormous sheets of plasterboard. We wanted to line the walls of our bathroom with insulated plasterboard – to create a flat surface for tiling but also to prevent damp and make the room warmer. The main exterior wall had been in a poor state when we bought the house because a broken guttering had led water to pour down it for many years. There had been such a volume of rainwater that it had even eroded a triangular hole in the granite window ledge.

We were pleased to see that the plasterboard we wanted was on special offer, so we resolved to return next day with the trailer to buy some. In another favourite DIY/garden centre place, we found some nice large bargain fruit trees to add to our collection of *fruitiers* in the back garden. We thought we could transport the trees and the plasterboard home on the same trip.

When we got home we had a belated lunch then sat in front of the fire together and went to sleep with our heads on one another's shoulders.

We were up bright and early the following morning and took the trailer to get the plasterboard. It was so fragile and awkward to handle that we decided the fruit trees and their stakes would damage it irrevocably and would have to wait until another occasion. At St Paradis we manhandled the metric '8ft x 4ft' sheets out of the trailer and into the barn where we stacked them against the wall.

In the afternoon Jack decided to be adventurous. In September 1994 the back garden had been completely overgrown with brambles and self-seeded trees. Chris and Michel had removed all the trees except one, which was quite tall. It seemed mean to chop it down so we pruned it back and spared it, although it was rather close to the back door. When we returned in April 1995, we found another tree a few feet further away.

"I planted it for you to provide some shade in the summer," said Paul. "That other one's no use – it'll just be in the way. You want to get rid of it."

He was right, but we'd never got round to removing the original tree which was, after all, just minding its own business and not doing anyone any harm. Things were also complicated by the fact it was nearly six metres tall and growing out from under a one-metre diameter lump of solid granite. Now we were thinking seriously about constructing a terrace at the back of the house and the tree would have to go. It was right in the way.

"I don't like to kill a tree deliberately," said Jack. "Let's move it down to the bottom of the field and transplant it. It looks as dormant as the ones we saw in the garden centre, so it might survive."

I'm just the labourer in these adventures so I do as I am told. The question "How?" doesn't pass my lips. Well – not for at least ten minutes.

Before we could dig it out we had to remove the big rock. Our part of the Limousin is littered with them and there are quite a few lurking on or just under the surface of our garden and field. We employed a massive ex-army crowbar, a smaller one and some logs to act as rollers, and after a lot of heaving, managed to move the rock a few feet out of the way. Then Jack dug a large circular hole round the tree about five feet in diameter, to expose the roots. Next we chopped through the roots until the tree appeared to be free, rocking it backwards and forwards until we could identify where the roots were holding and then cutting them. When it got

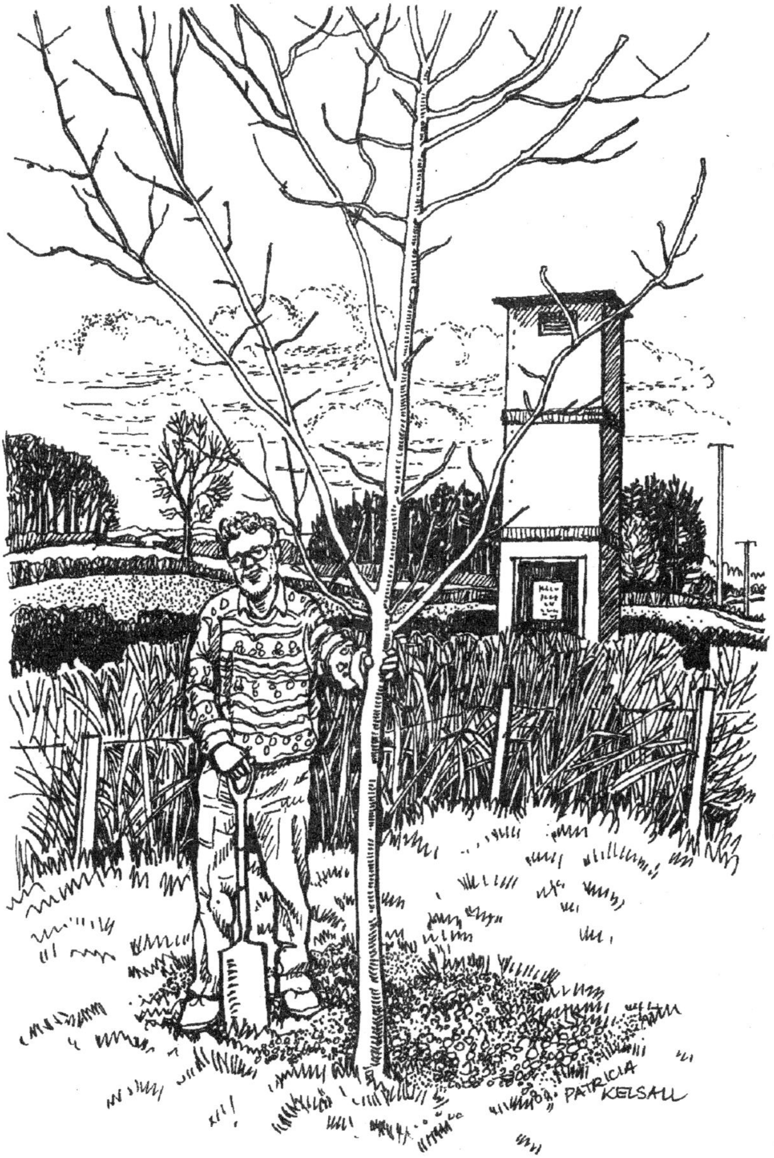

The poor tree eventually ended up being planted in a cement-mine. As we staked it and watered it in copiously, we hoped that there were some nutrients in there. We wanted it to hide the ugly electricity sub station behind.

to the point where we couldn't see any more attached roots, the tree should have popped out of its hole. But it was playing hard to get and stayed firmly in place. Jack then tackled it with a winch until the tap root finally yielded – and, lo and behold, we had a naked tree lying on its side, looking very sorry for itself.

Carrying and dragging it several hundred yards down the field between us was no easy matter, as the branches and roots anchored themselves in every irregularity in the ground and found all the old cowpats on the way. Eventually we got to its new home near the hedge. We wanted to plant it where it would help block out our view of the ugly electricity sub-station on the other side of the lane. The tall white concrete structure hasn't been connected to anything for years and is just an eyesore. We've often wondered about persuading one of our farmer friends to accidentally back his biggest tractor into it but it is so solid it might well win. We fantasise about getting EDF and the *Mairie* to agree to ask our good friend Georges the *maçon,* from our twin town of Mornant, to bring some dynamite to demolish it. Some years ago he and his wife Chantal decided to build a house for speculative sale and bought a large plot on a steep rocky hillside. He then blew an impressive hole in the ground and used the rock that came out to build the house over the hole, which became an enormous garage-cum-*cave*.

Jack was now in digging mode and because there had been a lot of rain over the winter, it wasn't too arduous. He dug a five-foot radius hole in which to replant the tree and the first spade's depth was a doddle. When he tried the next spade's depth he could hardly make any impression. We examined the soil on the spade. It was grey powder instead of brown earth, with the appearance of semi-set ready-mixed concrete – like a mixture of ground granite and wet sand. We'd never seen anything like it before. However having half-dug his hole, Jack was loath to start again somewhere else, so the poor tree eventually ended up being planted in a cement-mine. As we staked it and watered it in copiously, we hoped that there were some nutrients in there for it to live on. Only time would tell if the transplantation had been successful.

That night we rang Alex and Auntie. Things were as awful as ever with Mother.

As 'tree fans' we worry that the French don't take the task of replanting their trees seriously enough. The Limousin was once a wild area of forest populated by wolves and sorcerers – if you believe the guidebooks. Indeed, the famous Limousin novelist Claude Michelet writes of wolves being found here in 1900. There would be nowhere for them to live around St Paradis now. Because every household uses wood to fire its stoves, hundreds of trees are felled every year, but they are not replaced. Now our 'bit' of the Limousin is scantily wooded and Jack and I want to make our tiny contribution towards restoring the old landscape.

The next morning, a Sunday, we walked down to 'our' wood and looked for small saplings in the thick undergrowth to replant along the field edge. We earmarked some to dig up and then turned our attention to our pond, which backs on to a very old *fontaine* dedicated to St Paradis. It was once a paved *lavoir* where the women in our part of the hamlet did their washing but now it is a stagnant mess. A fallen willow tree lies across it and we need to remove that before we can tackle any kind of drainage work to recreate it in its former glory. We eyed up how we could best saw through the trunk, so that it wouldn't come into leaf and could be dragged out with a tractor in the summer when the marshy ground all around would be drier. It was currently far too wet to get any heavy vehicles near enough.

On the way back to the house we admired the daffodils which were growing round the base of the big chestnut tree by the gate. Its roots have long been covered with stones, to protect them and to keep farm vehicles away from the trunk, so it was hard to find some meagre Creuse soil in which to plant the bulbs the previous October. To our delight, they had flourished, and we intended to leave them to naturalise and spread over the coming years.

In the afternoon we tackled the Triffids – a jungle of tall hollow-stemmed bamboo-like plants which infested the bank at the side of the house in spite of poisoning, scythes and general maltreatment. As they hadn't started to grow seriously after being 'marmalised' in the autumn, Jack thought he would attack them when they weren't looking. While he dug out the roots, he asked me to do some scavenging. We have always found lots of broken bottles and glass on and just under the surface of the soil here, and in the beginning someone told us that it was where the local drunks would sit and later abandon their bottles of cheap plonk. But the more we investigated the more we decided it had been the rubbish tip for the farmhouse in the days before the commune provided a refuse collection service. We cleared what we could see every time we came to St Paradis, but there seemed to be an inexhaustible supply of junk working its way up from some subterranean cache. This time, I found a white enamelled colander, a red pot, fragments of window glass (some pieces seemed very old and were more than a centimetre thick) and some old shoes, together with large numbers of veterinary ampoules, old wine and medicine bottles and broken crockery. We had rarely found anything worth saving but it was a necessary exercise because the broken glass was dangerous. I often wondered what the Xaviers would think of me sifting through the detritus of their long-gone daily life.

We spent the next four days in Charente-Maritime, visiting Geoffrey and Joan Morris. Geoffrey is one of our Léonie Press authors, writer of "Only Fools Drink Water". At this point, we'd brought him the final set of proofs and I was due to print the book as soon as we returned to England. They are a delightful couple, almost eighty years old, and frustrated that they can no longer be the madcap "senile delinquents" they were once nick-named by their son. Geoffrey has been made an honorary member of the Foreign Legion in tribute to his wartime exploits in the 8th Army and has been nominated for the Legion of Honour, though he reckons he will have to live to be 150 before the bureaucracy catches up with the nomination. He and Jack have a lot in common, including a passion for DIY and all things practical. They are both radio amateurs, and Geoffrey showed Jack a TV satellite receiver and dish he had bought for a bargain £80 from Castorama, who were selling them cheap because they hadn't got any intelligible instructions and no-one could get them to work. After hours of fiddling about, he now had 250 worldwide TV channels to choose from! He had become an expert in distinguishing and discriminating between the various Arab TV stations.

We had a fascinating time with the Morrises exploring the Marais Poitevin, driving down the Atlantic coast, sightseeing in La Rochelle and dining out on regional specialities in some very nice restaurants.

On the way back to St Paradis I began to be very sick and decided I'd picked up a bug somewhere. There was a listeria scare throughout France and I had been a bit self-indulgent, sampling a host of unpasteurised cheeses when we were enjoying our traditional Charentais lunches. Instead of spending the return journey doing touristy things and visiting Beryl and Geoff, we came straight home. I had a temperature, was terribly thirsty and drank two litres of bottled water in the car. I went to bed, feeling dreadful, while Jack drove off again to do some very basic shopping so that we'd got some food in the house. When he came back I had a taste of soup and breakfast cereal, then curled up and went to sleep.

In the morning I felt better but weak. We decided to go to Stoc to do a proper 'shop' so I went over to Paul and Elisabeth to see if they needed anything. I was amused that they had noted that something was wrong because Jack had been out on his own the previous evening and neither of us had gone across to say "hello". It was nice to know that people cared enough to monitor our movements like that. I supposed we did the same for them, subconsciously. In a tiny community you are aware of the smallest things happening around you and you sense when the situation is not as it should be.

Jack got out the lawnmower and cut the grass in front of the house and round the back, where we were trying to tame some of the field and make it into a lawn. Unfortunately the holes made by the cows, when they grazed in the meadow and their feet sank into the mud, were ankle-turning hidden hazards. It was not exactly a croquet lawn, though we did tease Georges by telling him we were going to have a cricket pitch there.

After a light lunch Jack got kitted up in his fluorescent orange chainsawing gear and we went to the pond. He cut the main trunk of the fallen tree away and removed the smallest branch which was growing out over the mud. We discovered that another big branch was under water and would have to be left for the time being until the water level dropped in the summer. He didn't fancy sub-aqua chainsawing! We cut off as many vertical shoots as we could reach, then put rooting compound on them and stuck them in the ground a bit further down the field in the hope that they might grow. It was so marshy that we couldn't stand in one place for more than about ten seconds because we would have sunk down in the goo to above our ankles. I recorded the squelchy sound-effects on our camcorder. We certainly needed our wellies! The old *lavoir* itself was pretty noxious, too, with methane bubbling to the dark brown surface if we disturbed its depths.

Jack was in the mood for chainsawing and frustrated because he couldn't do any more to the willow. So he went round the trees on the perimeter of the field and cut through the stems of the ivy which was growing up some of them, and in some cases smothering them. Some of the stems were six inches thick. We hoped that killing the ivy would let more light get to the trees and improve their health.

It started to rain so we went into the barn and cut up some of the wood that we'd gleaned on the afternoon's perambulations so that it fitted into the Godin. Then when the rain stopped, Jack had a bonfire with the remains of the Triffids, which had been drying out since we went to the Morrises. He soon got a good blaze going. The hollow Triffid stems banged like machine-gunfire as they burned.

The news from Cheshire about Mother was not good when we had our regular phone call with Alex and Auntie that night. I felt in a strange state of numbed limbo.

Next morning was Easter Saturday and we decided to go shopping for food and DIY materials in the nearest city in spite of radio forecasts about dire levels of traffic as all France went to visit its granny for the weekend. There were few of the international juggernauts which usually dominated the road, but there was a nose-to-tail stream of cars coming the other way. As a diversion we started to note the *départemental* codes on their number-plates and during the 40-minute journey we spotted vehicles from practically every part of the country.

When we were back home having a late lunch, our friend Virginie came to ask us for dinner the next night. She and her husband Guy live in Lyon but spend most of their spare time at St Paradis in a house Virginie inherited from her grandmother. They are keen gardeners and DIY enthusiasts, and after years of hard work their property is now beautiful.

We were still in the throes of making ours beautiful. The next task was to put up the insulated plasterboard in the bathroom. The big sheets were very hard to handle and there was no way we could get them up the stairs, so we had to measure everything and cut them to fit with a handsaw downstairs on the kitchen table. We discovered by trial and error that it was best to vacuum up the plaster and polystyrene dust as we went along, with me holding the nozzle of the cleaner alongside the saw blade, like a dental nurse with a saliva-sucking tool. Otherwise the white powder clung to everything – clothes, hair, furniture and carpet tiles.

We made up the glue to attach the sheets to the wall in a black plastic bucket, using special powder stirred into water. It was easy to achieve a nice creamy consistency and Jack applied the resultant stuff in blobs on the scored backs of the plasterboard sheets every 20cm or so – a lovely, messy job reminiscent of playgroup. Once we'd got each piece against the wall, we had to tap it with a mallet to spread out the glue and then wedge it in place with a piece of wood until it dried. This was the hardest part and as the afternoon wore on we found ourselves having to climb over more and more clamped lengths of random bits of wood taken from the workshop.

We were pleased with the result. The bathroom had once been a bedroom and there were marks on one wall where a bed-head had scraped for many years. The existing plaster was in a poor state and had long ago been painted pink, brown and black with lime-wash. I had applied several coats of stabilising solution to it over the years without success, and eventually washed it off with soap and a sponge. It had been my *bête noire* – but now we were well on the way to having a lovely even surface which would support tiles and keep in the precious heat. I hate cold bathrooms!

After more work in the bathroom during the day, we spent Easter Sunday evening very enjoyably with Virginie, Guy and their teenage son Lionel. They had other guests staying, a couple from the Jura and their two sons, and a friend who worked as a senior member of the British Consulate in Lyon. Paul had mistaken him for a burglar the previous year, when he had tried to pay us a visit while we were away on a twinning visit. An enormously sophisticated and entertaining man, who spoke impeccable French, he had the remit of encouraging trade with Britain in the 18 local *départements* for which he was responsible. It currently stood at a staggering two billion pounds-worth per annum. And while we were talking big numbers, he added that four million British visitors passed through his patch each year – mainly on their way to and from the Mediterranean. Some of them did very silly things and had to be rescued by the Consulate from their folly.

Before they left to go their various ways home, we asked Guy, Virginie and their guests to come for an *apéritif* with us at noon the next day. We showed them round the house and they were very polite about it.

While we were in the garden, Virginie turned to a stone ornament that had always been half-buried, near an equally subterranean broken stone trough, and asked: "Do you know what that is?"

"Yes," we replied. "It's a bird bath. We grow the mint in it so that it doesn't spread everywhere."

"No, I don't think so!" she replied. "It looks like a Roman sarcophagus for a funerary urn containing cremated remains. They are quite common round here, and lots of people have a bottom or a top. But it could be quite valuable if you can find a lid to go with it."

We were rather chuffed. We had never been able to imagine what a stone bird bath had been doing in a former farmyard.

We continued to work on the bathroom, now resplendent with two plasterboarded walls and bereft of its 'buttresses'. The main task was running a pair of cables from the bathroom back to the fusebox in the kitchen. This entailed taking the cover off the ducting high up on the kitchen walls, which carried a cat's cradle of wires from all the sockets in the house. We'd had severe doubts as to whether we could squeeze any more in, but we just succeeded. It would have been helpful to have had an octopus as an assistant! Our success meant that we could now wire up two bathroom-friendly heaters – one to act as a fire and a smaller one to form part of a Loader-designed towel rail.

Jan and Beatrice came for supper, but after a mix-up over times (our fault) they arrived an hour early when Jack and I were both in our working clothes and before I had even started cooking the meal. As good friends, we laughed it off and everyone filled in the time with *apéritifs* while they watched me prepare a *pintade* and do the vegetables. They had brought Grisette and Gamine and we had great fun making a fuss of them. From our first wedding anniversary onwards, until very recently, we had always had at least one Irish Setter and were completely dotty about them. Jan and Beatrice's *épagneuls français* (literally 'French spaniels') – a prize-winning mother and daughter – were of a similar breed and genuine scatty temperament and we adored them.

In the morning we squelched around in the swamp again, planting more willow whips and generally tidying up the area. I was in charge of bramble cutting. I'm not a good gardener at all but I do enjoy a bit of unskilled chopping-down. Armed with thick gloves and sharp secateurs, I was in my element. We made a big heap of the prickly cuttings, so they could dry out before being burnt.

After lunch we had a very messy time trying to stick some flexible cable ducting in a channel cut into the back of various pieces of plasterboard under the window in the bathroom. This was a job requiring two octopus helpmates because the board kept springing off the wall when we weren't looking. The buttresses were back with a vengeance. Jack ended up covered in glue and I had to wash his shirt before it set solid.

When we had our daily chat with Elisabeth and Paul, we were sorry to learn that he was shortly going to have to have his sixth eye operation in three years. He'd suffered a detached retina in 1995, as well as cataracts, and his poor eyes had been getting progressively more painful and troublesome.

Back home we checked our e-mail and were delighted to receive a message from Chris and Linda. They said they had resigned from their jobs with Ericsson and were now working out their notice before starting at Alcatel. They'd had their bungalow valued the previous Saturday and the first person to view it had decided to buy it: the whole thing had taken just seven days! We were thrilled to have some good family news at last.

The following day I had a nasty shock when I took two films of our Charente-Maritime experiences to be developed and printed at a "one-hour while you wait" place attached to a big hypermarket in the city. I needed at least one atmospheric photograph to go in the front of Geoffrey's book, which was due out in May, and thought that it would be quicker to get the pictures done in France than wait until we got home. Worrying about Mother had made me a bit erratic and when I saw the prices displayed in the photoshop I thought they were 37FF for a 36-exposure film. At the current exchange rate that would have been about £4 – roughly what I would have paid using my normal postal developing/printing service in England. When I went back to collect the photographs I nearly fainted. I had missed a decimal point in the price and misinterpreted what it meant. It was 3.70FF *per photograph* – nearly 40p each. And I had 72 photos! So my pictures of Charente-Maritime cost about £28 instead of £8.

Jack was in seventh heaven because the reason we were in the city was to buy a cement mixer – a piece of equipment he had much lusted after for years and could now finally justify buying in the light of the plans for the terrace. We were now the proud owners of a bright orange electrically-driven *betonnière*, which we took home in the trailer and stabled in the barn. We had been very taken with Geoffrey Morris's theory that the best wedding presents for a French couple were a filing cabinet (to cope with the bumph generated by bureaucracy), a photocopier (to make copies of all their replies to the bureaucrats) and a cement mixer (to facilitate their later home improvements).

Then it was back to the plasterboard. A different type this time, coloured green and intended to prevent damp on outside walls. It was more easily broken than the polystyrene backed variety and we had to be very careful with it. We got the last piece glued wearily in place at 1.30am.

It was Thursday, April 8 – two days before we were due to leave – and we were expecting some new friends, Stuart and Pat Ahier, to visit. They had contacted us after reading "A Bull by the Back Door" and it turned out that they had a holiday home not very far away. We had invited them to come over and see St Paradis for themselves.

While I prepared some lunch, Jack planted horse chestnuts around the edge of the field, and replanted little hawthorn whips, which had been growing in the field, into gaps in the hedge. He chatted over the hedge with one of our elderly neighbours who was walking past along the lane. Her doctor had recently prescribed a daily 'constitutional' for her, and during this holiday we had often seen her striding past, stick in hand and scarf round her head. She was a tall thin woman in her eighties, always dressed in dark widow's clothing, and to see her walking purposefully down lanes normally frequented by cars and tractors rather than pedestrians, made her a timeless figure. She could have been setting off for market a hundred years ago.

We enjoyed a leisurely lunch with the Ahiers, and after showing them all over the property, swopped French house-owning experiences. They had had theirs for six years. It was in a hamlet about as tiny as St Paradis and they both found it a haven from the pressure of their busy lives in Britain.

At 7pm Georges, Angelique and the baby came round for an *apéritif*. The baby was now 15 months old and growing rapidly. With dark eyes, a ready smile and sparkling eyes, he was the image of his father. We told Georges our plans for the terrace and he said he would get us some rocks for the foundations. We also mentioned that we planned to mark out a proper garden area at the back so that we could keep the animals off it. We could have hugged him when he offered to use the augur on his tractor to put some fence posts in for us before we returned in the summer, if we would mark out the boundary with string. That was a wonderful bonus, because the ground is so stony that it would have taken

Jack hours to dig post-holes by hand. In addition, Georges said he'd help us pull the willow tree out of the pond when the land was drier. We were very grateful to have such kind friends.

In the morning, with our minds concentrated on thoughts of the new garden we might soon have, we went to the local agricultural merchants to buy some string. We were quite amazed not to find any at all, so we settled for a large ball of orange baler-twine type electric fence wire instead. Jack said he felt like a real French *paysan* now that he had his own electric fence wire and a *betonnière...*

We pegged out a rectangle 17m x 33m, which stretched out from the end of the barn and ran the length of the back of the house and outbuildings. It measured a mere 560sq m, which we thought should be enough to be going on with. Jack mowed the enclosed grass with the lawn-mower as it was still quite short from its last cut, and he wanted it to be shorn as low as possible before we left it to go home to England. We had no illusions about how much it would have grown when we returned in July.

Jack had a further 'go' at the Triffids and then gave the transplanted tree at the bottom of the garden a generous watering. We'd been going down there with a bucket full of water most days, to try to get it established in the strange grey powdery soil.

In the evening Elisabeth and Paul came over for their ritual 'last night' supper with us. We had learned not to give them too much to eat because Paul was used to having a cooked lunch at midday and couldn't cope with a large evening meal as well. We showed them a video of some of the jobs we had been doing.

It was the usual rush to pack everything up the next morning, but fortunately the weather was nice enough for Jack to park the trailer outside the front door so he could carry things straight out from the house. If it's raining he has to leave it in the barn, which entails a much longer walk with all the tools.

We went round closing the shutters, unplugging the electrical equipment and shutting off the gas to the cooker. It's a sad process each time, but at least we know we can come back again soon.

We said goodbye to Paul and Elisabeth and set off at 1.40pm.

As we reached the border of St Paradis, I said to Jack: "Dear old Mother – after all my precautions, she's proved me wrong, hasn't she?"

But I still had a very profound premonition that I would never see her again.

At Orléans we stopped as usual to go to Carrefour for some wines and Castorama for a 'nosy'. We wanted some more electric convector heaters but they didn't have any left. We should have looked the previous autumn, when the store was full of them. Friends had often told us that the time for bargains was at the beginning rather than the end of a season for selling something. April, for instance, was the beginning of the garden furniture season, and with this in mind we had been looking for a glamorous wooden-framed parasol to grace the terrace (when it eventually materialised). We hadn't found anything we could afford, until we had spotted a special offer in a Bricomarché flyer pushed into Geoffrey Morris's letterbox. Just the beige cotton parasol we wanted, for only 130FF. The problem was that the store didn't have any branches in our neck of the woods.

Deciding to go through the city of Chartres rather than round the ring-road we suddenly saw a hoarding advertising the DIY chain, and we made an instant detour. As usual, the *"Bricomarché à cinq minutes"* announcement was wildly inaccurate and after at least a quarter of an hour it was one minute to closing time when we arrived. We dashed into the store, expecting – from our lunchtime eviction experiences – to be chucked out without any ceremony. But the staff were very laid-back and after we'd found our parasol on display they went off into the nether regions to find us one without any fuss. As we packed the bulky cardboard box containing the Chinese-manufactured parasol into the back of the car, we couldn't believe our luck. This silly spontaneous purchase had made our day.

Finding our way back to the Rouen road without retracing our steps involved some challenging map-reading and took us through some pleasant countryside we hadn't seen before. Our diversion had taken up quite a lot of time, so Jack was forced to drive a lot faster than usual to get to Le Havre by 10pm for the 11pm ferry.

We booked in at the port entrance and joined the end of a fairly long queue. At 10.30pm as we were sitting, idly chatting and watching the lorries being marshalled into place, the mobile phone rang. We looked at one another with speechless alarm.

It was Alex, to say the nursing home had rung to tell him that my mother had just died.

I was shocked, but immensely relieved – grateful that at last she had been granted her release from confusion and fear. Mother hadn't been afraid of dying, but in the end, Alzheimer's Disease had made her terrified of living.

My mother was cremated in Cheshire after a funeral at the local crematorium attended by the immediate family, close friends and several nurses from the nursing home. They said she had been one of their favourite patients and that they had admired her fighting spirit. Then we took her ashes home to Spalding and held a memorial service in the church where she had been a stalwart and much-loved member of the congregation for many years. She now lies at rest in her parents' grave in the leafy peace of Spalding Cemetery.

Mother had a very matter-of-fact attitude to death and always said she "didn't want any fuss". I found out afterwards that she had been preparing for it for years, neatly annotating all her personal treasures so that I would know when the time came just how precious and significant they had been to her. This was a wonderful gift, because it enabled me to remember her as she really was, and not as the sad and confused Alzheimer's sufferer. Before she was struck by dementia, Mother faced the prospect of dying quite happy in the knowledge that she would be reunited with my father, who had died at the sadly early age of 68 – just at the beginning of the retirement they had hoped to share together.

So I knew she would have been highly amused by the fact that after I collected the casket containing her ashes from the undertaker, I carried it in a discreet shopping bag round the local branch of Marks and Spencers – her favourite shop for dress-buying dilemmas – in search of some last-minute purchases before we set off for the memorial service.

Chapter Six – June and July 1999
A Retiring Individual

After 30 years' service as a research scientist and information technology expert, Jack retired from ICI on Friday, June 25, 1999. He was just 55 years old. The prospect had been hanging over us for so long that it seemed unreal when the day came.

During the previous couple of years, the company had been haemorrhaging with early retirements and redundancies as ICI departed from its old role as a manufacturer of heavy chemicals. It became easier and easier to get a place in the car park at the vast complex of the Chemicals and Polymers HQ in Runcorn which had once employed four thousand people.

Jack's remaining colleagues were having a presentation ceremony for him that lunchtime, and the secretaries kindly asked me to go along. This was quite unusual and I was very flattered that they understood how important our marriage was to him. We're pretty much inseparable. Since we first started going out together in 1963, when I was 15 and he was 18, we've been known to our friends by the all-embracing collective noun of "Jacknanne".

Jack was astounded to see me. In his speech he said that he'd had to change what he was going to say because I was there. (I still don't know what the original version was!). He told everyone that he was now going to join me with the book publishing venture and to my embarrassment even referred them to some publicity leaflets he just happened to have brought along…

After some generous tributes, he received an official retirement certificate signed by ICI chief executive Charles Miller-Smith, some expensive woodworking equipment and a superb framed caricature showing him St Paradis-style with a bobble hat, hammer, nails and bottle of red wine. He'd chosen the woodworking stuff but had no prior knowledge of the picture. I had secretly provided various photographs for the artist to work from.

He was also given a photograph album containing pictures of all his colleagues and signed messages from them. It was a very touching souvenir.

After saying goodbye to everyone, he loaded up his favourite battered equipment trolley into the back of the car – which would have gone into the waste skip if he'd left it – handed his security swipe card in at reception, and (I quote from his diary entry) "drove off into the sunset to the strains of Dire Straits, to live happily ever after..."

That night, a beautiful evening, there was a big party at a local hotel, paid for by ICI. Employees with Jack's length of service were entitled to a lump sum to spend on a 'do'. Some used it to pay for a lavish meal for a group of special friends, but Jack decided to hold a buffet for all the people he'd enjoyed working with over the 30 years. Nearly 90 turned up and the occasion functioned as a massive reunion – many former colleagues had not met for 20 years. They were 'treated' to a short video of our progress at St Paradis, on the grounds that Jack had bored most of them rigid with stories of the place over the years, and now they could see what he had been talking about!

The hotel venue was geared up for nuptials, so all the guests stood in serried ranks – like a French wedding party – on the steps outside for a souvenir photograph taken by Chris. He and Linda had come over specially. Alex and Michelle were there too, looking after Jack's 90-year-old mother. We had a raffle and raised £160 for a group of Kosovon refugees who had been given shelter in a former old people's home nearby.

The next day felt a bit like a turning-point. I had sold my former company car, an H-reg Cavalier, which I'd had since it was new and had later bought when the lease expired, in order to buy Michelle's Peugeot 106. I loved the Cav, but it seemed silly to have two big cars when both Jack and I were at home together. The young couple who'd bought it earlier in the week came in the morning to pay over the money and I waved it a sad farewell. We'd travelled 98,000 happy miles together over the years.

But the bombshell occurrence took place in the afternoon, when Jack – inspired by another glorious sunny day – donned his straw hat, took out our sun-lounger, *put it on the lawn in the shade and went to sleep.* This was so out-of-character that I took a photograph of him. The dogs were mystified and kept going to check that he was still alive. I can assure you that it has never happened again.

We departed for France on Wednesday, June 30, leaving Auntie in charge of the dogs and of Granny Loader next door. We missed all the traffic hold-ups and made it to Portsmouth easily at a steady 60mph all the way. We were particularly looking forward to this trip because during it we would be going to the Vendée for a big family gathering to celebrate Annette's 70th birthday.

On the ferry we discovered that it was the last night of 'duty-free' and there was virtually nothing left in the shop, which was due to close at midnight. We couldn't buy the usual presents for Elisabeth and Paul, so we left empty-handed, wondering how the ferry company would use this space on the ship in future.

The journey down to St Paradis the next day, in beautiful sunshine, was equally relaxing and Jack declared in the evening that he had decided that Thursday, July 1, 1999 was the first day of his new life. In spite of his snooze on the lawn the previous Saturday, he had found it very difficult in the intervening period to stop working at the high-pressured pace he was used to. He'd had a problem with the modem in the laptop computer he had been given when he left ICI, and he'd been tearing his hair over it as if it were something which had to be fixed in a normal working day. In the peace of St Paradis he'd realised that it didn't really matter any more.

After unpacking we went over as usual to see Paul and Elisabeth and were sad to find Paul very unwell with heart problems. When we'd first met in 1994, the indomitable little man had told us he had "the heart of an ox". We desperately hoped he had not made himself ill by kindly doing all the heavy jobs he so enjoyed in our garden. One holiday we had arrived to find that he had single-handedly built us a beautiful rockery in front of the house, with stones it would take two normal men to lift – let alone an octogenarian.

Elisabeth told me that her son was working during the summer at a campsite *au natur*. I thought she meant a naturist camp and made a joke about how much he would enjoy it. Elisabeth looked puzzled, then laughed. *Au natur* did not mean a nudist camp, she explained, but one set amongst the splendours of nature…

To add to our pleasure at being back at St Paradis, we discovered that, true to his word, Georges had put oak fence posts for us all along the lines we had marked out with electric fence wire. He had done a superb job and they were rock-solid. We saw Angelique and the baby passing outside and gave her the bottle of Pastis we had brought as a present for Georges. She said we didn't owe him any money for doing the work, which was very generous.

Even more pleasurable was the discovery that thanks to a Millennium project across France, the bells in our nearby church were now tolling the hours and half-hours between 7am and 7pm, and the Angelus three times a day. It brought a new dimension to the background sounds at St Paradis and made the sleepy hamlet somehow come alive again.

Our euphoria was marred a bit when the phone rang and Auntie told us that we had mistakenly brought the keys to the garage, my office and Jack's workshop over to France instead of leaving them with her in Hartford. Apart from anything else, she couldn't get into the office to see if any faxed orders for books had arrived overnight. We promised to post the keys back in the morning.

After Jack's 'new life' declaration, we celebrated at suppertime by opening a bottle of Foreign Legion wine that Geoffrey Morris had given us. It was very nice – made in Provence by old legionnaires.

"To the future!" said Jack, raising his wine in a toast. We clinked our glasses.

"Jacknanne" looked forward to a new phase in the happy partnership.

The following day was even hotter and our digital thermometer registered 27°C outside at 11.30am. Inside it was a very comfortable 23°C. It seemed funny to think that this was what we had achieved earlier in the year thanks to the big Godin. The natural heat was different, somehow.

We went shopping at Stoc and bumped into a surprised

Virginie, who had just received – but not yet opened – a letter from us telling her we were coming. They were just about to leave! She invited us round for coffee at 2pm and we sat in the shade under one of their trees, admiring their rose collection. The garden was ablaze with colour and looked magnificent. We could quite believe it when she said that 40 per cent of their time in St Paradis was spent gardening.

They had just had a new window put in the side of the kitchen and the mason had done it beautifully. When the mortar had dried completely it would blend in unnoticed. We had seen some old houses where windows had been added as an afterthought and they looked awful.

When we got home at 4pm we struggled upstairs with a new 'antique pine' wardrobe which I had bought with some of the money Mother had left me. I also wanted to use some of it for an 'antique pine' dresser to put in the kitchen, where it would look very much in keeping with our deliberately old-fashioned décor. I hadn't found what I liked in England at a reasonable price, so we decided to search French furniture stores for one. Mother had loved France so much that I wanted to feel that part of her was at St Paradis. The wardrobe would only just go round the bend in the steep stairs and we 'oldies' were pooped after we'd manhandled it into position in our bedroom. The bed looked inviting, so since Jack was now retired and we were on holiday, we cuddled up on top of the bedclothes and went to sleep until the temperature had cooled down a bit outside.

At about 6pm Jack started to tackle the garden. As we'd feared, the enclosed area, which had been like a proper lawn before we left in April, was now covered in grass and weeds growing three to four feet high. The Triffids had once again failed to be impressed by our brutality. They were eight feet high and as thick as ever. Jack strimmed the relatively short grass in front of the house with the brushcutter and then turned his attentions to the back.

Summers in our part of the Limousin are notorious for their thunderstorms and we could hear rumbles in the distance. As we ate our supper the electricity failed but came back on again about 30 seconds later. There must have been a lightning strike somewhere. We hoped that the glorious weather would hold while we were at Annette's birthday celebrations over the next couple of days. On the way back, we planned to drop in to see the Morrises and give Geoffrey a box of copies of his book, which had come out as planned in May.

We packed everything into the car and managed to leave at 10am for the Vendée. As we walked out to the barn we saw the village dogs playing with something which turned out to be the corpse of an animal that resembled an extremely large rat. It had a long pink tail, big pink feet and a very coarse coat. The dogs had bitten off its head, so we couldn't imagine what that was like. We wondered where on earth they could have found it and hoped it hadn't been poisoned. We didn't want our canine friends to be poisoned in turn.

As we drove across to the west coast, via Poitiers, it clouded over and rained a little. When we reached the Vendée, the skies were ominously grey. We could see signs everywhere for the Tour de France, which was coming through the area the next day. We thought it might be an interesting phenomenon to be embroiled with, but our more cynical French friends warned us that the crowds of spectators and closed roads would be a pain.

The massive birthday party was to be at 'Le fief des forêts', Annette's 'country house' – a bungalow in a little wood which she and her late husband had constructed when they were young as a rural refuge from their apartment in a block of flats in Nantes. Over the years it had been extended and improved and all her children regarded it as their home from home.

I'd looked up *"fief"* in the dictionary many years previously and found that it meant "fief" as in "fiefdom" or medieval stronghold. I never knew if it was an ancient name for that plot of land, or a new one that the couple had given it themselves – their own little fiefdom away from the hassle of the city and the car factory where Annette's husband worked.

Marcel, her eldest son, had invited us to the party and booked us into a nearby hotel on the main road. Like everyone else, we were sworn to secrecy. Annette had no idea that anything exciting was being organised. We went straight to our room at the hotel, washed, changed into several layers of what we deemed to be smartly casual clothes and set off for the bungalow at about 5pm, confident that we knew where we were going. We soon got hopelessly lost in the network of narrow lanes. Fortunately we bumped into Marcel, who was on a mission to bulk-buy bread, and followed him.

Virtually everyone else had already arrived, and the wood was dotted with tents, caravans and camper-vans. People's pet dogs and cats pottered about, occasionally pursued by toddlers. It was lovely to see everyone again. Nearly all the family who had been at Sophie's wedding were present, as well as some others we hadn't seen for ages. David was there too, with Ann's widowed cousin Christine. Ann had not been able to come this time.

Annette was overwhelmed, not only to see so many members of her French family there, but also that the English side was represented too.

Before she arrived in the afternoon for what she expected to be a very low-key weekend, her children and their spouses had been busy behind the bungalow, setting up five gazebos (*tonnelles* in French), complete with balloons, lighting, sound amplification, tables and chairs, where people would sit to eat during the forthcoming evening meal. There were flowers decorating each table and yellow bunting strung around which read "Happy Birthday!"

In the meantime, everyone milled about outside, chatting. Jack and David played *boules* with Jacques. After a pathetic start, worthy of any Loader playing a ball-game, he leapt into second place. Jacques won, of course. Afterwards, Jack told me he had at last worked out the basic rules of *boules* (in spite of having played lots of times before, in a large team, as a willing but bemused participant who just aimed for the *cochonnet* and hoped for the best).

His explanation, completely devoid of technical terms, was: "To start, someone throws the little ball and then has their first go trying to get as close to it as possible. Everyone else then has a go. The next go is then done in order starting with the person who was furthest away with their first *boule* and finishing with the person who was the nearest. The person who is closest after the second turn wins and gets one point. However if his second *boule* is second-nearest he gets another point. The first person to 13 wins

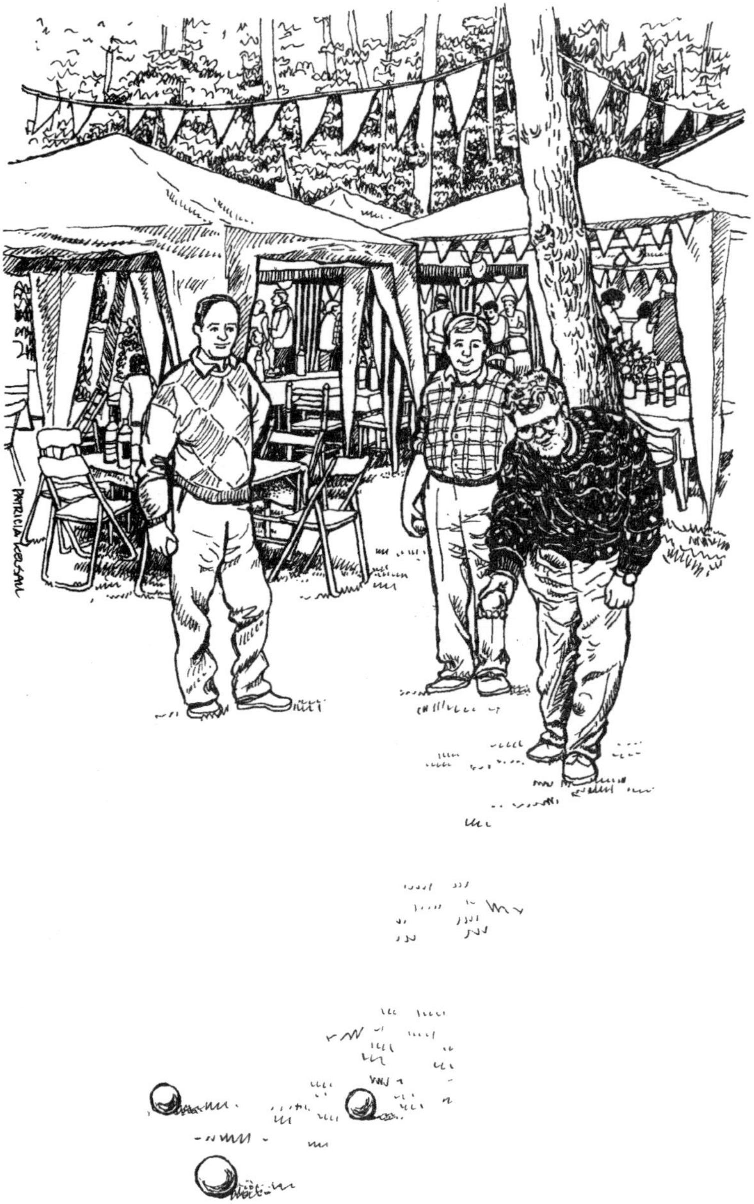

After a pathetic start, worthy of any Loader playing a ball-game, Jack leapt into second place in the game of boules.

the game."

Fifty-two people, including Annette's grandchildren and assorted relatives' babies who seemed to be in the great-grandchild generation, and two neighbouring couples who were old friends, sat down at 8pm to begin the meal. It was served as a colourful buffet of salad, *charcuterie* and fish, spread out on tables along the back of the bungalow, and the Birthday Girl's family had contributed all the expertly-presented dishes. Guests had paid a nominal amount each to cover the cost of the food and wine. We could soon see that there was enough to feed 102!

Annette has always been especially proud of her English maternal roots and is jocularly and almost universally known to the younger members of the family as "Granny" – and occasionally, we discovered, as "The Queen Mother". Since her retirement she had been busily researching her family history, and she and David enjoyed comparing notes.

As at all the previous family weddings we'd attended, singing played a major part in the proceedings, in particular songs which had been specially written for the occasion by her daughters, who seemed to have a special talent for composing appropriate lyrics. After entering the scene to the tune of "God Save the Queen" (which we mistakenly assumed was in honour of the Brits and then realised was for the honorary 'Queen Mum'!), an ad hoc choir of daughters and grandchildren burst into *"La Chanson pour Granny"* which our song-sheet said was based on *"un air de P. Bruel"*.

I'll quote it in French because it's sweet, and I'm sure French-speaking readers will get the sense of it better than if I translated the words into literal English. A couple of explanations: Annette spent her childhood at Rochefort sur Mer and *le coeur batte la chamade* means "the heart beats wildly".

Refrain 1
On s'était dit rendez vous en Juillet
Avec le soleil c'est écrit
Pour les 70 ans de granny
C'est la fête au fief des forêts.

Couplet 1
Le jour est v'nu tout le monde est là
Granny ne s'y attendait pas
Toute la famille est réunie,
ainsi que ses meilleurs amis.
Ses frères et soeurs, ses p'tits enfants
Qu'elle veut voir devenir grands,
Dans l'émotion des retrouvailles
II va falloir sortir l' mouchoir.

Refrain 1

Couplet 2
Avec ses cours de généalogie,
Elle peut r'prendre le cours de sa vie
On n'peut pas faire 70 ans d'histoire
Sans que Ie coeur batte la chamade.
Le Fief, Nantes, et Rochefort sur Mer
Et sans oublier l'Angleterre
Elle à déjà vu du pays
Mais rien n'est tombé dans l'oubli.

Refrain 2
Et si on se donnait rendez vous en Juillet
Même jour même heure dans 10 ans,
Avec granny pour ses 80 ans
Ce sera Ia fête au flef des forêts
Ce sera la fête, ce sera la fête!

We certainly agreed with the last verse, and promised to come back for her 80th birthday!

Then there was the giving of presents, and the family had gone to great lengths to come up with something personal. The gifts included two wicker chairs (in the hope that the ever-busy Annette would treat herself to an occasional rest), a watch, a hand-painted plate depicting the *fief* and a special coat of arms in the form of a painted shield showing Rochefort, Nantes and the *fief* set amongst its trees.

As we sang, drank, ate and talked, the rain fell from time to time and we were glad of the shelter under the illuminated *tonnelles*. Between courses, the choir entertained us. In the background, one of Annette's sons-in-law, a big gentle bear of a man with the most delicate touch (he'd painted the coat-of-arms), was sporadically indulging in his hobby of catching moths. Armed with a butterfly net, he had a white sheet and a bright light under one of the trees, where he was capturing and identifying them expertly. Apparently the *fief* woodland was a good site. I didn't get too closely involved. I have a 'thing' about moths and butterflies which is quite irrational, but I really can't stand them. I think it goes back to walking through a cloud of Cabbage Whites when I was a small child, and feeling them fluttering against my face and mouth.

At the end of the savoury courses, the birthday cake was brought on, candles flickering. It was a most beautiful concoction of sponge, cream and strawberries, complete with a diamond-shaped flower and fruit arrangement, and the flags of Great Britain and France. Like Sophie's wedding cake, it really seemed a shame to eat it. Annette huffed and puffed until she had blown out all the candles and then it was chopped up into small portions. She made a little speech and we toasted her in bubbly. She richly deserved her moment of glory. Her husband had died when they were quite young, leaving her with a step-daughter and five children of her own to bring up on a nurse's pay packet. Life had been a struggle, but she had never let it daunt her. Now it seemed she was as busy being a peripatetic Granny as she had ever been as a resident Mummy.

We departed with David and Christine at about 1am. They left their car in the wood. Hitching a lift with us meant that they could enjoy the wine without worrying about being breathalysed. The local red that was being served was especially nice and was called, appropriately, *"Fiefs Vendéens – Domaine St Nicolas"*. We hadn't come across it before and promised ourselves we would try to find some in the shops.

Back at the hotel, we were amused to find that our single beds had green hairy counterpanes and we wondered if they would come alive and gobble us up in the night.

In the morning we had breakfast with David and Christine in the hotel dining room, which was also used by commercial travellers and other passers-by for their *petit déjeuner* and a perusal of the daily paper.

We went back to the *fief* just after 10am and chatted to people, intending to go at about noon after doing a wee. However, a queue of 48 people put quite a stress on the single combined loo/bathroom in the bungalow, so we hadn't got in by the time lunch appeared. It was the leftovers from the previous night, and consequently excellent – much better than the McDonald's we might otherwise have had somewhere en route. We eventually made it to the loo and finally left Annette and the family around 2pm, by which time serious rain had set in. Saying goodbye to everyone involved kisses and hugs outside the gazebos, and getting very wet!

We took the coast road down to the Morrises to avoid the Tour de France. The rain seemed to have brought all the holidaymakers out for a jaunt in their cars, and it was quite busy. Some of the seaside towns had massive caravan sites which reminded us of the Lincolnshire coast of our youth, around Skegness and Ingoldmels. One had a collection of colourful all-plastic huts described as 'chalets', which we imagined must be appallingly hot and sweaty in August. We could quite see why the inhabitants of Geoffrey's unspoilt fishing village were snooty about the annual influx of *estivants* – summer tourists – from the holiday resorts.

After a cheery greeting and a cup of tea, we chatted with the Morrises until supper-time. Joan said that the animal we had seen the day before was a muskrat, a bit like a coypu. After a simple but delicious supper, including some gorgeous ham home-cured by Joan's butcher, we went to bed about 11pm, which was just as well after the previous evening's jollifications.

We left about 10am and drove south to La Rochelle where we had fun in a *bricolage* chain we hadn't patronised before, lusting after a miniature tractor for tens of thousands of francs and actually spending 150FF on a 130m drum of nylon cord for the brushcutter. Then we headed towards Rochefort to see the famous copy of a 16th century sailing ship which is being built there using traditional methods. The heavens opened and it rained so hard that it was impossible to contemplate getting out of the car, let alone walking anywhere. The water standing on the road was so deep that it would have swamped the sandals I was wearing and we couldn't have got round to the back door of the estate car to grab our coats without being soaked to the skin. We gave up and returned home via Cognac, Angoulême, Limoges and Bourganeuf. We had our own rain cloud which kept more or less ahead of us all the way. It was quite uncanny because we could see the rain start a few hundred metres in front of us. Every time we drove beyond the cloud and rejoiced that it had stopped raining, it would catch up and the deluge would start again a few minutes later. We didn't know what we had done to deserve a Loader microclimate on this particular trip, when by rights the summer weather should have been dry and sunny.

The sad news next morning was that Paul was due to go into the local clinic for about a week to be treated for his heart condition which was making him very poorly. Only a year previously he had been in fine health, planting rows of sunflowers, pumpkins and haricot beans for us, and digging the rest of our back garden into submission under the blazing sun.

We went into the nearest town to have a preliminary look at opening an account with the Crédit Agricole bank there. When we'd bought the house in 1994, we had accompanied our estate agent to a Société Générale bank in Limoges (we suspected he had a friend there!) and arranged to open an account at the nearest branch to St Paradis, which was in the *départemental* capital. This had been fine and we'd always had an excellent service from them. But it was a long way to drive to pay in Travellers Cheques and to take money from the cash dispenser when we needed it. Now Jack was retired we hoped that coming to France would become a way of life and not just a holiday, so having a bank on the doorstep would be much more convenient. Our recce showed that the neat little bank, with its smart architecture and plate glass windows, had a hi-tech cash machine and was manned daily. We resolved to apply for an account another day, when we had nerved ourselves up for the linguistic challenge.

At home I made war on the cobwebs which had colonised everywhere in the house since our last visit. There were some very large and nasty ones complete with dead inhabitants – both prey and 'hosts'. Jack attacked the jungle in the back garden and was annoyed when a small part of the brushcutter broke and he had to make a time-wasting lash-up repair with impact adhesive.

We were amused to be the centre of attention for a group of sightseers complete with rucksacks and sensible boots. They visited the famous old well on our boundary and then stopped outside Paul's barn, which they examined in minute detail whilst also looking closely at the stonework of our own house when they thought we weren't watching. We gathered afterwards that they were doing a conducted tour of the best stone buildings in the area. I wondered afterwards if I should have invited them in to have a look at the interior of the house, which has been changed very little structurally over the last 100 years, unlike many similar farmhouses which have been 'done up' and had their original layout obliterated. If I see a similar group outside again, I will do. I'd like to pick the brains of the person conducting the tour, too.

Hugo and Harriet came over after visiting Elisabeth in the early evening, bringing with them an adorable golden pup whose name appeared to be "Peachy". She raced round the kitchen like a whirlwind and perched squirming on our knees to be petted. At five months her teeth were like needles and we soon had the scars to prove it! We looked back with pleasure to the time when our own puppies were bundles of joyful energy like that.

When they'd gone we walked down the field and gave the transplanted tree a large bucket of water. It didn't look very happy and had hardly come into leaf. We hoped it would have recovered from the shock to its system by next year.

The Virginia creeper had survived well and was climbing up the wall near the *salon* window. Unfortunately, the wisteria at the end of the barn had spread across the ground and grown lots of tendrils but hadn't made it up the wall. I did some 'first aid' by attaching it to the old mortared bits in the masonry with large staples but these 'toe-holds' were very precarious.

Opening the doors to the barn next day, on the way to move the car, we heard a strange "clack clack" noise, as if of machinery. We wondered what tool we had left turned on. Then it transpired that the sound was being made by little brown birds with vivid orange breasts. A chick was on the floor as Jack walked in, but it flew away into the rafters when it saw him. We could hear it "claaack-ing" high above us and then watched another of the little birds weaving in and out of the gaps in the eaves. The barn echoed to their strange song and we hoped the feral cats that lived in the hayloft wouldn't get them.

I helped Jack to put his ICI presentation woodworking machinery together, and after lunch we tackled the back garden – Jack cutting the grass while I raked it up and made a miniature haystack. The sun shone all afternoon and it was a pleasant task. From time to time, we sheltered under the shadow cast by the remaining small tree in the back and tucked into ice cream cornets and ice lollies. I was sitting back in my folding plastic chair, enjoying the view, when there was a crack and I found myself in a heap on the grass. On inspection, the chair leg seemed to have been stressed by the uneven ground. Jack teased me unmercifully, especially as we had tried to follow a regime of living on salads and eating less food.

At 6.30pm we went round to our neighbours, the Lebruns for a drink. The patriarch of the family, to whom we had given our unwanted 'burnt house' years before, and his wife were there with their daughter Bernadette and son-in-law Pierre, who were our age and also on the verge of retirement. We liked them very much. When it was too late we realised we must have mistaken the time and we were much too early. They politely glossed over this. We arranged to meet Bernadette and Pierre when they came on holiday to Britain with some friends in a few weeks' time.

Madame is always a great fund of local knowledge and it was with great interest that we learned that the little road between our properties was called the *Route des Morts* because that was the way coffins were taken from a neighbouring hamlet to the church in St Paradis, before the current metalled road was constructed. The bearers put their burden down for a rest at various little crosses along the way. Madame said she had hidden in the *chemin* when one of the nearby roads was full of refugees being strafed by Italian planes in 1940. She had been staying with her mother in the house. She and her husband were living in Arras and she described the subsequent complications of getting passes in the zones *libre, occupé* and *interdit* during the early part of the Occupation.

When we returned home it was a beautiful evening with a clear bright blue sky, so we ate our supper on the table outside the back of the house. All the swallows were out catching insects, so the flies were keeping a low profile and it was all very idyllic.

I must confess that we enjoy shopping, and the following day was given over almost entirely to the pursuit of Mammon. We went to the city, mainly in search of a pine dresser for the kitchen at St Paradis and a new kingsize Dunlopillo bed for ourselves in England – these seemed to be much cheaper in France and we planned to ship one home in the trailer. We looked in three of the main furniture superstores and as always were staggered that the French could have such superb taste in some matters and not in others – dining suites in shiny pink plastic veneer and imitation blue marble, and some quite amazingly garish and uncomfortable-looking sofas. We found exactly the bed we wanted, in two of the shops, but it was on two to three weeks' delivery and we would have gone home by then. It was very frustrating. We didn't see any dressers we fancied.

We compensated by buying some tools, a convector heater and a bargain PAL/SECAM video recorder. We had my mother's old television at St Paradis for some time and used it for playing back video direct from our camcorder. Jack had a theory that we could receive French TV on the video recorder and then use the SCART link to display it on the English screen.

Back home we had a late lunch and went to sleep until 6pm. We'd decided that a siesta in the heat of the day was a very civilised institution. Afterwards we did some more clearing up and I made hay while the sun shone.

It was misty, damp and overcast when we got up, with the thermometer registering only 16°C outside at breakfast time. We pottered about indoors for a while and I was annoyed to see that the spiders had busily respun all the webs I had removed two days before – in spite of the spider population having been sucked up into the depths of the vacuum cleaner. Perhaps they had all trooped out via the still-attached hose during the night and set to work again.

By 10.30am the sun was shining brightly and the temperature outside was 29.6C. We took down the old barbed wire fence which had originally divided part of the garden from the pasture beyond but which we had adapted five years before to protect our four fruit trees from being eaten by animals using the field. The new garden boundary started some 10 feet further away and the old barrier was no longer necessary. Wearing thick leather gloves, we removed the wire from the old fence posts, rolled it up roughly and put it on one side to take to the tip. Then we pulled out the posts. One, cut from a piece of the tree that Jack had removed from the pond the previous year, wouldn't come out. We discovered that it had taken root and was putting out shoots and leaves. Jack's aunt, who had left us the money we'd used to buy the house, had often done this to establish horse-proof fences at her riding school, so it seemed somehow appropriate. We were sad to have to pull it out.

Working outside we became aware of the idiosyncrasies of the newly activated church bells. They were controlled from a central point together with all the other bells in the national Millennium scheme and Georges had mentioned that there had been a bit of a problem with a relay. We noticed that they had struck eleven times at 10am and ten times at 11am. At noon, the Angelus seemed to go on for ever. It didn't matter. It was so heartwarming to hear the sonorous peals ringing through the little community and somehow unifying it. Everyone loved it, even Mme Echelle who lived nearest to the church and whose counterpart in England would probably have got up a petition against it by now.

Jack inaugurated his woodworking equipment by making a stand for the new video recorder. I held bits of wood and was generally helpful. We were in the barn and watched with curiosity while the randy Milord had sex outside in the road with the new little bitch, whose name we now knew as Ophélie. She was crying out in pain. We'd spent most of our dog-owning lives preventing this happening rather than encouraging it, so we weren't very *au fait* with the canine equivalent of *The Joy of Sex*. The act was certainly 'athletic' – they were back to back and stuck fast together for ages, in spite of the fact that after a time they both looked as though they wished they weren't. We'd read of this phenomenon, of course, but couldn't get our minds round the actual logistics of it. The thought made your eyes water.

After supper we walked down to the pond and were disappointed to find that the tree was thriving happily in spite of its trunk having been cut right through. The downward-pointing branches had simply rooted themselves in the pond, which was as noxious and gloopy as ever. Working out how to remove it looked like the ultimate military or management training exercise! Maddeningly, the willow cuttings we had planted did not seem to have taken in the primeval mud.

It was a beautiful evening, so we went back, weeded the front garden and dug up some of the mint that had colonised the corner of the big flowerbed Paul had made for us. We planted it in some green ornamental plastic pots we had brought from home and this reminded us to have a look at the urn Virginie had identified in the back garden. We hadn't inspected it closely before apart from manhandling it a few inches out of the way when Jack had been laying the drains for the bathroom and *arrière cuisine*.

I pulled at the mint growing in the urn and all the contents came up together, held by the mass of mint roots. We had never seen inside before, having simply added compost to the existing soil when we planted the mint. There was a neat cross carved in the bottom, which made the hairs stand up on the back of our necks. Being told by Virginie that such urns were commonplace had made us blasé about it, but the carving brought home to us that it had once contained a real person's cremated remains. We resolved to look for the lid.

Out shopping in the nearby town next morning we went into the *tabac* / newsagent which always has a good choice of local books and a few videos. Faced with a choice between the latest blockbusters and some random touristy films, we chose a video showing life in the Limousin in times past, telling the proprietor we had just bought a *magnetoscope* and wanted to try it out. When we explained where we lived he was very friendly, saying that he knew the house well and that his family had lived at the Lebruns' dairy next door.

Jack sprayed his *magnetoscope* unit matt black and when he installed it under the television stand, it looked very professional.

We spent the afternoon gardening and Elisabeth came round for supper that evening. We had been in daily touch since Paul went into hospital and his stay had been extended until the middle of the following week. After our meal we showed Elisabeth some photos of my mother's and then settled down to watch the Limousin video. It was very interesting, if a bit of a cheat in that there was no archive movie film (which we'd been expecting), just very clever still camerawork – zooming in and out and panning – on old black and white photographs.

There was some rain in the night – enough for a passing car to disturb us by splashing through puddles on the road – and it rained during the morning, so we decided to do some work on the bathroom. Jack had been putting this off, on the grounds that he was enjoying himself outside, but he had run out of excuses. We worked out where we were going to put the shower screen for the bath and the exact dimensions of the false wall which was going to hide all the pipes behind the loo, bidet and washbasin.

In mid-afternoon, it was dry enough for Jack to venture out and cut Elisabeth's lawn, and then trim ours again now that it had been tamed into submission with the brushcutter. I turned the hay in my haystack, which had got all wet. We didn't want it to go rotten, as we hoped it might eventually be of use to animals grazing in the field, or even to Dirk and Pieter's donkeys.

In the evening we went for a barbecue to Jan and Beatrice and were pleased to find that Dirk was there too. Pieter had gone back to the Netherlands for a few days to see his family. We sat on a newly paved area that they had created at the far end of their hilltop garden, which was sheltered from the wind, and admired the view. There was the noise of shouting and machinery behind us in the wood and we saw three men moving logs which they had obviously recently cut down. Jan and Beatrice knew them well as neighbours and invited them to join us for a drink. They clambered over the fence and were soon accepting a *coup*. One asked for red wine and Beatrice mistakenly thought the other two wanted whisky and poured two large glasses of it neat. One declined and requested a *peu de rouge* instead while his friend downed both whiskies in quick succession. We hoped he wasn't about to climb back into the wood and operate a chainsaw.

It turned chilly, so Jan cooked the food on the barbecue outside and we ate it round the dining table. Beatrice had made the kebabs herself with beautifully tender meat and they were served with salad. The dessert was apricots in vanilla ice cream from Stoc which actually tasted of real vanilla pods and was completely unlike any English 'vanilla' (i.e bland, white and 'industrial') ice cream we had ever eaten.

In return we invited everyone, including Pieter, round for a curry at the weekend. We left fairly early, as we had a long drive ahead of us in the morning. We had arranged to go and see Grace McKee, author of the Léonie Press book "Où est le 'ping'?", and her husband Phillip, at Larroque, their old farmhouse in Gascony.

Chapter Seven – July 1999
Après nous le déluge!

Excited at the prospect of visiting a new part of France, we left home at 10am and drove to La Souterraine, where we joined the motorway which passes through Limoges. It was 35°C on a clear, sunny day with clouds in the distance. The *autoroute* was packed with Dutch cars towing caravans or trailers and heading south for their holidays. There were far more Dutch vehicles on the road than French ones. We reckoned that as it was a Monday morning, all these people must have set off at roughly the same time from Holland over the weekend.

It became hotter and hotter. We stopped for lunch and a rest in an *aire* then continued on to the current end of the motorway. With everyone else, we took the Route Nationale to Cahors. There had been an accident on the steep descent into the town, which blocked part of the road and caused an enormous traffic jam. We crawled a few metres every five minutes for about an hour, thankful for our straw hats and open sunroof. The thermometer in the car registered 45°C and we just didn't know what to do with ourselves. We vowed that the next car we owned would have air conditioning. After we had eventually crossed the town, we got stuck in another jam trying to leave the by-pass, but this seemed to have been caused by our old M6 friend "sheer volume of traffic".

We had been looking forward to sitting outside in the evening sun with Grace and Phillip but as we got nearer to their home, set amid rolling hills planted with cereals and vines, it went dull and thundery. When we drove into Larroque's former farmyard, two simultaneous thunderstorms started on either side of the horizon. The heavens opened. It poured with rain as hard as it had at Rochefort. The 1999 Loader microclimate had struck again!

We looked round the lovely old house and sat together in the kitchen as the rain beat against the windowpanes, talking about the forthcoming book – which we were producing thanks to the wonders of fax and e-mail. After some time, they told us sadly that they had decided to sell the house after owning and loving it for seven years. Phillip, a world authority on skin pathology, and Grace, an internationally-known pathologist specialising in the diagnosis of breast and cervical cancer, had the year before moved to the United States where Phillip was a professor at Harvard Medical School. Grace was a pathologist at Massachusetts General Hospital and an assistant professor at Harvard. They only had three weeks' holiday a year and realised that they would not have the chance to come to Larroque regularly any more. The air fares were enormous and it seemed foolish to pay a mortgage on a property in a different continent that they could rarely visit. It had been a sensible but heart-breaking decision to sell the property, and we grieved with them, especially as they had originally intended to spend their retirement there. But they were so dedicated to their profession that we couldn't see them retiring for a long time – if ever.

We went out later for a meal at their favourite pizzeria in nearby Condom (I'd had to be careful to keep references to the town out of our e-mails for fear of them being defined as pornographic by some Worldwide Web censor). In the morning we had a rather wet conducted tour of the outbuildings and land, and a simple French lunch of tomatoes, eggs and onions with bread and cheese. We left at 2pm with Grace and Phillip facing the sad prospect of a 5pm meeting with their estate agent and builder to discuss prices and final renovations.

Our personal microclimate persisted. It rained all the way back to the Creuse, in varying degrees from moderate to torrential. At times we could hardly see where we were going. Our French fellow motorists of course made no allowances for the wet conditions and we came across two recent accidents. One near Villeneuve-sur-Lot had caused a traffic jam of Cahors-like proportions, so we followed a local white van driver who did a swift three-point turn out of the queue and headed for the side roads. We stuck with him and by-passed the accident. Later we saw where a little black sports car had taken a corner too fast and ended up in a ditch. Three accidents in two days! We hardly ever saw them on ordinary roads in Britain.

It stopped raining around Limoges and it was lighter at 9pm

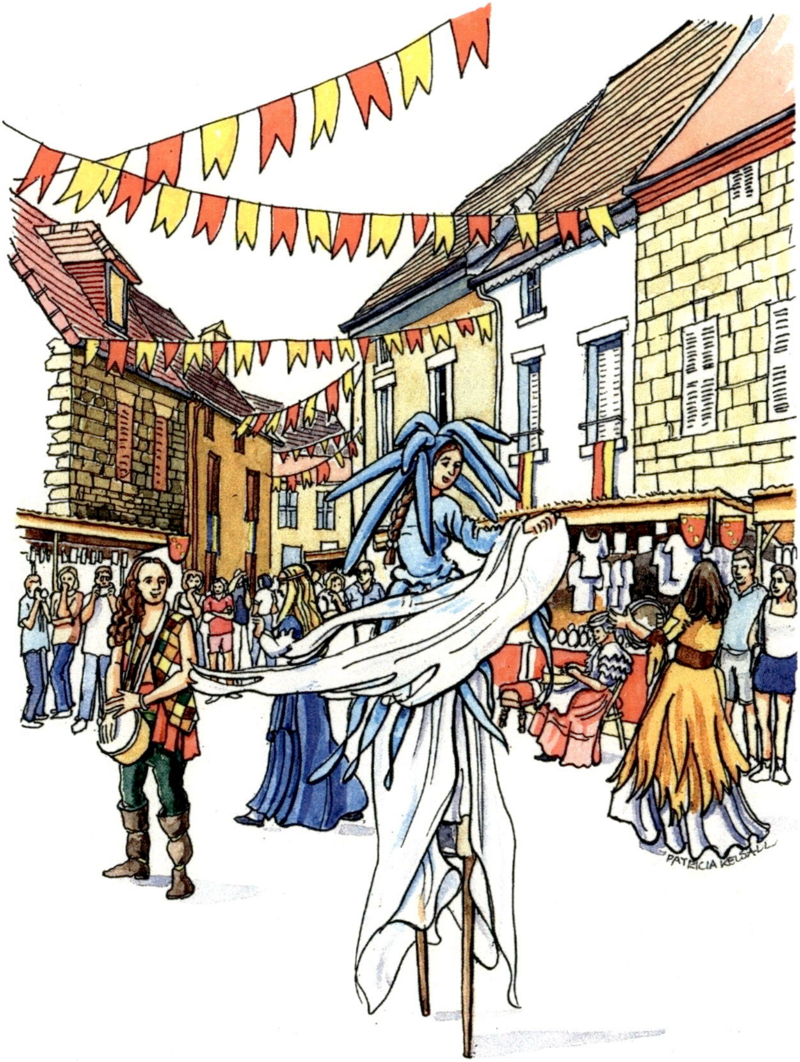

At the Marcheville medieval fair, drums and wind instruments heralded the arrival of a street theatre troupe, complete with a 'hunchback', a fool, a woman with an extraordinary headdress who was amazingly graceful on stilts, and various medieval characters.

than it had been at 4.30pm. But as we drove into St Paradis at 10.15pm, it was pouring again and flashes of lightning were illuminating the north eastern sky.

"Après nous, le déluge!" commented Jack, before we collapsed exhausted into bed.

Next day was *le quatorze juillet* – Bastille Day. We consulted the rain gauge in the garden. There had been 6mm of rain.

We drove down to the town for the ritual of the annual *brocante* (antiques-cum-junk fair) which was being held as always at the *salles de fêtes*. Jan and Beatrice had bought some really nice bargain pieces there, over the years, which now adorned their house as ornaments. We had never been before, but I wondered if it might be a good place to find a dresser. At least we could see if such an item of furniture existed in France.

We paid 10FF each at the entrance to the *salle des fêtes* and went in. The *brocante* was divided into two distinct parts. Inside were some authentic, beautiful and very expensive items – furniture, china, silver, eastern rugs – and some other pieces of furniture which even to my untutored eye looked to be too tarted-up to be worth the very high price tags on them. There were *armoires*, tables, bookcases and cupboards which seemed to have been stripped down, stained and revarnished with a modern polyurethane finish which was too red and garish to be quite right. They didn't have the patina of age and careful polishing. One ugly thing in dark brown wood was very odd. Its label stated that it was a 19th century cupboard incorporating doors made from 15th century carvings. We couldn't imagine the circumstances in which it had been made. Where had the carvings originated and who had vandalised them like this?

Outside, gazebos were dotted around the grounds, protecting their owners' stalls. At the very bottom of the market, sellers simply spread their wares on the grass. There was more furniture, of a lesser quality, and collectors' items like lovely old clothes, postcards and pictures, but it was mostly pure flea-market material. Stallholders were charging quite a lot of francs for broken and wormy stuff that even we would have thrown away (and we don't throw much away!). We wandered around under an umbrella, for it was drizzling with rain, which didn't really put us in the mood to buy anything.

We were disappointed – it would have been nice to have put a French dresser in the kitchen at St Paradis, but there was nothing like that available.

In the evening we walked down the field to water the transplanted tree and when we got back we found Georges had pushed a note under the front door inviting us to the annual village summertime meal, to be held a few days after we had left for home. Jan and Beatrice had often told us how much fun these communal events were and it was a shame that we would miss it.

While Jack worked next morning in the bathroom putting *lambris* on the airing cupboard and making a frame to support the shower, I dipped into two *Almanachs François* that we had found on the floor with lots of other old books and papers when we first took over the house. I had given them to Mother to read shortly afterwards and she had kept them in two paper bags inside a Boots polythene carrier bag labelled in blue biro "Anne's French books – funny ones". I had found them when I was going through her neatly annotated things.

The first was dated 1926 and was provided by a chemist in the nearby town, while the second was from 1938 and had been obtained from a pharmacy in Treignat, Allier. Their names had been overprinted on the front cover. Inside there were national advertisers, especially manufacturers of quack medicines, who sponsored the various bits. They were both essential reading for hypochondriacs. In the 1926 version the main ads were by sellers of purges, cough medicine, cold cures, piles treatments and medication for *menstruel coliques*, toothache, ulcers, anaemia and intestinal infections. There was even a very long dictionary of maladies and proprietary cures starting with *abees* (pus which forms in the tissues) to *vers* (worms), via *corps étranger dans l'oesophage* (foreign bodies in the oesophagus) and the purgative *Tisane des Quakers* (which, as a one-time Quaker, intrigued me).

Usually around July 14th there was a communal celebration in the town, and from our reading of the forthcoming events in a leaflet which Jan and Beatrice had shown us we expected there to be a medieval fair being held in the centre. We thought we would go down and have a look. When we got there, we found little evidence of it apart from bunting and some wooden stalls with thatched coverings. In the baker's we picked up a freesheet guide to summer in the Limousin and discovered that the fair was to be over the next two days.

Disappointed, we set off to one of the nearby bigger towns to buy some more *lambris* and the ingredients for the supper for Jan, Beatrice, Pieter and Dirk on Sunday. The branch of Stoc (bigger than our normal one) had a big sign in the foyer saying that opening hours had been extended from 9am to 7pm. We nearly had a heart attack. A French store in a provincial town that was going to be open during the sacred lunch time? Surely the end of the world was nigh?

We went to the *bricolage* next door first and then left it deliberately until after 12 noon to go into the supermarket, so that we could experience 'a first'. The shop was full of customers. So much for the universal retailing dictat that it isn't worth opening at lunchtimes because all French people are at home eating their meal. We hoped other stores would follow suit.

As we loaded our stuff into the car we watched two elderly men dismantling a heavy generator that they had just bought at the *bricolage*. They were attempting to reduce it to a sufficiently small number of pieces to fit on their two mobylettes. Jack thought that this looked a very dangerous exercise and would have offered immediately to transport it home for them, but decided not to on the grounds that the linguistic exercise would probably have been too much for everyone concerned.

In the afternoon we made a big policy decision. Ever since the plans first germinated in our minds for creating the bathroom, we had imagined it with tiles covering the walls completely. We had bought enough rectangular marbled beige tiles to do this in 1995 and they had lived in boxes in the barn ever since. We'd initially discovered a beige bathroom suite at a bargain price and everything else – the light brown floor tiles, wall tiles, beige soap racks and other ceramic extras we'd found in the meantime, had been bought to co-ordinate with it.

Then while I was watching Jack finish fitting plywood on the false wall hiding all the pipework, I had a flash of inspiration. I suddenly envisaged the bathroom as a shiny tiled box, quite out of keeping with the old house. I didn't like the prospect at all. It was much too modern and clinical. Was Marguerite trying to get through? She'd made her views very plain, telepathically, when we had planned the 'wrong sort' of light fittings in her old bedroom. We couldn't buy them anywhere. It seemed as if she had swept them off all the *bricolage* shelves. But we had immediately come across a sale of mock oil lamps which looked exactly right and they were at a price we couldn't miss. The bedroom had looked twice as nice when we had installed them.

I suggested to Jack that instead of tiling it, we should cover the bottom half of the wall in varnished *lambris* to match the airing cupboard. The pine would be equally waterproof and would have a much more rustic ambiance. He could use his woodworking tools to make a decorative wooden dado rail to cover up the join with the tiled surface.

"You might have said that before," said Jack. "We've just driven all that way to buy the *lambris* and we haven't got enough now."

He went downstairs to the workshop for a tool and came back smiling.

"I've found two more packs of *lambris* that were hiding behind the parasol box," he said. "We've got enough, after all."

Thank you, Marguerite!

Next morning was clear and sunny. I painted the inside of the airing cupboard with white silk emulsion after washing the old pink distemper off the wall. It looked very nice and clean.

Then we plucked up our courage to go to Crédit Agricole to open an account. The bank manager was charming and it was all quite simple. We beamed when he and his assistant said that we spoke French very nicely. They asked us to go back the next day with some bills addressed to ourselves to verify our address, and said that as we were due to leave the following week, they would send our cheque-book, card and PIN to England separately. We discovered that they had a marvellous machine in the foyer that would provide all sorts of information and print out bank statements at the touch of a finger. It was much more user-friendly and hi-tech than anything we had back in Cheshire.

At home, I went into the spare bedroom and found a lizard scuttling on the floor. Before I could do anything, it had vanished into a crack under the skirting board. I hoped it would be all right. I propped a thin plank of wood up against the open window so that it could climb out when I had gone. The gloss paint under the window was too shiny for lizards to get a grip on and they sometimes fell into the room if they were exploring the window ledge. They lived in the crevices in the front masonry.

At 5pm we went to the medieval fair, just as it started. There was plenty of space to park in the market place but it was filling up rapidly as we walked into the ancient heart of the town. Everyone had entered into the spirit of the occasion and we were delighted to see that flags had been strung across the front of a big house near the market place which has been empty for years. It's such a shame. Old photographs show it in its splendour as the home of a moneyed *bourgeois* owner, but now it has been divided into two and the unoccupied half is dingy and neglected, with peeling paint and missing window panes.

We bought a programme from the stall run by the organisers, the Friends of the Old Town. The old words were lovely, with resonances of long ago, promising *bateleurs* (tumblers) and *saltimbanques* (travelling acrobats). The attractions included street theatre, medieval music and dance, folk songs, craft exhibitions and demonstrations, and a big firework display on the last night. The literature said that the Friends had been founded in 1975 and since then had put up old-style street lamps, repaired the wooden panelling in the church, restored a 19th century *lavoir*, reconstructed the wells in the market place, and rescued a 15th century house which they were in the middle of restoring. In addition, they had organised 12 medieval fêtes, eight night-time extravaganzas and three medieval markets – which made one major event a year since their inception. It was all a remarkable achievement for the inhabitants of such a small place.

We felt quite out of style in our 20th century summer clothes. A large number of adults, children and even toddlers were wending their way to the fair dressed in approximations of medieval garb

– with incongruous touches such as glasses worn under wimples, and mobile phones being operated by men in short velvet skirts and tights.

The narrow streets of the medieval centre were lined with thatched stalls, selling local produce from the farms, beautiful crafts, especially jewellery of all kinds, and some wonderful hand-made lace. It was a nice contrast with the 'tat' which was usually for sale at the twice-yearly horse fair. All the stallholders were in costume. We bought a big jar of honey from a beekeeper from a nearby village who syphoned samples from plastic containers on to tiny spoons for us to taste, and some local apple juice after a *dégustation* from several good-sized glasses of different varieties of *pommes*. I hung my nose over some pretty bead necklaces. Everything was refreshingly non-commercial.

Drums and wind instruments heralded the arrival of a street theatre troupe, complete with a 'hunchback', a fool, a woman with an extraordinary headdress who was amazingly graceful on stilts, and various medieval characters including a large lascivious dame in a shapeless brown dress obviously unsupported by any modern foundation garments. They all descended into the crowds of spectators who had gathered where the road widened out in front of the church, to elicit audience participation. We thought this could be embarrassing for us, as we didn't understand a word but could gather that the plot of the play was extremely earthy and anyone singled out was expected to say something rude and witty. Our confused contributions would not have added to the general hilarity, so we stood behind a woman with a frightened Alsatian on the grounds that the players wouldn't venture too close in case it bit them. We weren't the only ones hoping not to be drawn into the badinage. A prim-faced resident of one of the old houses marched straight through the crowds, looking neither to the right nor to the left, aiming to get home without being tainted by the frivolity. She didn't know that the 'fool' was following in her wake, making faces and gestures at her.

It all looked so authentic in the medieval setting of the church square. There was bunting everywhere and painted heraldic signs on many of the buildings throughout the old quarter. We were impressed by the trouble and expense that people had gone to.

The local theatrical costumier must have had a field day. One mother was there in full costume, hand-in-hand with her small boy who was dressed as a Crusader, complete with painted silver sword.

After the strolling players had moved on, the local children stood on the steps of the church and sang traditional folk songs. Householders had created taverns in their outbuildings which, though empty at 5.30pm, we guessed would be full and raucous at midnight.

It was all quite magical. In spite of the many incongruities, we could imagine similar scenes in the town 500 years ago. Human nature hasn't changed that much...

On the way back to the car, we stopped off at the *Syndicat d'Initiative* (tourist information office), which we had rarely seen open, and had a long chat with the woman in charge. I picked up samples of all the relevant leaflets and we bought a video about the attractions of the Creuse, which we thought we could leave for friends who might stay at the house and were looking for ideas for visits.

Back at home, I began to read about the history of the town which was detailed in some of the leaflets. It was fascinating, especially as I could now imagine it in pseudo-medieval mode. It was extraordinary to imagine so much happening in 'our' much-loved but seemingly insignificant little place.

I won't mention the town's real name because I desperately don't want to 'do a Peter Mayle' to St Paradis. For the purposes of this book, let's call it "Marcheville" – a town in the Marche area of the Limousin. I think the history is worth sharing because most of us British (me included) don't know anything about how French political history affected the ordinary people, who were pawns of royalty and the land-owning aristocracy, especially in the Middle Ages. The poor citizens often had a pretty bloody time – in all connotations of the word.

Marcheville was described as an old and important fortified stronghold where a town developed around a defensive promontory, which still exists. In aerial photographs you can see clearly where the original settlement was. The Comtes de la Marche had a *château* there and they constructed the church in the 13th century. In 1265 the inhabitants obtained a charter from Comte Hugues VII de Lusignan, defining their rights and duties, and this was confirmed by Hugues VIII in 1279. All was not well though. A large part of the town was destroyed by the English during the Hundred Years War and was rebuilt by Bernard and Jacques d'Armagnac. In 1424 Jacques II de Bourdon, Comte de la Marche, King of Hungary and Sicily, gave the vast forest of Marcheville to the town, which was then surrounded by ramparts flanked with six towers and pierced by four gates. King Charles VII visited Marcheville in 1441.

The 16th century was obviously a time to be well away from Marcheville. In 1545 the town was devastated by a fire and in 1564 it was ravaged by the plague. In 1573 it was pillaged by Swiss mercenaries during the Wars of Religion and in 1592 it was put under siege for six months by the troops of Henri IV.

The 17th and 18th centuries, by contrast, seemed to represent its heyday. Marcheville developed its role as a commercial and 'distribution' centre because it was handily placed at a natural geographical crossroads where products and services were in transit from the south of France to Paris, and from east to west. From this area industrial products, cattle and the famous masons travelled north, together with wines from the Auvergne. The bi-monthly fairs were renowned nationally and regionally. It was also an administrative centre with a brigade of mounted *gendarmes* and served as winter quarters for the military. It had a post office for letters and was a stopping-off point for stage coaches. Marcheville accommodated 700-800 souls who formed the bourgeoisie of *prévôts*, state prosecutors, barristers, *notaires*, and bailiffs – some of whom were Freemasons.

After the Revolution in 1789 much of its administrative role was transferred to another ancient town some 20 kilometres away. At the beginning of the 20th century Marcheville tried to maintain and develop its commercial activities and looked to the improvement of public health by providing a water supply. In 1902 the famous horse fairs were started which are still the most important in France today.

It made our English home-village of Hartford seem quite boring in comparison. It does have Roman origins, being like

Marcheville on a historic main road. Hartford was mentioned in the Domesday Book and was the site of a skirmish in the Civil War, but after that its main claim to fame is as the first village in England to have street lighting powered by electricity, and as an almost colonial 'company town' for ICI management in the early to middle 20th century. Rape, pillage and siege have never been mentioned, though I suppose the inhabitants suffered during the Black Death like everyone else. Come to think of it, I do remember reading of murderous Welsh brigands infesting nearby Delamere Forest during the 14th century... Perhaps medieval life everywhere was traditionally 'nasty, brutish and short'.

Our appetites whetted by reading the history, we decided to round off our day by watching the video we'd bought at the *Syndicat d'Initiative*. It had pretty photographs on the box and we were looking forward to a colourful educational trip round the region. We were rather disappointed. The content was fascinating and the background music catchy, but whatever we did to it, it came out in black and white. Jack was sure that it shouldn't but admitted that his calculations about the relationship between the video recorder and the English TV set might have been wrong. We smiled that we had been so foolish as to buy a real black and white film as our original experiment, so that the problem had not been apparent.

Next morning, in bright sunshine, we drove down to the bank with a collection of official documents to prove that we lived at the address we'd said. The bank manager photocopied them but also took them as an indication that we wanted to have them paid by direct debit from the new account. He filled out the appropriate forms for us, and although the debits were currently being done for us by Société Générale, we signed them and paid a lump sum of money into the account to cover the next lot of them that we expected.

Jack worked on the bathroom and I pottered about. After lunch he bent over the woodworking machine, with no exertion whatsoever, and felt his back 'go'. This was very frustrating and he lay down on the bed for most of the afternoon to try to ward off any ill effects. It was ironic that he never hurt his back, which was pretty vulnerable nowadays, doing anything strenuous.

We were delighted to see Paul being brought home from hospital and went over to see him after allowing an appropriate length of time for him to have a rest. We'd been keeping in regular touch with Elisabeth and it was lovely to see him back in his kitchen garden with his son, chatting and picking some of the vegetables which had been maturing in his absence. He was relatively full of beans – certainly in comparison with how he'd been when he went into the clinic. Later Hugo, Harriet and Anne-Marie arrived, and we left after a decent interval so that he didn't have too many people to deal with at once. St Paradis never seemed complete when he wasn't there.

In the late evening we drove down to Marcheville to watch the free firework display which was the culmination of the medieval celebrations. The sky was pitch-black. We weren't sure where the display would be let off, or where the audience would be, so we parked on the outskirts of the town on the edge of what must have been the medieval moat and started to walk in. Then we saw a lot of people just sitting down along the side of the road beside their cars and decided to follow suit. Jack's back was pretty uncomfortable and the thought of a long trek both ways – just to get a bit closer to fireworks which we would be able to watch in the sky anyway – was not appealing. In the distance we could see a constant stream of many hundreds of people, perhaps even a few thousand, walking through the medieval centre, across the moat and then sitting in rows on the curved embankment on the other side, as it reached round to the left and out of our sight. This snaking procession of spectators continued unabated for nearly threequarters of an hour. Some of them were in medieval costume which lent the scene a timeless atmosphere.

At about 11.15pm loud drum and tambour music eerily filled the air. The drumbeat could have come from anywhere across the world and was almost primeval. It made the hairs stand up on the back of our necks.

For the next 15 minutes, the commentator worked up the crowd and got so excited sometimes that we thought he was going to reach the heights of sexual ecstasy. The fireworks, when they started, were very spectacular and must have cost the little community a fortune. There were lots like the ones at Portsmouth the previous year, which shoot up into the sky with a whoosh and then burst into a sparkling coloured ball. The accompanying music included *Land of Hope and Glory, Summertime, The Ride of the Valkyries* and extracts from *Cosi Fan Tutte*, all played full blast on a public address system with a fabulous mellow tone. We were too far round the old defensive promontory to see the fireworks being let off but we could see a fiery glow from the low-level ones and imagine how they must look against the medieval backdrop.

Sitting on the edge of the road, watching the figures in the distance bathed in the light from the fireworks, we thought of the siege, fire and pillage that the ancient town had suffered and the people who had died there through wars or pestilence. The cheers and shouts from the crowd in response to the announcer could have belonged to their forebears listening to a rabble-rouser in the 1500s. It was a strangely moving and spooky experience.

The spectacle lasted about 25 minutes and then the mass exodus began. We were pleased that we had only to step back into the nearby car and drive home to bed. As we drove past the fields of cattle, we wondered what they had made of all the noise. Our dogs would have been terrified.

We were cutting wood in the barn at about 10am when Michel hurried across and said urgently: "There's something wrong with Paul!"

We followed him over to Paul's garden and found him leaning against the gate with his eyes closed, his right hand over his heart and his left arm out at a funny angle against the gate. We all thought he'd had a heart attack. I took his left hand gently, stroked his cheek and asked if he was all right. He opened his eyes, smiled and said that he was just having a little sleep. Poor Michel was enormously relieved. I'm sure he thought he had lost his old friend. Later in the day, Paul came across to the house dressed in his smartest clothes, asking if we would have some of the *haricots verts* which were now ready in his vegetable garden. He also gave us some plums and a lettuce. Our St Paradis friends were so generous with their fresh produce in the summer that there was often no need to buy any vegetables in the shops.

We worked on the bathroom and out in the garden, where I turned the hay we'd cut earlier. By noon it was 37°C on the front wall but there was also a slight breeze which made it very pleasant to sit out in the shade at the back of the house.

When I went up into our bedroom, I discovered a lizard under the wash basin. I wondered if it was the same one I'd seen before, which had ventured deeper into the house rather than climbing back up the plank. I didn't want it to starve, so I managed to shoo it into a big cardboard box and took it downstairs to show Jack. He went down the back steps and released it into the garden.

A moment or two later he came to me, looking worried.

"I've just realised that I've done something silly," he said. "If that was the lizard that came in through the spare bedroom window, it'll be a 'front lizard' and I've just put it in the back garden with the 'back lizards'. Do you think it will ever be able to find its way home?"

As the day wore on the weather changed. There was the unmistakable feeling of a storm brewing with lots of thunder and a massive wind that whipped the winged seedpods off the trees and sent them swirling everywhere like miniature helicopters. No rain arrived to break the spell.

Jan, Beatrice, Pieter and Dirk came for supper. Jan and Beatrice brought us a delightful lavender sachet, while the men handed me a gorgeous bunch of dark red and yellow dahlias just picked from their garden and a jar of apricot jam homemade by Dirk.

I'd cooked a green lime curry but it wasn't as good as the ones I do regularly at home in England because I couldn't obtain all the ingredients I needed. We had goat cheese, sliced tomatoes and cucumber, served with vinaigrette dressing, for starters; curry for the main course; a big choice of cheeses next, and champagne sorbet and ice cream for dessert.

As it was the first meal Pieter and Dirk had eaten with us, I wanted it to be a nice occasion, especially as their stylish hospitality was legendary. I didn't want to let the Loader side down. I used my mother's best cutlery for the first time – it was a fine bone-handled set that she had inherited from her own parents and had been a retirement gift to my grandfather. It's lovely but there are only six place settings and I could have done with some more forks. I had to keep collecting them up and washing them in the *arrière cuisine* between courses. I was sure my mother had used them for dinner parties with more than six guests, perhaps she and Daddy had done a 'family hold back' exercise and surreptitiously used the everyday cutlery themselves. In France, we usually use a stainless steel set from IKEA augmented by other cheap cutlery bought for our caravan in the days when we took the boys away to canoeing competitions each weekend. We also didn't have enough matching big plates or middling-sized plates for starters. The crockery we had at St Paradis consisted of the 30-year-old remains of our Wedgwood earthenware wedding present service, augmented with bits and bobs of different designs from other long-defunct dinner services. Pieter and Dirk offered us some extra plates they had at home, from the days when they'd organised working parties of friends to help them clean out the house and had needed to feed a dozen or more people at a time.

They invited us round for coffee in the morning to meet the donkeys and look at the house. We confirmed that they were about a couple of years younger than us: Dirk was almost 48 and Pieter was 53. Dirk continued to work part-time in the Netherlands for the Dutch Government, commuting from France for half the week. To anyone living in Britain that was a mind-boggling concept, but the excellent continental train services made it quite possible. We learned it was cheaper to buy a return ticket from La Souterraine to The Hague than from Hartford to London – and Dirk got a sleeping compartment thrown in for the price, as well.

After they'd gone, we did the washing up and Jack scraped the label off the oven door. It had only been on there for five years! We had forgotten to take it off before we used the oven for the first time and it was well and truly baked on. Then, as it hadn't rained, he took the bucket of waste water out to the geraniums on the kitchen window ledge and the clematis by the donkey stable. As he poured the water into the geranium planter he felt something under his foot and wondered what squashy thing we had dropped in front of the window. As he raised his foot to see, there was a scuffle and a very large – and very upset – toad lumbered away as fast as it could and hid behind the stone seat nearby.

At 12.30am it was still 24°C outside and very sultry.

When we woke at 7.15am, after a night spent sleeping under only a sheet, it was raining and we could hear a lot of thunder as interference on the radio. When he checked the digital thermometer, Jack found that it was 21.3°C outside and 22.6°C inside, both the highest temperatures we'd noted at this time in the morning. The relative humidity was 67%.

The rain continued and we worked on the bathroom. It had been so dry previously that even 5mm of rain did not wet the ground significantly.

At 11.30am we went round to Pieter and Dirk, armed with carrots for the donkeys. We were absolutely bowled over by the house, which is of course their main residence now rather than just a holiday home. It has been built into the side of a hill and they think it dates back to 1830. It was in an awful state when they bought it, but it had once been loved and had been 'done up' about 40 years previously, when central heating had been installed. Under the ownership of the two Dutchmen, it has been exquisitely renovated by skilled local craftsmen and furnished with great taste. We could only marvel at what they had achieved. They told us that many years ago, pigs had been kept in what is now the kitchen and that the space between the upper floor and the ceiling had been full of dead rats and husks of corn. The attic had been dreadful. Everything everywhere had been filthy – much dirtier and more repulsive than our dear old house which had at least retained its dignity under the cobwebs and grime. We had bought a basically handsome house with an existing strong character, while they had bought a more ordinary house in a beautiful setting and created a stunning character for it.

We met the two dogs, a fox terrier and an elderly white Jack Russell with a sweet little face, and the two cats, one tabby and one black and white. The tabby had been thrown out of a car in Holland when she was seven months old and pregnant. Pieter had found her and given her a home for the night, then put her out again. Dirk had said: "I liked that little cat..." and, as if she had known, she came back again. Then she began to fill up with fluid. The foetuses inside her had not developed properly. Pieter and Dirk saved her life by paying for her to be operated on by the vet and then kept her. They were obviously very good with pets – one of their previous cats had lived to be 22 years old! The black and white cat was the boss of the household and Pieter said she had recently beaten up a dog which had been pestering the Jack Russell.

The doves lived in a big cage in an old building which had been used as a garage until very recently when Pieter and Dirk had bought a large stone barn on the other side of the narrow lane to the right of the house. Their property now occupied a complete T-junction, overlooking the lake. On the left, their land was bounded by a river, which had been dammed a thousand years before to form the lake. From time to time, the owner would harvest it in the traditional way by 'pulling the plug out', emptying the lake and removing the fish. The big ones would be taken away in a lorry while the small ones went into a special reservoir, presumably to be returned when the lake refilled. On the other side of the little river from their boundary were the remains of a watermill, without its wheel. From the roadside it looked like just another farm building, but closer inspection revealed that it went down a long way and still had its mill mechanism inside.

We walked up the field to talk to the donkeys, two young females of different breeds. The pasture was divided into three by an electric fence, to optimise the grazing. The smaller of the two donkeys was frightened of strangers and wouldn't take the rather rubbery carrot from my hand, but the larger one was happy to be bribed to say 'hello'. I thought of the donkeys which were for sale at the Marcheville horse fairs. They always looked so vulnerable and tugged my heartstrings. Perhaps we would renovate and reuse our own donkey stables…

Dirk showed us his garden where he grew vegetables, herbs and flowers. This was where the dahlias had come from. He gave us some garlic bulbs that we could divide and sow in pots in our own relatively primitive garden.

Then we all sat outside admiring the peaceful panorama, drinking *kir* that Dirk had made from their homegrown raspberries and eating a cake that he'd baked that morning. Afterwards, Jack and I immediately agreed that it was one of the most lovely places we'd ever been. The two Dutchmen had created a perfect haven.

No wonder Dirk didn't mind commuting all the way to The Hague.

We worked in the bathroom and garden over the next couple of days. It was vital that at least the bath should be useable when some good friends came to borrow the house in a few weeks' time, so we had to knuckle down seriously. At this point we had a wash basin in our bedroom which the occupants there could use, and a sink in the *arrière cuisine* for the person in the spare bedroom – or a china bowl and jug if they preferred to revert to prewar sanitary arrangements. The loo downstairs served everyone.

On the third day, in spite of intermittent rain, we tackled the fencing using the posts that Georges had so kindly put in for us. It was surprisingly easy to fix the barbed wire – a job we hadn't done since we had worked at the riding school with Jack's cousin Joyce as teenagers. Jack anchored the wire to a big tree on the right-hand side of the back garden, and then to the corner post at the other end, put in a tensioner, tensioned the wire with a hammer and attached it to the posts, then screwed up the tensioner until it was taut. Then we turned the corner back towards the barn and did the same again. We had positioned the wire 113cm high off the ground and then we just stapled it on to the split oak posts at this height. We did the same with the next strand, 37cm below the first one. It was all nicely neat and the task was very aesthetically pleasing. We continued until we had run out of wire. As it stood, a calf could duck under the wire, but a cow couldn't. One more strand was needed all round at the lowest level.

Then we went over to the wood where we selected two tall thin trees, about 14ft high, to use as a temporary barrier across the new garden entrance until we could fit a proper farm gate. We dragged them through the wood and loaded them into the back of the car for easy transportation. While we were doing this, there were the most hilarious squirting, wind-breaking and peeing 'noises off' from the cattle in the neighbouring field as they were uniformly and constantly incontinent – 'firing on all cylinders' you might say. The funniest thing was that we couldn't see what was happening – as country people we wouldn't have found that amusing, just natural – it was the Monty Pythonesque sound effects which were so side-splitting.

And talking of comical things: we christened the bath that night. We had got the bathroom to the point where there was tiling around all the parts where water might be splashed. So we waited until 12.30am for the grout to dry between the row of tiles round the bath, and I climbed in. I was a bit reticent because we had no curtains and I felt psychologically exposed. Jack teased me unmercifully. Did I really think that the assorted perverts of St Paradis and district were going to line up at the bottom of the field after midnight for a fleeting glance at my naked body? Actually, they needn't have bothered, they could just have waited for the film to come out and posted it on the Internet.

For as I luxuriated in the first bath at St Paradis in five years, I heard the landing floorboards creak and looked up to find Jack peering round the door, video camera in hand.

"We have to immortalise this historic moment," he said. "Stick a flannel over your boobs and move your knee a bit and then you'll be quite decent!"

We left the water in the bath and then drained it away into the back garden the next morning via some special yellow plastic pipe we had 'liberated' from the skip when our next door neighbours in Hartford were having their house improved. The ground just soaked all the water up greedily, leaving barely a trace. The soil must have been extremely dry.

We went to the *départemental* capital to do some shopping and bank visiting, then on the way home on the main road we saw a man standing by his car at the end of a lane on the left and some *gendarmes* on the right. A few yards farther along was another man, also beside his vehicle at a road coming in from the left. Then we saw small groups of people strung out along the road wherever there was a house or a crossroads. We wondered if we should wave grandly as we went past and became more and more consumed with curiosity. When we got home we looked up the regional diary of summer events and discovered that it was the *Tour Cycliste National de la Creuse*. Presumably the cyclists had been due to race by shortly after we passed.

After lunch we went out into the garden and finished the

fencing with a roll of barbed wire we'd just purchased. Now, not even the smallest calves would be able to venture into the garden.

We had lots of neighbours visiting to say goodbye, as we were due to leave at lunchtime the following day. Jack mowed the 'lawn' at the back so that it should be as short as possible when our friends arrived, and we looked proudly at the wilderness we'd tamed.

Paul and Elisabeth came round for their customary 'last night' supper. Paul's improvement had continued and it was great to see 'our French father', as we called him, in such good form. He was almost his old self again. He was very polite about the vegetable soup I had made for him using the vegetables he had given us from his own garden, and chuckled at the carefully-posed video of me in the bath.

It was hard to pack up and go back to Cheshire. We couldn't stay any longer because I was due to do some part-time temporary work for a local borough council for seven weeks while their press officer was away. It was a job I enjoyed and the money would be handy. Jack was going to hold the fort for the publishing venture while I was away.

Thanks to Jack's retirement this had been our longest visit to St Paradis and we felt as at home in the Limousin as we did in Hartford. It was as though we had two parallel lives – an English life and a French life – and we could slip effortlessly between the two. We longed for the day when the French life could be extended to at least six months of the year.

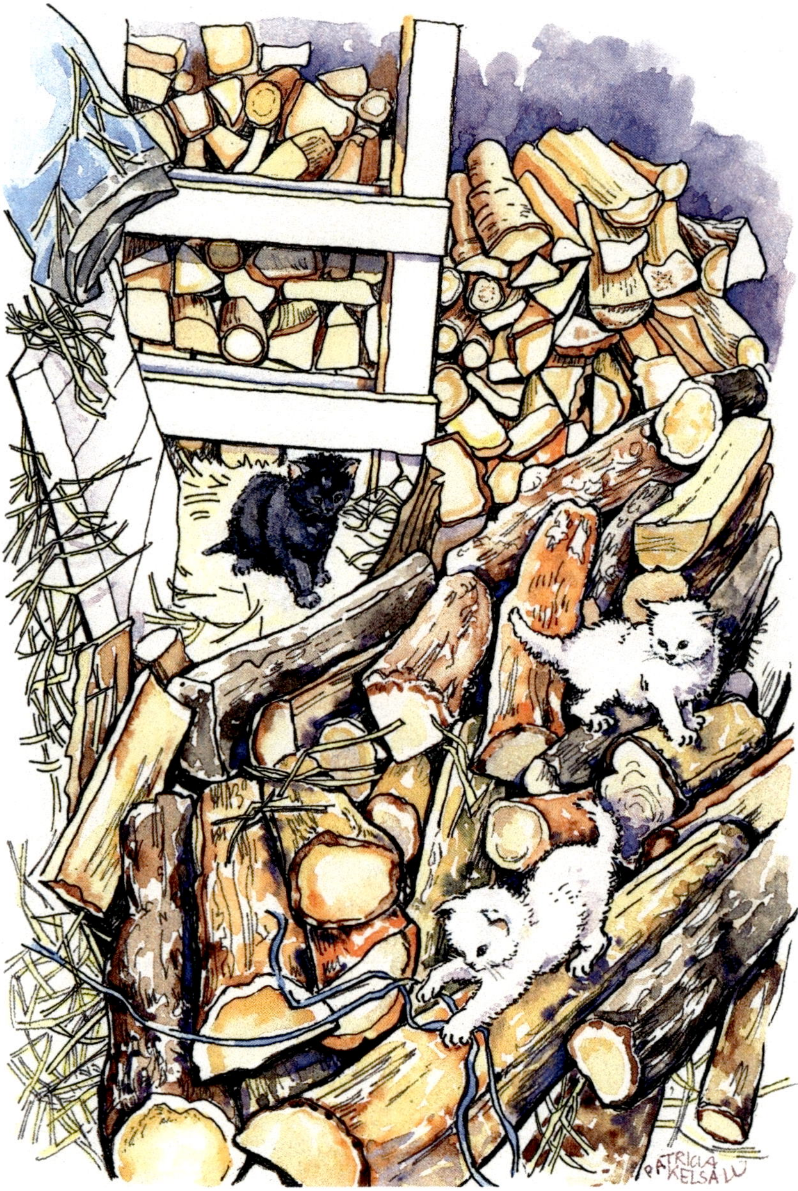

We're not 'cat people' but we couldn't help but be captivated by the delightful little kittens who had made their home in the barn.

Chapter Eight – October 1999
Happily in Harness

Poor Jack. On July 26, the day I started at the borough council, and the first day of his non-French 'new life' he was confined to bed, unable to move. His back had 'gone'. It was a result of driving 1000km home from France with a spine that was already grumbling pretty loudly about having its warning twinges ignored. I had to set off at 7.45am leaving him in bed with a portable phone to ring the osteopath and a notepad to take Léonie Press messages. I felt guilty and disloyal.

Everyone said that it was a direct result of retirement and extremely common. The build-up to retirement, they explained, is so great that when it actually happens the body allows itself to have all sorts of things go wrong that it hasn't had time to suffer from before.

Jack disputed this stoutly, but it took him a fortnight before he was right again. He had a relapse after a week when he took his trousers off at bedtime and collapsed in an agonised heap on the bed.

It was a very strange role reversal to have him as a 'house-husband' with no salary coming in, and me going out earning, leaving home at 7.45am and getting back at about 2.30pm. He is very self-sufficient but he had never spent much time alone in the house without me before. I was horrified to discover one day, when he remarked that he'd had a very nice lunch of *pâté* and salad sandwiches, that the *pâté* was some I had bought for Auntie before we set off for France a month previously. I hadn't realised that she had left it in the back of the fridge, uneaten. We hoped he wouldn't get food poisoning to add to his problems.

When his back was better, we went on a spending spree with a little of his early retirement money. We bought a new turbo vacuum cleaner, a Panasonic breadmaker (on Chris and Linda's recommendation), a new stair carpet, an antique pine Welsh dresser for St Paradis and a new king-size bed for Hartford, comprising a hard and a soft single mattress, side by side. A soft mattress made Jack's back worse, and a hard one made my back hurt. The vast new bed – which measured 6ft across – was the answer and it had added room for any dogs that might want to join us in the mornings.

We still didn't really feel right about his retirement and our partnership in Léonie Press until I had finished my temporary job and we were at home together all the time. Then we breathed a big sigh of relief and settled down happily in harness.

In August, while we were in England, our friends Peter and Vivien Wilson, and Vivien's mother 83-year-old Lenna Bickerton, borrowed the house at St Paradis for a holiday. Lenna was our first Léonie Press author and she had always wanted to see the places I had described in the St Paradis books. She loved the hamlet and the peaceful, welcoming atmosphere of the old house. Lenna died suddenly a few months later but photographs of her enjoying herself at St Paradis are published in a memorial edition of her first book, *Memories of a Cheshire Childhood*, and in her second book, *We'll gather lilacs...*, which was published posthumously. We were very pleased that she was so happy there.

In September we went to Biot, near Antibes, to stay with our old friends, Roger and Eileen Williamson, in their mobile home. It was another case of *"après nous, le déluge"*. They'd had a glorious heatwave until the day we arrived. We managed to fit in one swim in the campsite pool, then it poured with torrential rain non-stop for three days. We were beginning to get a complex about our effect on the French weather. Nevertheless, we had a lovely holiday just being tourists and sightseers. At St Paradis we simply felt like householders and were ashamed of our ignorance of most of the local beauty spots.

We left for the Limousin for another two and a half weeks on Tuesday, October 5 – the day of the Paddington rail disaster. We were due back on October 22 for Jack's ICI 30 years' long service dinner that night (his 30 years had been up in April but the dinner had been a trifle delayed!). Auntie couldn't come because she was waiting for a hospital appointment and Jack's mother, now

91, maintained that she would be quite all right on her own. Alex promised to visit her at the weekends when he came home from Kent, and the neighbours were on full alert. The pups went off as usual to our dear friends who usually look after them, and their mother Sally was deputed to keep Granny company.

We had a stress-free trip to Portsmouth with the trailer but were surprised to be stopped on the docks for a security check, for the first time in all our years of travelling to France. We were asked if it was our own car, if we had packed it ourselves and if we were carrying offensive weapons such as knives, guns or CS gas. We declared ourselves as pure as the driven snow but afterwards Jack wondered if he should have mentioned the chainsaw! We were mightily relieved not to have had to unpack the car or trailer.

Once on the ferry, we dumped our bags in our cabin and went to see what had happened to the old duty-free shop. I bought an embroidered tee-shirt in a sale in the boutique that I'd fancied on previous trips, pleased that the price had been reduced. Then we had a look round the main shop and were very disappointed. There was an awful lot of rubbish in there and the alcohol was only being sold VAT-free when the ship was outside British waters. Even then, the prices were merely comparable with those we would have paid in French supermarkets.

It was dark when we disembarked at 7.10am at Le Havre and we soon encountered thick patchy fog. It didn't cause us any real problems but brought a very rapid and strange dawn – above the fog the sky was completely clear but it was thick enough to obscure the sun completely. We drove into enveloping fog in the dark and when we emerged the sun was fully up and it was very bright, so the change from apparent night to day was very fast.

At Orléans we stopped at Carrefour, where a man was going round the cars begging. Perhaps unkindly, we pretended that we didn't speak French and walked on. I wanted to buy some new crockery. During this holiday we would have three friends staying with us to help Jack start to build the terrace, and I wanted to have a complete matching dinner service so that the meals looked attractive. Pieter and Dirk had given us about 20 old dinner plates, as they'd promised, but I wanted something a bit better for our guests.

While Jack searched for a beard trimmer (I'd forgotten his again), I scanned the shelves for a pretty design and found exactly what I was looking for in attractive thin porcelain. The pattern depicted ripe autumn fruit on a sky blue background. The price was more than I had intended to pay but the quality was so good that the 30-piece boxed service was a real bargain at 599FF. There would be five of us, so we would have one of everything spare, I reasoned.

It was a beautiful day but at 17°C just a comfortable temperature for long-distance travelling. We arrived at St Paradis at 4.45pm to find that Paul had opened the shutters and some of the windows, and had lit a fire in the Godin so that the kitchen was warm and cheerful.

As we unloaded the car and started on the trailer, Hugo, Harriet and Peachy turned up to visit Elisabeth and Paul. When we'd finished we went over to join them. Paul was cheerful and pleased to see us but his skin had become paper-thin, like my mother's, and he had to be careful not to let the young dog scratch him. He was pleased that the doctor had said he could drink two glasses of red wine a day, and poured us some, too.

After a quick supper of chicken in white sauce, potatoes, *flageolets* and baby carrots, chocolate *éclairs* and a glass of Cahors wine, Jack set up the laptop computer and tried to send some e-mails. It was essential that we keep in touch with everyone at home, not only because of the book sales, but because we wanted to monitor how Granny was managing.

In the morning the alarm went off at seven but we went back to sleep until eight. It had been a cold night with frost on the field and a heavy dew. We had grown to like our ultra-wide bed at home in Hartford but it was nice to cuddle up in the middle of a conventional one again, especially one that had been warmed up by an electric blanket. We hadn't got round to installing such a luxury on the mega-bed, but it would be very necessary when we returned to England at the end of October.

After a late breakfast we measured up outside for the dimensions and depth of the terrace and Jack did some quantity surveying.

We decided it was too late to go to the local Stoc (which didn't open at lunchtime) and neighbouring builders' merchants so we cleaned up the corner where the new Welsh dresser would go, when we had assembled it, and vacuumed up some of the worst cobwebs in the kitchen.

We noticed that the kitchen window seemed to be very smeared, so I went outside with some glass cleaner to remove the marks. While I was there I heard some mewing from the barn and saw a tiny tortoiseshell kitten by the hole at the bottom of the door to Jack's workshop. It was sweet but disappeared in a furry brown flash as soon as it saw me. Paul had mentioned the previous evening that there were five kittens in the barn, and when Lenna and her family had returned from their holiday she had spoken of a wild white one that had hissed at them. Their mother was a feral white cat which we often saw prowling in the field and less often spotted high in the hayloft where she lived.

Lunch was pretty meagre as we had banked on shopping during the morning and had very few ingredients. At 2.15pm we set off for the builders' merchants, then Jack discovered we had left the exercise book containing his list of materials in the kitchen. We had passed Mme Echelle's son by the church talking to two friends and done the usual greetings, then we had to drive past him again a few minutes later, waving and pointing to the book, and feeling rather silly! This was a different merchant from the one where we had finally obtained the stainless steel flue, and he specialised in bulk things like the sand, gravel, breeze blocks and cement that we required. We were immediately delighted to see that he had two English Setters, a mother and daughter, who made a fuss of us, and a yapping Westie that wouldn't come near. He and his wife were very helpful and promised to deliver our order within the next two days.

Then we went to Stoc where we bought enough food to last us about five days. At the end of one aisle we gave way to a French woman and her very elderly companion. Afterwards we heard them talking about *"les étrangers"*, which was rather a blow as we had only said: *"Après vous, Madame…"*. Perhaps native French people don't give way with such diffidence! At the checkout we remembered that we had forgotten to buy some ice cream, so Jack went back for it while I wheeled the trolley out and packed the car. A tiny old man who was leaning against the next car in the car park struck up quite a long conversation, initially asking what our GB sticker meant and if the country was a member of the European Union. Eventually he said I spoke very good French, and his charm made me feel ashamed because at first I had wondered if he was a beggar. I thought it would be funny if he was waiting for the woman who had made the remarks in the store! Even he knew about the Paddington rail disaster, which had apparently been top of the French news bulletins.

At home I unpacked all the shopping while Jack mowed the grass at the front so that the house looked respectable once more. I'd made him take some homeopathic arnica tablets, as recommended by the osteopath, to protect his back, before he began. When he went round to the back garden the mower gave up and refused to start, then the brushcutter went on strike too. He began to feel the victim of a conspiracy but eventually after the application of some "Loader engineering" the wayward mower worked again and eventually transformed the pasture-like area into a semblance of a lawn.

Before we went to bed, Jack put all the ingredients into the breadmaker to bake a wholemeal loaf by 7.30am, and switched on the timer. We had used the machine we bought with his retirement money every few days since we had purchased it and it had become a fixed part of our daily lives. We had brought it with us to France so that we could have fresh bread for breakfast without having to drive into the town to buy it, or wait for the *boulanger's* van to call. Its products were delicious – much nicer than anything we could buy in England. I had declined to get involved with this mechanical breadmaking, on the grounds that it was chemistry, rather than cookery, and thus not within my remit. Why have a PhD on hand and do it yourself? Jack enjoyed experimenting with the proportions of different flours and ingredients, and usually his efforts were excellent.

We woke up to the intoxicating smell of fresh bread permeating up into our bedroom from the kitchen through the gaps in the floorboards. Outside it was getting pretty autumnal, with a temperature of 5.9°C but the kitchen registered a very acceptable 19.1°C and the fire had kept in all night in the big Godin.

We had our nice new bread for breakfast, finding that the only problem was the bread knife. It was one we had received as a wedding present in 1969 which we had rejected in Hartford for being too blunt. It could saw through crusty French bread quite well, but wasn't suitable for a moist new-baked wholemeal loaf. Scratches on the door and excited whimpering meant that we had our usual breakfast-time visitors, Gitane and Soupette. They knew we were a soft touch for something appetising. We gave them some cereal which had gone off during the summer and they were very pleased. Then we went out to the barn and cleared a space in the left-hand side so that the builders' merchant could put sacks of cement in there, where it was dry. The barn is of a standard Limousin design, with haylofts over cattle stalls on either side of a high central part, where the farmer could fit a threshing machine or a large cart loaded with hay or straw. We keep the car in this big middle bit, and the logs for firewood are stacked against the wall at the back. On this occasion there was an additional pile of logs in there which had been delivered in our absence by a farmer friend of Hugo's to supplement our stocks. We buy it by the *corde*, which in the Creuse is four cubic metres, but in other parts of the country the volume represented by the expression is different.

We saw two little white kittens and a black one, playing on the pile of new wood. We'd mentioned the kitten I'd seen the previous day to Elisabeth and she'd told us that the litter was about two months old. We're not 'cat people' but we couldn't help but be captivated by the delightful little creatures. We stayed still and quiet so that they didn't see us as a threat. They ventured off the wood and darted round the car and the lawnmower, jumping off and ambushing one another. We became concerned when we could see that the smaller of the white ones was in very poor condition – it was a bag of bones with a sparse coat and sore pink-edged eyes. We wondered if the eye problem had been caused by all the dusty old straw in the haylofts, or if it had an infection. Perhaps it was just the runt of the litter.

"We can't do anything," I said to Jack. "Apart from the fact that the kittens wouldn't let us catch them, we can't really interfere with the balance of nature. They are wild, after all, poor little things."

But I had a horrible sneaking thought that if it had been a puppy I would have spent hours catching it and then taken it to the vet. I consoled my conscience with the fact that there was no comparison between the two species. There were feral cats everywhere on the farms, but the dogs were all firmly domesticated. If I ever succeeded in catching the kitten, it would be terrified. We decided to put milk and food out for it (and its siblings) in the hope that a sure food supply in the short-term might build up its strength and help it to recover.

While we were watching the kittens, Michel came past on the way to his vegetable garden. He said Charles had a bad leg and that his own leg wasn't too good, either. Afterwards we spotted him several times, chugging around the village on his favourite 1950s tractor at his usual enormous speed of about 3mph.

We raked up all the grass from the back garden and put it in a hollow where we hoped it would rot down and make a leaf-mould filler. I collected a basin of conkers from the chestnut tree so that we could walk round the field boundary and plant them. We were still determined to do our bit for the tree population of the Limousin.

Our priority over the next few days was to make the house suitable for our three guests, who were to arrive shortly. Jack's former immediate boss, Phil, had taken early retirement about six months before Jack. Knowing about Jack's fragile back, he had kindly offered to come over with his wife Lynne, to help us build the terrace. Then he asked if his friend Bob could come too. They had worked together on DIY projects since their early twenties, and made an excellent team, he explained. We were happy for Bob to come, naturally, but it meant that we needed to rearrange the bedrooms. We had a double bed and a single bed in each of the two main bedrooms, and, as I've mentioned before, the third bedroom was a study. We couldn't expect Phil and Lynne to share their bedroom with Bob, so we took the single bed out and put it in the study, at the same time removing the desk, computer and printer into the corner of their room where the bed had been.

We also had to finish the bathroom to the point where it could be used practically, even if it was not aesthetically complete. We couldn't ask our three guests to do their ablutions in the *arrière cuisine*, and we certainly couldn't expect all five of us attend to the needs of nature at the same time in the sole downstairs loo.

We knew the couple would understand the 'work in progress' state of the bathroom. They had their own *maison secondaire*, a former tin miner's cottage in the Lake District, at the tip of Ullswater, where we had shared a very happy weekend with them. They had only just finished constructing their own shower-room, and Phil was always busy doing something or other to improve the house.

After lunch we had a 'set-to' in the bathroom, installing the washbasin after two or three hours of thought and action. When it was all joined up and plumbed in we had a ceremonial video/photo of water gushing out of the tap.

While I wasn't needed as a holder of things or a supplier of ideas, I made up the bed in the study, with a single electric blanket and two duvets, a single one and a 10.5 tog double feather and duck down one which had not been out of its plastic bag in the linen trunk for five years. It had a rather potent pong which I hoped would wear off before poor Bob came to sleep under it.

When all this was finished I went over to Paul and Elisabeth to ask if they would like Jack to mow their grass, which we could see was getting rather long and unkempt. Harriet and Hugo arrived while I was chatting to them. Paul wasn't very well at all and his eye was troubling him again. It looked as if he was about to have a fifth eye operation.

Elisabeth's apple tree had fallen down in a recent gale with the weight of apples on it. Paul gave me a bag of them and some unfamiliar leaf vegetables with thick white stalks from his kitchen garden with explicit instructions on how to cook them. We had them for supper and they were very tasty. I still don't know what they are called in English… Perhaps we don't have them in England.

Next day I cleaned the spare bedroom and re-arranged the furniture while Jack began to prepare the pipework for the bidet. At about 11.30am the builders' merchant arrived with his lorry-load of materials. He took one look at the field entrance and said he couldn't go in or he would get stuck on the mud and slippery horse chestnuts. He was probably right, as there was virtually no tread on his lorry tyres!

He and Jack unloaded eight 50kg bags of cement into the barn manually, and then using the hoist on his lorry he lifted off the pallet of 84 breeze blocks and put them as far back as he could reach into the main part of the barn. It was at this point that we had a major traffic incident.

All morning a couple of tractors and trailers had been moving loads from the direction of the church past Michel's farm. By Sod's Law, with the builders' merchant's lorry taking up a major part of the road outside the barn, both tractors turned up outside the house going in opposite directions at full speed at the same moment. Both hit the anchors! The uphill empty one backed up a bit and went down the Route des Morts while the loaded one reversed, repositioned himself and then squeezed past with inches to spare.

The lorry driver decided that, with his vehicle now being about a tonne lighter, he would try to back into the field. We put down a blue tarpaulin by the side of the donkey stable and then he tipped the sand and gravel onto it. As he was now blocking the road even more completely than he had been outside the barn, I kept watch round the corner ready to stop allcomers, but no-one appeared this time. When he had gone we restacked all the breeze blocks by hand a bit further into the barn so that we could close the doors.

After lunch we went to the *départemental* capital to buy food for our guests' visit, some booze and an electric blanket to warm the spare double bed now that the nights were getting chilly. I also wanted some net curtain for the bathroom window. It was fine when we were on our own for Jack to joke about people watching me in the bath from the bottom of the field, but now we were about to have other residents at the house, we needed to ensure that there wasn't a clear view of nude bathers and loo-users from the garden below.

When we got home Jack turned off the water and fitted the pipes to the bidet, cut *lambris* to fit over them and drilled holes in the floor tiles in order to anchor the ceramic bowl by bolting through into the wooden floor. The water was then turned back on and to our relief there were no leaks. Another piece in the bathroom jigsaw was complete.

While we were upstairs, I went into our bedroom and saw a herd of about 30 cows wandering down the road and milling about in front of the house. They were not quite as organised as the original Bull by the Back Door and his wives, and kept stopping for a mouthful of grass or to follow a diversion into one of the little side tracks. Eventually they all went down the Route des Morts. Michel and his family were watching them quite happily from their front steps a couple of hundred yards away, so I concluded that the cattle must have had someone leading them from the front who had disappeared before I got to the window. It was, however, unusual not to have had a person or a dog chasing up the stragglers at the rear.

In the evening, Alex rang to say that he had come over from Kent to find that Jack's mother's osteoporosis had returned with a vengeance and she had taken to her bed. She gets occasional 'attacks' when her bones start to disintegrate or move around, and she is in a lot of pain. The only thing to do is to stay in bed, take painkillers and wait for things to sort themselves out. This can take several weeks. Alex had coped splendidly, calling the doctor, getting the district nurse lined up, ordering the home help service to come in and booking Sally into some nearby kennels.

We both had baths so that we would be clean while the visitors were with us. I'm afraid we belong to the generation that had a bath once a week, as children, 'whether we needed it or not' (as Joyce would have said when she was particularly covered with horse manure). The only hot running water provided upstairs in my parents' old house was via a terrifying geyser which belched flames and fumes over the bath and was to be avoided at all costs.

The new bath was very slippery, indeed we were seriously worried that someone might hurt themselves. We had bought a rubber anti-slip mat but it was a disappointment. It clung to the bath like a limpet when we wanted to adjust it and slipped murderously sideways when we were trying to climb out while balancing precariously on one leg.

Our friends were due to arrive late the next night, so in the morning we started to get things ready. Beforehand, however, we went down to the horse fair to have a look round. It was such a big local occasion that we didn't feel we could miss it. We thought there were not as many animals as last time. On the way back to the car we explored a former dairy building which had just been converted into an antiques shop. Unlike the *brocante*, it had some really nice pieces, including a magnificent grandfather clock which would have required a very high ceiling to accommodate it. The floor was paved with square red tiles of a type which were once used locally to cover attic floors. We were busy studying and comparing tiles, looking for inspiration as we hadn't decided how to pave the terrace. These would have looked very nice, and some friends had a barn stacked high with ones they'd removed from their *grenier* which we could probably have bought, but we thought they would not stand any frost.

Among the market stalls we met Charles and his wife, who said that Madame le Maire had had the old *fontaine* on our boundary tidied up. We stopped to look when we were nearly home, and there it was, transformed: the stonework had been repointed, the statue of St Paradis replaced and a new glass screen fixed over the front of his little shrine. Gravel had been spread around the base and the whole thing was superb. All that needed to be done now was for us to tidy up our murky bog behind it.

In the *arrière cuisine*, I opened the big box containing the new dinner service with the six sets of everything, so that I could wash the new crockery ready for our evening meal for five. I took it all out, removing the individual wrappings carefully, pleased once again with the pretty design and shape. At the bottom of the box were two large plates wrapped in cardboard. I tried to lift them out and couldn't. They were smashed to pieces. I could have wept! The service was a Carrefour own brand and at that time there were no Carrefour stores in the region. We would have to take them back to be replaced on the way home to England. My plans for a nicely laid table were foiled.

I then did the washing in the twin-tub while Jack bit the bullet and tackled the job he had been dreading for five years – installing the lavatory in the bathroom. He had been very worried about getting all the joints of the soil pipe glued so that were at exactly the right angles and also watertight. The special glue sets on the plastic pipe so quickly that there is a maximum of five seconds to make any adjustments. His worries proved groundless and everything went together without any problems. Fitting the washbasin had been much more of a pain.

However, when we turned on the cold water, it started to drip out of various places on the lavatory itself, which was decidedly unsporting. The tank appeared to be leaking, so he took it apart and remade all the joints with a liberal coating of silicon rubber.

While this was drying, we put up the lace curtains, which had an immediately civilising effect. I'd bought too much material and cut off the bottom segment which made a sort of tray cloth to go over the rather grotty windowsill. A vase of flowers on top made it look quite attractive.

Then we screwed some cup hooks into the door frame and hung a thick heavy curtain, which normally covers the back door in wintertime, across the space where the bathroom door would go if it hadn't been leaning against a wall on the landing. It needed to be resized to cope with the raised floor in the bathroom and there was no time to do that before our guests arrived. I vacuumed most of the mouse droppings and cobwebs out of the base of the curtain, found a piece of white cardboard and a piece of string, and wrote a sign saying *"Occupé"* and *"Vacant"* which I hung from the curtain with a safety pin. It could be twisted round to show whichever word was appropriate.

I christened the bathroom by washing my hair in the basin and installing a mirror, hand towel and glass for tooth-cleaning or pill-taking.

Jack raked up the loose grass and disturbed another toad. He wheelbarrowed a load of logs into the *atelier* and then fitted a convector heater in the bathroom. His last task before Phil, Lynne and Bob arrived at 9pm after a long drive from Charles de Gaulle airport in a hired car was to try to kill some of the many flies which seemed to be congregating on the landing. Perhaps they were admiring the bathroom, too.

Before everyone went to bed, we mentioned in passing that we had earlier switched on the electric blankets in the spare beds to keep them aired. Phil had said that he couldn't stand electric blankets. He liked to climb into a cold bed – though he didn't have much choice tonight. Lynne, it seemed, had been through married life without trying one. She'd declared in the morning that the warm blanket was wonderful and resolutely switched it on each evening of their stay!

Chapter Nine – October 1999
Working Party

After a leisurely breakfast, Jack put the ingredients for the first of many wholemeal loaves in the breadmaker and switched it on. We took our guests for a conducted tour round the outside of the house, down to the bottom of the field and then to the fountain and the wood. When we'd finished, it was after 11am so we all jumped into the car and drove to Stoc to do some food shopping. In spite of the fact that they had come to work, Phil, Lynne and Bob were determined to share the costs of their visit and were very generous with their purchases. Phil and Lynne hadn't been to France *en famille* before, so they had fun wheeling their trolley round the shop, popping in 'new tastes' and things they'd tried in restaurants. Phil was particularly keen to sample some fish soup. They were not Francophile – Austria and Germany were their usual European destinations and they could speak German quite well – so our different affiliations were a source of much mutual teasing during their stay.

Jack, Phil and Bob made a fine matching set, and you could imagine them being for sale in an auction as a job lot. Not only were they all in their fifties, superbly practical, mechanically-minded, safety-conscious and sensible, but most importantly, they all had grey beards.

However, Phil and Lynne were different from Jack and me in that they were very fit and very well travelled. Their recent holidays had included walking in Alaska and 'doing the Inca Trail' in Peru. Apart from our Riviera trip with Roger and Eileen, we spent all our holidays 'doing the *bricolage* trail' at St Paradis and this either kept us fit or clobbered Jack's back! And that was why they had so kindly offered to give us a hand with the hard labour involved in digging out the foundations for the terrace and getting the project on its way.

The extrovert Phil and the quiet, witty Bob were like chalk and cheese. Both engineers, they'd met when they'd taken up their first jobs after leaving university and complemented one another perfectly, each bringing out the best in his friend. Bob was still working, but Phil was having a great time in retirement, buying several smart new flats in Chester and becoming a landlord for yuppies. As an ICI manager he'd been plagued by the corporate structure and said the best aspect of 'doing your own thing' was that he and Lynne could make major financial decisions whilst chatting in bed, without having to make a single presentation or write a report.

Lynne was a retired teacher and it was through her that I had started what became the Léonie Press. She had been teaching creative writing to a daytime class at a local college of further education and had asked me to go along to talk to the students. At the time of the invitation, in 1995, I'd been a newspaper editor. When I came to do the talk, in 1996, I was very much an ex-newspaper editor looking for a new role in life. I tried to think of a subject which would be of interest to a group with widely varying ages and abilities, and decided that the one thing they had in common was their humanity. So I decided to talk about writing autobiography. It's my favourite literary genre. I looked in my bookcases for some good samples from the scores packed on the shelves – James Herriott, Lilian Beckwith, Dirk Bogarde, Edward Blishen. Then I thought of two amateur autobiographies I'd been given to read and had longed to make full use of while I was a journalist. One was Lenna Bickerton's *"Memories of a Cheshire Childhood"* and the other was about the early life and young adulthood of the current Mayor of Crewe, Les Cooper. I sidelined the famous autobiographers in my talk and concentrated on the two unknowns. The students loved them, and the germ for Léonie Press was born. I was enormously grateful to Lynne for being the unwitting catalyst in all this.

After lunch we all went outside to contemplate the patio problem. The first step for the male workers was to move the rocks, the granite sarcophagus (which we all referred to as "the urn" for short) and the broken trough, and roll them further down the garden away from where the edge of the terrace would go. When they were dug out they were much more massive than we had expected and required a lot of sweat and effort to shift. We left them on one side for Jack to clean up with the pressure washer at a later date.

There was considerable debate about the actual size and position of the terrace. Jack and I had already worked it out in our heads but when we marked the sides with string according to our original measurements, and the patio furniture was laid out where we wanted it to go, the area didn't seem big enough or in the right proportions. When it was lengthened by 60cm it was better but still felt too asymmetric to be visually satisfying, though on paper it was symmetrical. Eventually, although the back door steps were not mathematically in the middle, the assembled 'committee' felt that the terrace plot was just right visually.

The next issue was to work out the levels, using some water gauges that Jack had bought some time previously for the job. It turned out that the old farmyard dropped so much that one of the corners was very high and would have looked quite strange, as well as using up a lot of materials for infilling. The men reduced the height of all the sides by 20cm and then lowered the field end by a further 5cm to give a very slight slope to allow for drainage.

After all this surveying suppertime came along very quickly. We had roast lamb followed by various cheeses and ice creams, and then we all sat round the table talking and listening to the Dubliners on our old hi-fi system until it was time for bed.

Next morning was fine and bright after a misty start. The bathroom was coping well, though people preferred to use the downstairs loo for times of contemplation – mainly because of the 30 or so books we had in there expressly for such occasions. They had a mixed pedigree. Some were surplus to our bookcases at home in Cheshire (where there is one in every room including the bathroom), some were from my mother's house (which explained the presence of various royal biographies), some were English-language books bought in error by Jan and Beatrice from a library sale in Amsterdam, some were paperback novels in French and the rest I had obtained for a pound or two at charity shops in Northwich. There was something for everyone, from a vast learned analysis of the bombing of Pearl Harbour which Jack had been ploughing through for years, to a well-thumbed copy of

Ruth Rendell's latest crime novel. The expression "I'm just going to pay a visit to the loo" soon became "I'm off to the Library..."

Phil and Bob started on the footings. Bob methodically moved umpteen barrowloads of the sand and gravel from the gateway to a spot near the back of the house, while Phil did the digging. He was a phenomenal digger and had excavated the first neat trench in no time. Jack woefully recalled that it had taken him two days to dig a parallel one a few years before, to take the drains from the kitchen to the septic tank – although he'd had the disadvantage of meeting large rocks along the way which had needed to be split apart with a powered hammer drill, cold chisels and a sledge hammer. He wheeled the new cement mixer round from the barn and started to connect up the water hose from the exterior tap behind the *arrière cuisine*. Unfortunately the only right size jubilee clip we possessed was damaged, and we decided that we two would leave the other workers, take Lynne for the ride, and go to Espace Emeraud to buy another clip. We also needed a new pick-axe handle to replace one of Paul's which we had broken.

When we returned from our errand, Phil had dug the footings along the edge nearest to the barn and had discovered a fascinating old semi-cobbled stone surface about 20cm down, which sloped gently towards the field. We joked that if only Phil would dig up the whole of the old yard, we needn't construct a new paved terrace at all! I took several photographs and fantasised that it might be the remains of a Roman road. Jack and I agreed that we must ask Michel if he recalled there ever being a paved *basse court* behind the house.

Phil and Bob christened the cement mixer. Soon it was producing barrowloads of cement which went into the footings trench and had breeze blocks placed on it immediately. We wrote the date and all signed our names with a black spirit pen on the first breeze block, then photographed it for posterity.

After a time Jack decided that the two friends intuitively worked so well together as a team, after 30 years' practice, that he was *de trop* and might as well get on with a job on his own. So he dug out a hole to make a sump for the bathwater and then excavated a trench to take the extended yellow pipe we'd rigged up at the end of our previous visit.

It was such a nice day by 1pm that we had lunch outside around the patio table on the 'lawn' by the new fence. Mme Echelle's dogs were intrigued by this new phenomenon and we had their company throughout the meal. But their education was sadly lacking because unlike our own dogs in England who were experts at licking the last drops from a yoghurt container, they weren't pampered at home and couldn't really get the idea of cleaning out the small plastic pots which had contained our puddings.

Jack caused great hilarity by innocently asking: "Does anyone want a 'little pot' to finish with?" Phil, of course, wilfully misinterpreted this as an invitation to smoke a 'joint' and pretended to be shocked.

After lunch, work continued. Lynne and I were deputed to carry breeze blocks round from the barn, which was a truly boring task. The men could carry two or more at a time, but we could only manage single ones and we traipsed round with a total of 20 each clutched to our bosoms during the afternoon. They were soon swallowed up in the foundations.

By the close of play, Phil and Bob had done a superb job: all the footings and one course of breeze blocks were in place. While they were busy, Jack had buried the bathwater drain at an increasing depth as it got further from the house.

It was as well that Jack had sorted out the crude soakaway, as the bathroom came into its own when the workers had finished. The Loaders stayed grubby, ready for a wash at the hand basin in our bedroom at bedtime, while the others had baths – having been solemnly warned about the slipperiness of the tub. Nobody had turned a hair at the rather primitive curtain arrangement. It was just necessary to remember to turn the *Occupé* sign the right way round and make a discreet noise to indicate one's presence.

Lynne cooked a delicious pork casserole for supper with more than a kilo of meat, which had been cut up very expertly by the butcher in Stoc, mixed with aubergines, peppers, leeks and carrots. We sat round the dining table in true French mode and talked for hours as we worked our way through the various courses.

After two days' toil, we decided that the visitors should have some time off so the Wednesday of their stay was dedicated to *bricolage* visiting in the city and a trip to Evaux-les-Bains. It was raining from time to time, so working outside would not have been pleasant anyway.

We started off in the DIY superstore on the western outskirts of the city where we found some plastic plant ties we'd been searching for, and Phil got some brass brushes to use in his hobby of ornamental blacksmithing – he's very good and has made some beautiful objects in his forge at home in Cheshire. Then we tried the *bricolage* in the town commercial centre where he and Lynne were very taken with a hexagonal gazebo at a bargain price. As it was three minutes to lunchtime, the staff wouldn't serve them. We went on to our favourite hypermarket where we did the main food shopping and as a culinary experiment bought some delicate *chanterelle* mushrooms which cost an incredible 75FF a kilo – luckily they weren't very heavy. While we were there, Phil, Lynne and Bob bought me a beautiful enamelled cast-iron casserole which was said to serve between eight and ten people. I hadn't catered regularly for five hungry people at St Paradis before and had found that I didn't have a big enough container to cook and serve stews and casseroles. I'd been using two smaller ones which filled the two shelves of the bottled-gas oven and didn't allow me to get anything else in. I was most grateful for the gift, which would solve the problem perfectly.

We had lunch in the cafeteria attached to the shop. Jack and I were rather embarrassed that although the meat was nice the accompanying *frites* were past their best and had obviously been hanging around for rather a long time. We so wanted our beloved France to impress our Teutonically-inclined friends, and the country wasn't really showing its best side. We then went back to buy the gazebo, which came packed in a small but incredibly heavy box which the men lifted into the car. It just fitted across the boot.

Evaux-les-Bains was the next port of call. Its thermal springs have been used to treat complaints associated with rheumatology, *phlebologie* and gynaecology since pre-Roman times. Phil and Lynne told us that they 'collected' spa experiences and had been pummelled by grim white-coated attendants and pressure-cooked in foul-smelling waters all over Europe. They were keen to sample the local regime.

We found the massive establishment housing the baths without any problem and went in to see if they could go for a swim. Unfortunately we discovered that the baths were only open to the public between 6am and noon, as they were used for people who had booked medicinal 'cures' in the afternoons. Jack and I recalled that French friends were sometimes prescribed several weeks' curative stays in a spa on the French equivalent of the NHS. Phil and Lynne put their swimming togs back in the car, disappointed.

The rain had just started again when we decided to walk up to the town to have a look at an exhibition of watercolours advertised in a building near the church. As it was quite a distance, Jack drove the car up and I walked with the others past a public park where a herd of fallow deer was grazing close to the fence. When we arrived at the exhibition, the Loaders' embarrassment was increased when we read a hand-written notice announcing that there was a *fermeture exceptionnelle* for that day only...

"Oh dear: Austria 4, France 0," we thought.

We went into the church out of the rain and cheered up. The *abbatiale* was fascinating and had 11th century monastic origins. The interior design seemed to Jack and me to be very un-French. It was high and bathed in light, resembling our home-town parish church in Lincolnshire and most unlike many of the sombre dark French churches we had explored. We looked at the tall pillars and spotted that at least one of them was far from vertical and had a marked kink in it. According to the guide, the end of the building adjacent to this pillar had had to be rebuilt. There had been a fire in the 16th century when the church was pillaged (how like Marcheville!) and an accidental blaze in 1942 when all the internal wood had been destroyed – perhaps this accounted for the plainness of the walls. There was little trace of the most recent fire so presumably all the stonework had been cleaned, making everywhere seem so light and airy. Outside there were cloisters and an attractive little square with a fountain, and at the front a most unusual porch with a five-storey bell-tower topped by a little spire. We really enjoyed looking round and felt that the church had been well worth visiting.

When we left it was still pouring with rain so we decided that

La Belle France was obviously not trying to make a good impression and that we might as well go home.

It was too wet to do anything outside when we reached St Paradis, so our guests explored the cellar and fixed the maximum-minimum thermometer on the wall so that we could measure the long-term stability of the *cave* temperature.

For supper I used the new casserole dish to do guinea fowl in white wine sauce, accompanied by the *chanterelle*s, which I cooked in butter. When the meal was finished we listened to extracts from *The Secret Policeman's Ball*, and other stuff from our 'yoof', by candlelight. We were very lucky. The pretty silk flowers and artificial cherries making a decorative ring round one of the candlesticks caught fire and it was only Jack's lightning reaction as a former research chemist that stopped things being nasty. He immediately poured the remains of the jug of water we'd served with the meal over the flames before they ignited the plastic table cloth. If we had all got up from the table and turned our backs on the candle we could have had a serious fire on our hands. Since then, I have always removed any floral decorations from a candlestick before the candle in it has been lit. The rings of flowers look attractive but are a very real hazard.

Thursday was a dull damp morning but at least it wasn't raining. After breakfast Phil and Bob got stuck into the terrace building, and Jack, Lynne and I agreed to go and fetch some hardcore from one of the piles in Hugo's garden. Naturally, the words "hardcore" immediately provoked a "little pot"-type reaction!

Whilst Jack got the trailer out and reinforced the wooden floor, I raked up the horse chestnuts and their spiny husks so that the slope into the field from the road wasn't as slippery as it might have been. We didn't want the car to get stuck again. As we were doing this, Pieter drove past, saw us over the hedge, and stopped for a chat. He said that it was Dirk's last day at his ministry job in The Hague and that in future he would be working for himself from home. We said we thoroughly recommended it!

After he drove off, the three non-terrace labourers went round to Hugo's. He and Harriet asked us in for some tea or coffee and then we loaded the trailer with anything from the hardcore heap

– the stuff we had rejected in the past as being lumps of concrete, old tiles and odd-shaped stones. We asked them to come for an *apéritif* in the evening after their daily visit to Elisabeth.

The drive back into the garden was easy and Jack was able to get the trailer near enough for us to take the hardcore out of it and throw it into the breeze-block 'box' that was emerging on the ground.

From time to time we saw – and heard – a man driving a tractor with a big hedge-cutting slasher on the side. The commune paid for the hedges bordering the roads to be cut, and this was a useful service although not one carried out with much finesse. We were concerned that our young oak trees in the hedge at the bottom of the field might be slashed to pieces, so I dashed down with some white plastic carrier bags which I tied into their branches as a signal that they were not to be cut.

After lunch outside on the grass again, we saw Paul walking slowly down the road with a stick so Jack and I went to talk to him. We asked him to come and look at the work in progress. He said he'd have to go and get a bottle of good wine first for the workers! He also told us that he had fallen during the night and showed us his bruised and still bloody head under his cap. When he came back with a bottle of Côtes du Rhône and was introduced to Phil, Lynne and Bob, he was very polite about the works. While I popped over to see Elisabeth, the others opened the bottle and drank to his health with very small glasses of wine as they didn't want to be sleepy or tiddly during the day – but equally didn't want to make light of our old friend's generous hospitality.

We made another trip to Hugo's and loaded a little more into the trailer than we had done in the morning. When Jack drove over our grass the trailer tyres made much deeper tracks, so we decided that we had reached a sensible load limit. We emptied the rubble into the 'box' in a sort of human chain, with Lynne and me filling buckets and giving them to Jack to tip over the breeze block wall. There would be time to spread it out neatly later.

Jack prepared a broken length of sewer pipe to go into the corner of the terrace nearest the church so that we could use it to take the upright pole of a rotary drier. As he dug a hole for it, he hit the old cobbled surface, which must have sloped down quite steeply

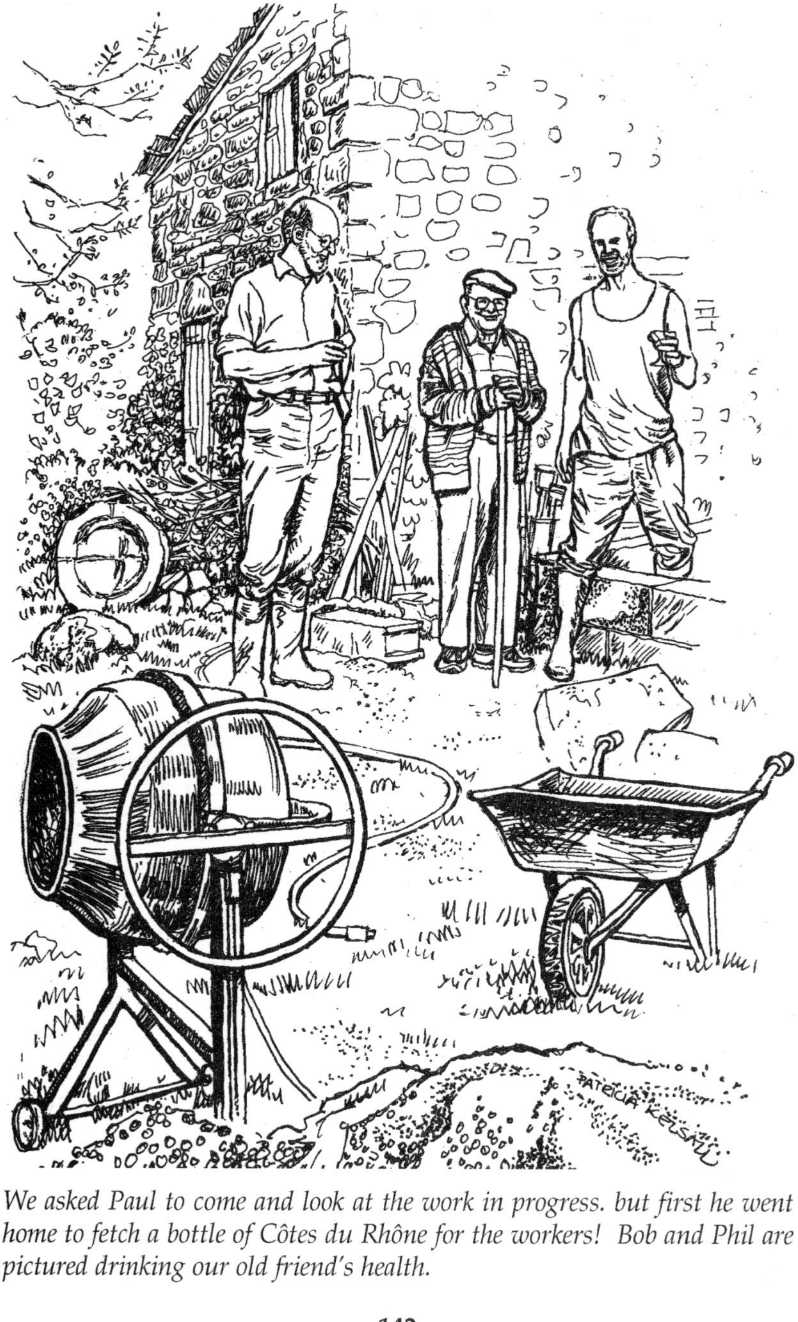

We asked Paul to come and look at the work in progress. but first he went home to fetch a bottle of Côtes du Rhône for the workers! Bob and Phil are pictured drinking our old friend's health.

from the house. Bob and Phil put large fillets of concrete into the corners of the breeze block 'box', and into the middle of the side by the chicken building, to strengthen it.

Our two efficient and skilled workmen had done the basic job on the terrace in a fraction of the time it would have taken Jack and me. We were immensely grateful. It now remained for the two of us to lay the hardcore, gravel and sand properly and then put down a paved surface.

Everything was then hosed off and we were almost cleaned up when Hugo and Harriet arrived with Peachy.

We designated the next day, Friday, as another rest day, as the major project was now completed. We decided to go sight-seeing and terrace tile-hunting. Phil drove us to the *départemental* capital in their hired Megane Scenic, and we found some interesting square brick setts in one of the *bricolage* yards. I went to enquire the price and was told that the factory making them had closed. I didn't have the heart to ask why the tiles were still on display! There were also some nice quarry tiles with irregular colouration and glaze, but they were very expensive.

Then we went to the tourist office to see what special events were on. Phil spotted a poster for an open day at an arboretum specialising in spectacular autumnal maples, and Jack hung his nose over information about the local astronomy centre and telescope that we always meant to visit and somehow never got round to. We walked through the city square and down the pedestrianised streets to the church. Everywhere was virtually deserted and we wondered, not for the first time, how any of the shops actually made any money.

A trip to the Continent hypermarket for us to buy a 30FF cake slicing utensil resulted in a spending spree among the wine shelves with a combined bill of 1700FF shared between the five of us. We had lunch in the smart Crescendo restaurant attached to the shop where the food was thankfully much better quality than the fare we'd had earlier in the week.

Afterwards we directed them to one of our favourite Creuse villages, Sous-Parsat, which we recommend to all our visiting friends. It's in a lovely woodland setting and the residents have gone to great lengths to make it beautiful and welcoming. There are flowers everywhere, lovingly-maintained stone houses, an artist's studio and waymarked footpaths. But our reason for loving it is the church, which must be unique. In a four-year project undertaken not long ago, and financed by public and private money, the artist Gabriel Chabrat has covered the entire interior of the stone church with modern biblical frescoes on a brilliant blue background, complemented by magnificent stained glass windows made in Limoges. The church has neither pews nor furniture, and the empty floor space concentrates the visitors' attention on the stunning walls and ceiling. When you turn the lights on, church music plays automatically in the background and the effect on the senses is overwhelming and emotional. I don't think it's somewhere I could pray because it's too stimulating, but it is somewhere which lives in the memory as an inspiration.

When we left the church we strolled round the village and followed the signs to a *fontaine* half a kilometre away, up through a wood with sweet chestnut trees overhanging the path. We filled our pockets with edible chestnuts which had fallen on the ground. Jack wanted to take them to England, plant them in pots and bring back any that had sprouted successfully into strong baby trees. Then we could replant them at St Paradis as part of our personal tree-planting mission.

Wandering back through the village, we looked out for the artist's studio. It was closed. Even today La Belle France was not going to yield up all her attractions. Not far away I saw a large round flat stone in someone's garden which was labelled as the cover for a gallo-roman funerary sarcophagus. It had a small hollow in the centre. Seeing the cover made me think of our own sarcophagus and how Virginie had told us that it was quite common to have the top or the bottom but not both. The flat stone in the Sous-Parsat garden reminded me of something. What was it? Suddenly I remembered. When Paul had made the flowerbed in front of the house using massive stone blocks that had been lying around, we had noticed that one of them was almost round, with rough bits on opposite sides – like ragged ears – which spoiled the chiselled curve. We had assumed that it was a grinding wheel, millstone or building block that a mason had discarded for some reason when he had nearly finished shaping it. I resolved to measure it when we returned home to see if it might have fitted on top of the sarcophagus.

We climbed into the Scenic and drove on to Moutier d'Ahun, another magical place in our estimation, where there is a Roman bridge over the River Creuse, a famous ancient church which was once part of a Benedictine monastery where we knew there were fabulous wood carvings inside and Roman remains outside, and a museum of rural tools which we were sure would fascinate our guests. The church was locked and the museum was closed. I was beginning to get a complex about what the visitors were missing! We sat on the broad low walls of the bridge and watched the river flowing underneath. It was quite turbulent because the bridge pillars are large and restrict the passage of the water. Interestingly they are shaped like the prow of a boat on the upstream side so that the water parts round them, and are square on the downstream side.

Back at Marcheville, we parked in the market square and went to look at the menus displayed by the two local hotels. Phil was keen to go out for a meal and both establishments had a good reputation among our French friends. We compared food and prices, and eventually booked at the one which had the fish dishes that most appealed to Phil.

There was a big mobile *bricolage* parked near us on the square – a large articulated lorry with sides that dropped down to reveal its shelves of wares. It visited various local venues regularly to cater for the needs of country folk who could not just jump in a car and drive to shops in the big towns like we did. We knew when it was coming because fliers were pushed under our front door a few days in advance. We've seen similar massive ones at fairs, with peel-back roofs. Jack was suffering from *bricolage* deprivation and bought himself some jubilee clips, much to the amusement of the others, who said it was quite impossible to go anywhere with Jack without having to stop off for a *bricolage* fix.

In the time before our hotel meal, Phil had a go with our chainsaw in the barn. He dearly wanted to buy one but, like most sensible people, was a bit frightened of the prospect. They are, after all, extremely dangerous if you don't know what you're doing or have a mental aberration. Mme Echelle's son had told us once how his father had nearly cut his own leg off when he absent-mindedly let go with one hand to get a hanky out of his pocket whilst leaving the saw running.

We got reasonably dressed-up and Jack drove us down to the hotel. The bar was quite full but we were the only diners. The restaurant was typically rural French, with no frills, probably like Paul's had been in the past. The couple who owned the place were very attentive hosts and we enjoyed a nice meal. Phil had *moules marinières* followed by salmon because he was determined to have as much fish as possible. As the hotel was so quiet the service was very rapid and we returned home just after 9pm. We settled down in front of the fire with some more drinks and attacked a very 'more-ish' monster bar of black *noir de noir* chocolate that had been among the visitors' purchases at Continent.

After a clear night it was a dull morning and a cool 10C. Phil and Lynne went for a pre-breakfast 2km jog 'round the block' in the village, setting what they decided was an all-comers' record of 19 minutes. There wasn't much chance that Jack and I would ever feel inclined to break it, especially as it involved climbing a hill which started at our house level and ascended over a couple of hundred yards to higher than the church spire. This was of course a mere nothing to residents of the Lake District and veterans of the Inca Trail!

During our fireside chat the previous evening, I'd told everyone about my theory of the sarcophagus lid, and when I measured the round stone which formed the corner of the front flowerbed I was thrilled to find that the 60cm circumference was very similar to that of the sarcophagus. The troops thus decided that they wanted to have a close look and do some more research.

The three men got together and raised up the round stone, which was lying flat. They discovered our very large and sleepy toad underneath which had to be evicted so that it wouldn't be squashed if the stone fell back. Under the stone there was a reduction in diameter which made it look very much like a fitted lid, and the 'unfinished ears' that we'd noted in the past now appeared to be ideally-placed handles. The 'committee' agreed that it should be taken round the back of the house to be compared with the sarcophagus.

This was easier said than done. We felt the only way that something of this weight could be moved such a distance without inducing hernias all round was to get it on the trailer. Jack hitched the trailer up to the car and backed down towards the *Route des Morts*. We took down the metal side which was nearest to the stone and then everyone heaved together to lift the trailer bodily across as close as possible to Paul's flowerbed wall. Thick pieces of wood were laid down from under the stone to the floor of the trailer and a rope was looped round the circumference of the stone. Everyone other than Phil pulled on the rope and Phil braced himself against the side of the wall and pushed. The stone came up the slope until it was over the side of the trailer and then the wood tipped and the rock and wood came on together. It was all reminiscent of those TV programmes where people re-enact the building of Stonehenge or South American temples. Jack then drove the car into the field, backed up the slope to the flat area in front of the hen-house and we discovered that by sheer luck (or Marguerite's good management – we always credited her with jobs on the house that went more easily than we expected) the stone was exactly over the axle so everyone was able to manhandle it to the side of the chicken building and then slide it off the back. We chocked it carefully with stones so that it was vertical and positioned it so that it could be seen from the terrace. Then the men rolled the sarcophagus so that it was alongside its possible 'lid'.

Jack pressure-washed both stone artifacts. The first surprise was that the urn had a square hole in one side that formed a continuation of the vertical piece of the carved cross. This had been made, we presumed, at some point in its life to prevent water being retained inside and freezing, thus cracking the hollowed-out granite. We moved it round so that the hole became vertical. As it dried we could see how neatly the outside of the stone had been carved into diamond-shaped lozenges.

I was in the kitchen preparing the lunch when Lynne called me. She looked a bit sheepish.

"Can you see anything on the lid?" she asked.

I looked and gasped.

"There's a cross scratched in it – and it corresponds exactly with the one in the urn!" I replied.

"Yes, that's what we thought," said Lynne. "We just wanted to check that we weren't imagining it."

We hardly dared hope that we had indeed found the lid. We examined the sarcophagus and spotted the remnants of some ironwork sunk into the granite around the top. Could an iron band have held the cover in place, we asked ourselves?

The only niggling problem as far as I was concerned was that the granite for the 'lid' and the 'sarcophagus bottom' were not from the same piece of stone. The colour was subtly different. They were both granite, certainly, but not from the same block. Jack thought that didn't matter. He imagined a gallo-roman stonemason matching together two bits of the same-sized rock and being thankful that he didn't have to do a more complicated job for his bereaved client.

While I was finishing preparing the lunch, Jack pressure-washed the back steps. Phil and Bob positioned two long narrow rocks to act as further steps down from the terrace, and dug out some of the other big rocks which had worked their way to the surface in different parts of the garden. They also rebuilt the flower-bed wall in the front where the sarcophagus top had been removed. It was marvellous for us to have this done by two strong willing men, for it would have taken us quite a long time on our own. Jack's strong and I'm willing, but I'm not a man...

We had a quick lunch and set off for the open day at the Arboretum de la Sedelle at Villejoint, between Dun le Palestel and Crozant. Their publicity material said they had invited a number of plant and tree suppliers, and local craftsmen, to display and sell. We eventually found the place, which was rather remote, and parked the Megane Scenic in a nearby field. It turned out to be a lovely community event reminiscent of an English garden fete, with most of the traders or amateur enthusiasts operating under the ubiquitous gazebos. These *tonnelles* were so popular everywhere, for umpteen different uses, that I wondered how the human race had managed before they were invented. I was dying to have one, although Jack said I couldn't unless I could think of a really good reason.

There were some fascinating kinetic sculptures in the centre of the area where the stalls were pitched, and a blacksmith who had some lovely decorative work on show. Phil talked to him for some time, in sign language and Franglais, with Jack acting as occasional interpreter.

Guided tours of the arboretum itself left every half hour or so from the entrance, and we joined one. The guide's French was too hard for us however and we continued on our own with the aid of a leaflet we had been given. The gardens were ablaze with hundreds of maples in different spectacular shades of orange, red and scarlet – we had never seen anything like it. We went past a wooden Japanese pavilion jutting out over a small pond and then followed a path that dropped down to the steep-sided green valley of the River Sedelle. At the bottom, fringed by ferns, white water was rushing over the rocks, creating eddies and 'stoppers'. There was the characteristic earthy and ozone-y scent of a racing river which took me back several years, reminding me how we had first met Phil and Lynne during our sons' canoeing days. Our two families had belonged to different Cheshire clubs, but our boys were of the same standard and we had attended the same weekend slalom competitions all over the country. Jack and I had been stalwart supporters, spectators and transport-providers for Alex and Chris, while Phil and Lynne had entered into the spirit of the thing and actually competed as well. It wasn't until many years later that Jack and Phil had worked together at ICI.

We left the narrow marked path after a time when it turned sharply back up the bank to the arboretum. Some fellow visitors, who squeezed past us from the other direction, recommended that we should follow the river along to *'le moulin'* a bit further along. The steep uneven bank became slippery with moss and fallen leaves, and I fell over, bruising my knee and hand. When we came to the mill it was well worth the detour and made Jack and me think of Impressionist paintings we had seen by various 19th century artists from the School of the Creuse at an exhibition in Dun le Palestel a couple of years before. The riverside watermill and its rocky weir had been a favourite subject for the painters because it was in such a picturesque situation.

On the way back, seasoned walker Phil took pity on me as someone hardly able to cope with Putney let alone Peru, and cut me a walking stick from a nearby tree. It came in extremely handy during the steep climb up from the valley to the site of the plant sale. I examined all the acers for sale very closely, looking for ones whose names I had noted down during the walk round the arboretum, where all the specimens were labelled. I'd particularly liked the *acer japonicum* and *acer palmatum* but the ones on offer were too large to get into the back of a Megane Scenic with five people in it. I settled for a foot-high *acer saccharum*, which was a smaller specimen but not, it transpired, cheaper. If the price had been on the label I might have chosen something else! When I came to pay, it cost 80FF and had been planted in the 1995-96 season, according to the grower. I took that to mean that it might make a height of four feet by the time I was in my dotage.

Phil purchased a flat white gourd which he was originally going to cook for that night's supper but eventually decided to take home to England. Bob bought some dried gourds. There were some beautiful ones on a stall where a craftsman had made them into little lamps and pricked out patterns on the hard parchment-coloured surface.

We came home via the M. Bricolage store in the *départemental* capital so that Jack could buy a tap for the hosepipe – a diversion which again caused great hilarity. While Jack was in the shop the rest of us stayed with the Megane while Phil filled it up with petrol for the trip back to Charles de Gaulle airport the next day. We had a long wait to settle the bill because the person in a white van in front of us drove off without paying so the cashier raced across the car park after him and then had to go through the rigmarole of reporting him to the powers-that-be. Bob waited for her to come back and put the right money down in notes on the little counter in the pay-out booth. The wind caught them, whipped them off and blew them away. Altogether it was an eventful transaction. We eventually drove back to St Paradis past Pieter and Dirk's house, which we were keen to show off on their behalf.

At home, I prepared *paupiettes de veau* in the new big casserole, with Paul's stalky things cooked with onions and herbs, potatoes and carrots, followed by apple *feuillités* and *crême fraîche*. It was very nice.

While we were in the garden we heard faraway raucous screams and saw hundreds, maybe thousands, of what appeared to be geese flying in V formations across the sky from east to west. It was fascinating to see how the birds formed up and filtered into line like good motorists joining an autoroute.

The guests were busy while I worked. They had been gathering in huddles for some time over the past couple of days, scribbling things down on bits of paper, and we wondered what they were doing. We soon found out. After supper they told us that they had written us a poem for the visitors' book, and proceeded to perform it:

ODE TO THE LOADERS

The bathroom is ready, they now can arrive;
A *périphérique* tour round Paris and then a fast drive.
We'd all read the book
Now come for a look:
St Paradis is real and the characters live.
A hot meal was eaten, the first *vin* was drunk
Then into warm beds we all gladly sunk.

The following morn we surveyed the estate
Then off for some shopping – the building must wait.
We basked in the sun
While Jack baked a large bun
Then planned out the terrace we're going to create.
The treasures of the attic we inspected with awe,
Old tools and beehives and bottles galore.

Now into work togs for a full day of action
We must build the foundations to Jack's satisfaction.
The gravel was shifted
The French earth was lifted
The footings were laid – said Jack "Move it a fraction!"
When finally happy, the breeze blocks were placed
For Jack to add rocks so they'd be nicely faced.
Now Wednesday is rest day because it is raining,

Bricolage visiting is our main bit of training.
The hot springs were *fermé.*
The art show was *fermé.*
But *bricolage* visits they kept on occurring.
The guests got a tent, the Loaders a pot,
Christened with a casserole – we enjoyed it a lot.

The next row of breeze blocks were now to be laid
Using loads of cement, a trowel and a spade.
We need more rocks
And not just breeze blocks
So the foundations of the terrace were finally made.
Ready for 'inspection' we followed the rule
Let's hope it's OK, 'cos here comes old Paul.

Our last full bright day, Phil and Lynne had their run.
We then looked around for more jobs to be done.
The urn needs a lid
In the rockery one's hid
So a heave and a ho, all five had such fun.
Completing the urn was a bit of a quest
Without Marguerite's help we would never have guessed.

The week has flown by, it's been a great hit
We'll all miss the 'library' where we had a good ... read
Our hosts were so fine
Like lords we did dine.
We can't come again 'til the third book is writ.
So it's *au revoir* to *bricolages* and all the cheese odour,
To Paul, to the dogs and to Jack and Anne Loader.

We rose at 6am, after waking several times during the night because we knew we had to get up earlier than usual. It was very dark and the Morning Star was shining brightly. Everyone was great: Phil was actually downstairs first, breaking all records. They had packed their stuff and were very organised. Various boxes of their wine, which we had arranged to bring home for them in the trailer, were stacked away in the spare room.

We all had *croissants* and *pain au chocolat* for breakfast and then by their deadline of 8am our friends were suddenly gone. I went "oomph!" and flaked out on the sofa. It had been a smashing week, and their rapid departure was an anti-climax. We would miss them.

Chapter Ten – October 1999
Winding down

While I caught up on some sleep Jack started to make the Welsh dresser, which we had brought over flat-packed in the trailer. We had bought it in MFI at Crewe whilst on our way to order one twice the price and half the quality from a speciality pine shop not far away. We had only popped into MFI to buy two blue velvet headboards for the new maxi-bed and were amazed to find exactly the dresser we'd dreamed of and fruitlessly searched for in posher establishments. The component parts were very well made and were all solid wood.

When I woke up we went outside and measured the new terrace 'box' – it was 5.5m x 6.85m including the area taken up by the stone steps, roughly 38sq metres, less the area taken up by the stone steps, which would take a lot of tiling. Then we levelled the soil and hardcore inside so that at its highest the filling was well below the edges of the breeze blocks.

I went over to talk to Elisabeth and Harriet after we saw Hugo driving Paul off for his regular Sunday fun with his friends betting on the Tiercé horse-racing system – a bit like a cross between the Lottery and the Tote. Harriet was planting tulips and daffodils in her sister's borders and Peachy was so pleased to see me that she smashed a pot of geraniums. On the way back I chatted to one of the neighbours who was beating a rug against Elisabeth's barn wall, still wearing her rollers, One of the little white kittens peeped at us out of a small ventilation gap in the wall.

Chaos in the house resumed as soon as the Loaders were on their own. Bits of the dresser rapidly took over all available spaces on the floor and table and there were also components propped up against the working surfaces. It was a beautiful day so we opted out of the kitchen chaos by having lunch in the garden, luckily without any problems with flies or wasps. There was a small queue of dogs for unwanted titbits, indeed the dogs were constant visitors all day, in their usual little 'gangs'.

Jack did some serious work on levelling the terrace. I cut back the brambles behind the sarcophagus and alongside the chicken house whilst leaving them growing thickly as a barrier between us and the Route des Morts below. I also cut up bits of fallen branches from the tall overhanging sycamore, as kindling.

We planted out the new *acer saccharum* and a red flowering shrub that we had brought from England, using some of the compost we had made in the plastic bin bought from the local borough council. The claggy brown contents weren't a patch on what Jack makes at home in a large concrete-sided space covered with a plastic sheet, which is a paradise for worms and such 'good stuff' that plants shoot up like proverbial beanstalks once they get their roots in it. He once won a bottle of whisky in a competition at work for growing the biggest ornamental cabbage without using a chemical fertiliser. His was as big as a football – twice the size of everyone elses's, thanks to our compost.

While we were working in the garden, Michel and his wife were harvesting apples from the *potager* opposite. Suddenly we heard a cry from his wife and metallic noises as the aluminium ladder slipped. We dashed to the gateway to check, but they were OK. Neither of them was of an age to fall off a ladder.

At about 7pm we heard all sorts of muffled bangs and there were hundreds more long-necked birds filling the sky, honking away eerily. As on the previous occasion, we were fascinated to watch them transforming themselves from an amorphous mass into orderly V-shaped battalions. Our neighbours came out to get a better view. I needed to walk round to the front of the house and bumped into Charles. He told me they were what sounded like *groos*, which I interpreted as 'grouse' (spelt the same in French) – not your common little Glorious Twelfth variety but big ones, almost like turkeys. We had once stayed at a *gîte* where an enormous stuffed specimen was displayed over the fireplace and dominated the room. Charles said they were from Africa and were a protected migratory species, supposedly safe from the French *chasseurs*. They flew over in the opposite direction in the Spring, he explained. We weren't too sure about the safety from *chasseurs*, as we were certain we'd heard some shots. I didn't fancy being hit on the head by a falling grouse weighing as much as a Christmas dinner.

It was not until a later visit that we discovered from a French friend who could speak English that they were actually cranes – *grues*. This was what I had thought Charles had said, but I'd immediately dismissed it as a mis-hearing on my part. I knew a *grue* was a mechanical crane because Paul had made his name in his younger days as the only man in the region with one, but it had never occurred to me that the words for a mechanical hoist and a stork-like bird could be identical in both languages.

A year or so afterwards, I was researching Creuse folklore and found out that in the past, when the discordant cries of cranes or geese were heard during the night and it was too dark to see them, it was called the *chasse-volante* or the *chasse-infernale.* Frightened listeners likened the howling sound to an army of neighing horses, miaowing cats and barking dogs. Some people attributed the unearthly noise to evil spirits, others to devils, the ghosts of animals or the condemned souls of the village dead, returning to circle the cemetery and curse those who had not prayed for them. Often big fires would be lit and folk would spend the night around them, making a great din of their own to scare away bad luck. To be conceived when the *chasse-volante* was going over was considered to be very unlucky – though one would have thought that one's parents would have been put off their *amours* by the racket!

While I was roasting some pork, Jack pressure-washed the new stone steps that Bob and Phil had installed, and the big square stone which had been over the roots of the transplanted tree. After supper, he assembled some more of the base unit of the dresser.

We tried the e-mail and discovered various messages, including one from Lynne, saying that they had arrived home safely.

We celebrated sole ownership of the new bathroom by using the loo and having a long soak in the bath. Belatedly, we discovered that the towels seemed to be very damp and that we needed to install a warmed towel rail. We were sorry if our guests had been putting up with manky towels out of politeness.

It was very misty the next morning, with the church spire only

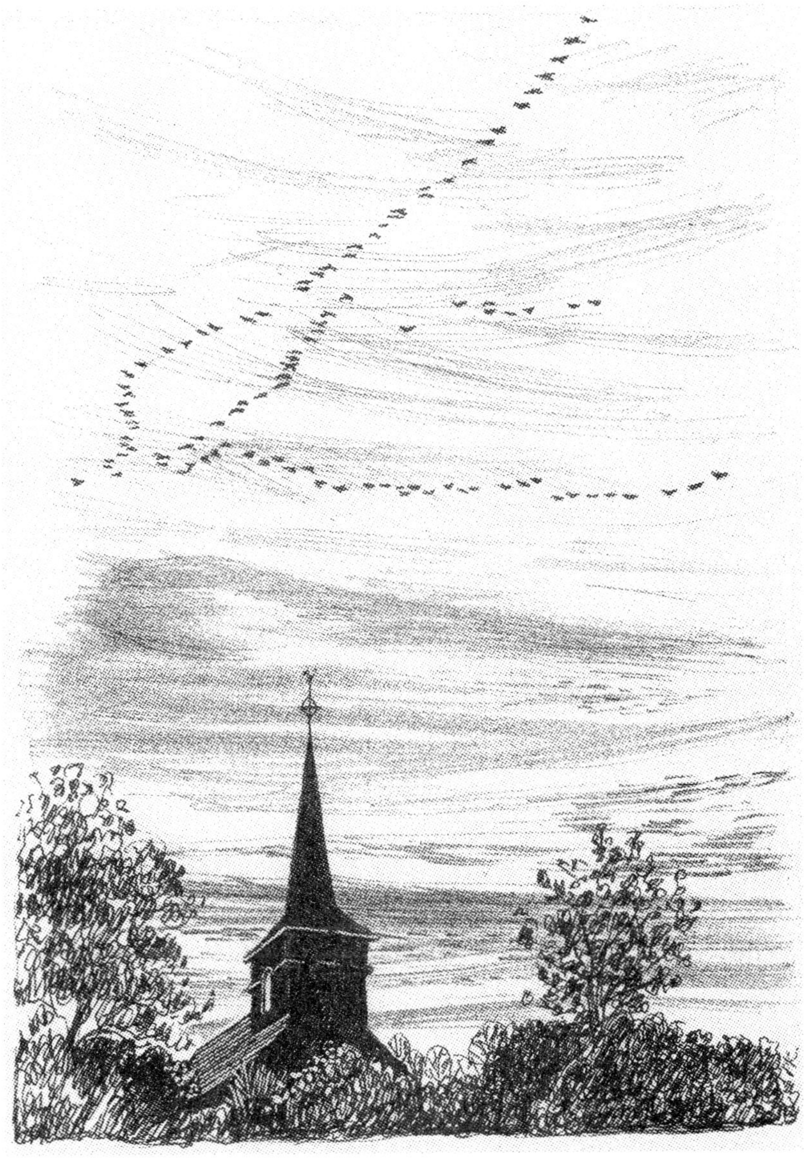

In the past, when the unearthly discordant cries of cranes or geese were heard during the night and it was too dark to see them, it was called the ***chasse-volante*** *or the* ***chasse-infernale.***

just visible from the back garden. The ground was very wet and the general miserable dampness developed into a dreary rainy day later on. The radio told us that back in England the London Eye was being raised into its final position and the Chinese President was starting his country's first state visit to the UK. It all seemed to be happening a long way away.

It was a good day to continue with the dresser. When Jack had finished his assembly work it fitted exactly into place between the electricity meter and the side of the kitchen window; indeed if we'd ordered the piece of furniture to be made to measure (and we'd toyed with the idea) it could not have been better. We soon filled the glazed cupboards in the top part with our new and old 'best' crockery and some ornaments. The only problem was to find homes for all the typically 'Loader-ish' things that had been kept on the table and set of wooden shelves which it replaced. These included three rechargeable torches, a phone and mobile phone, a digital thermometer and hygrometer, a collection of adaptor cables, a battery charger, maps, leaflets about local attractions, a camera, a video camera, two handbags, a telephone extension cable, an ultraviolet anti-insect lamp, two clear plastic boxes and a French-English dictionary… I'm afraid we'd never have our cluttered home portrayed in a Laura Ashley catalogue. We do intend to tidy up one day, when we grow up.

When we had finished we went out into the barn and added the new firewood, which had been dumped into the central part, to our neat stack at the back. It looked a simple job but took ages. During the course of our labours, we discovered that when the load had been tipped in by Hugo's friend it had disrupted our stock of 'woodworking wood' that was leaning against the side of the cow-stalls. At one point all these planks fell down, narrowly missing us. After we'd finished, we brushed up all the bark, straw and rubbish that had fallen out of the wood load and put it in sacks to add to a bonfire in the back garden.

As we were doing the wood-stacking, the sick white kitten came down from the hayloft. We gave it some rejected fish soup that Phil had left in the fridge, but the little cat shared his instincts by not being too sure about it. It sat very still in the straw by the water tap for a long time and watched us listlessly. We didn't think it would survive the winter.

Michel walked past, so we told him about Phil finding the extended semi-cobbled surface that we thought might have been a courtyard and he came round with us to have a look. He said that when he was a small boy the Xavier family had kept chickens in the area which was now becoming the terrace, and that he had no knowledge of any hard surface. While he was there, we showed him the newly cleaned sarcophagus. He laughed and remarked that objects like that were often used as pig feeding troughs in the old days. He'd got one himself. He added that perhaps we should give it to the local municipal museum. We didn't say so aloud, but both Jack and I recoiled at the thought. We didn't want our 'urn' to end up as a specimen on display – we felt strongly that it should stay at St Paradis. We had no idea if it had originated on our land or if a member of the Xavier family had obtained it from somewhere else to use as a trough, but we reckoned it was so heavy that it was unlikely to have been brought a long distance. We had our ghost from the twentieth century, it would be nice to think that we had links with the fourth century, too!

When we checked our e-mails we had a nice message from Bob, and a little later Phil rang up to ask if we could try to get him an electric chainsaw, as he'd found they were much more expensive in England than in the Limousin where they were everyday working tools.

Next morning we had arranged to go to see Stuart and Pat Ahier, who have a house in a tiny hamlet not far from Dun-le-Palestel. I nipped across the road first, to ask Paul and Elisabeth round for their usual 'last night' supper the following evening. Elisabeth was all ready for the chimney sweep to arrive while Paul was seated at the kitchen table, studying form and working on his Tiercé predictions.

At Marcheville, we took a convivial week's worth of empties to the bottle bank and dropped into the real bank to pay in a couple of cheques. In the *départemental* capital we tried to go to the *bricolage* department of one of the big hypermarket chains to see if they stocked the chainsaw Phil required but they were having their car park re-surfaced and we got embroiled in the chaos of a massive jam as impatient people attempted to manoeuvre round tar-sprayers and road rollers. After extricating ourselves with a multi-point turn, we tried another *bricolage* where we found a slightly bigger model of Phil's preferred saw at a bargain price, and bought it for him.

We found the Ahiers' home without any problems although there was thick fog on the way. The house is tall, built into the side of the hill and situated high above the road. There are two rooms on the ground and first-floor levels and a large *cave* which occupies the same area. The floor of the *cave* is well above road level and we climbed up to the front door via a steep flight of stone steps. At the back is a large garden with many fruit trees and to the side is an old wooden *hangar* which Pat and Stuart use as a wood store and outside seating area.

They had prepared a very nice lunch for us and we sat and talked at the table for a long time in the best French fashion. Afterwards we had a walk round the little community which has only one house with permanent inhabitants. It is a lovely place, and we especially liked the view across to an old watermill in a little valley not far away. One of the houses had been abandoned and was in a dangerous state, appearing to be held up by a course of bricks forming the lintel over a door, which was now badly distorted with a brick being squeezed out. We suspected that when the next good frost came after the brickwork had been wet, the ice would force the vital brick out and the whole thing would collapse. There was another house in a similar state but its demise was due to theft. Someone had stolen some carved stone lintels and this had left the building quite unstable. It seemed so sad that once-loved homes should end up like this.

On the way back to St Paradis we discovered an industrial estate on the outskirts of the *départemental* capital that we hadn't explored before. We found a big pseudo-builders' merchant selling doors, shutters, bathrooms, showers and tiles of all sorts. They had some rustic stone paving we really liked which would have looked wonderful on the terrace but it was prohibitively expensive. With more than 35 sq metres to cover, the slabs would have cost us several thousand pounds. Not far away was a similar establishment stocking outdoor tiles which was closed but we thought it would be worth a visit another time.

We returned to the store with the newly-laid car park, now finished, and while we were looking idly at special offer classical CDs, the mobile phone rang. Our hearts stopped, remembering the last occasion this had happened in France and hoping that Jack's mother was all right. It was Glenn, our next-door neighbour, saying that he had been into the house as usual and discovered the ceiling wallpaper hanging down in the hall by the front door and water dripping through from above. Something drastic had happened to the central heating pipes under the little bedroom floor. Jack told him where to turn off the water at the stopcock and how to switch off the central heating. We were pleased that Auntie was not in residence as usual, because she would have had to spend the next two or three days in the cold, with no hot water.

Our last full day was spent doing trivial jobs. After a wet night we put on our wellies and went out to measure the width of the entrance into the field. It was 3.35m – narrower than we'd expected. We had been surprised that the delivery lorry had found it such a tight fit as we had always envisaged it as quite wide. We thought we'd keep an eye out to see if there were any good quality second-hand gates that we could fit, instead of the poles from the woodland which were there at the moment.

Jack levelled some more of the terrace and filled the space with gravel which had been left over from the cement-making. Then we covered the pile of sand with a blue tarpaulin and weighted down the edges with rocks. I cleared most of the rampant mint out of the front garden flowerbed, pulled up any dead plants and tidied up the rest of the facade, while Jack sprayed the Triffids again with strong weedkiller. We planted tulip and narcissus bulbs along the roadside, under the horse chestnut tree and in the corner of the back garden.

I went down the field and removed the white plastic bags which had been flying like pennants on top of the little oak trees by the hedge. The tractor driver who had been flailing the hedges had respected the signals and left the young trees untouched.

They were now well above the new height of the hedge.

In the late afternoon Jack cut the grass at the back for the last time. It was quite a civilised procedure and only amassed the same volume of cuttings as a normal weekly lawn-mowing would have done in Hartford. It was annoying to think that the next time we came back, the grass would probably be knee-high again, and would require days of work to subdue.

We decided to pack the trailer in advance to give ourselves time to leave early the following day. We thought we might have to spend some time at Orléans dealing with the broken dinner plates and getting replacements sorted out. We had told our 'labourers' that there would be plenty of room for their booze and various other things in the trailer but Jack soon found that it was getting pretty full. It was soon even more packed when Paul came across with two massive home-grown pumpkins and a box of beetroot for us to take back. Previous gifts of giant pumpkins from him had taken pride of place at the local primary school's Hallowe'en celebrations.

Hugo, Harriet and Peachy strolled over to say goodbye and a little later at 7pm Elisabeth and Paul came for supper. We showed them the video of what we had been doing, and when Paul saw the cows wandering up the road on their own on a Saturday afternoon, he said they were obviously "going to confession" at the church!

Our old friends only stayed a short time and we could tell that Paul tired very quickly now. It was sad to see him getting old like this.

When they'd gone Jack cleared the table and I did the washing up, then we made a heap in the kitchen of all the things we wanted to pack in the morning. We were constantly pestered by flies. Jack kept walloping them with a folded newspaper but kamikaze reinforcements continued to arrive.

At bedtime we decided we should have a bath as there wouldn't be any hot water in England until Jack fixed the leak in the central heating. We laughed at the novel role reversal – we usually had a good bath in England to tide us over being dirty in France.

There was heavy rain during the night but it was a nice

morning with high cloud when we got up at 7am. After breakfast we finished doing the trailer and I packed the suitcases. Jan and Beatrice arrived to say 'hello' and 'goodbye'. We didn't recognise them at first. Their smart black Citroen was at the garage for a service and they had been given a courtesy car. It sounded terrible and was only just about running, which didn't give us much faith in the garage that had provided it!

Although it was October 22, the day became increasingly sunny and hot, with the digital thermometer registering 29°C at 11.30am. I was boiling in my 'English' outfit, which was designed to keep me snug on the ferry and during the journey from Portsmouth to Cheshire.

In spite of the fact that we had started early and had done lots of the packing in advance, we finally left St Paradis at 1.30pm, only half an hour sooner than usual. Parkinson's Law always seemed to apply on these occasions. We gave Paul a big kiss and hug, hoping that his health wouldn't continue to fail during the winter.

At Orléans, the customer service department was apologetic about the broken plates and we had no problems replacing them. We scanned the shelves, where the service was also stocked in individual pieces, and bought two more dinner plates, six small bowls and two middle-sized plates.

It took us four hours to get to Le Havre, including a half-hour stop for a quick meal. The ferry wasn't carrying many other cars but there were a lot of lorries. We normally return on a Saturday night and the clientele was quite different. Our uncharacteristic Thursday night trip was necessitated by Jack's long service dinner the next evening. We had a quick look round the shop which had replaced the old 'Duty Free' but nothing appealed to us and we went straight to bed in the cabin.

The crossing was made in Force 5 or 6 conditions, but we had flaked out and didn't feel any movement of the ship at all. When we disembarked the traffic was very heavy, as it was a normal working day, but this didn't make much difference to our stately trailer-towing 60mph progress.

When we arrived home at about noon, after a quick trip into the town to buy some food, we were confronted by a heap of carpet tiles in the hall and the ceiling paper hanging down in a soggy strip, but most of the wet had dried up thanks to Glenn's valiant efforts. Jack's mother was much improved and pottering about, although she was quick to accept the offer of an omelette for lunch. We found that her food stocks were seriously depleted. She appeared to have been living on some 'vegetable soup' that Alex had attempted to make for her the previous weekend from a saucepan full of carrots, cabbage, potatoes and brussels sprouts, stewed in water, which had been reheated several times and had stuck to the bottom of the pan. It smelled disgusting and we threw it away.

As soon as we'd eaten, I went through the 14 messages that had been left on the answerphone. Then we cleared the little bedroom and chucked everything portable into the spare bedroom at the back of the house. We dismantled the bed and carried it down into the hall, as Alex had said he'd like to borrow it, and Jack pulled up the carpet. He decided it must have been laid just when we'd treated ourselves to a new staple gun, as he had to take out umpteen staples which were holding down the underlay and thick grey lining paper.

While he took up the floorboards and delved in the bowels of the central heating, I went to collect Sally from the kennels to which she had been dispatched when Granny Loader was taken ill. She was very pleased to see me but also extremely annoyed about being shut up for so long in less comfort than she was accustomed to. She had barked herself hoarse and smelled very 'doggy'.

Next I went round to our friends who had looked after the 'pups' for us. It was hilarious. I was told that they had fallen out over a bone about a week previously and hadn't spoken to each other since. I bundled them, sulking, into the car with their sack of food, bowls, bones and various belongings, and drove home.

Jack had meanwhile discovered that one of the Yorkshire fittings in the pipework under the bedroom floor had split longitudinally – something he'd never experienced before. He had expected the problem to be in a nearby manifold. Fortunately, he knew the workings of the system very well, having installed it in

1971 shortly before Alex was born. It was the first time anything had gone wrong. He had to drain the system down further than Glenn had done to get the area dry and in doing so made the hall ceiling even wetter than it was already. We went down to an English *bricolage* to get some replacement bits.

We had set a deadline of 5.30pm to start getting tidied up and ready for an ICI taxi to come and collect us at 6.30pm for our glamorous night out. Jack hadn't finished the plumbing repair so our wash-basin ablutions had to be preceded by heating kettles of hot water – just like the old days at St Paradis! We climbed into the taxi in our glad rags feeling rather like scruffy imposters, knowing that we would normally have taken a lot more trouble with our appearance.

Chapter Eleven – March 2000
The Tempest – and afterwards

In December 1999 everyone seemed to be getting quite hysterical about the advent of the new millennium. Jack had been involved for a couple of years in pre-empting any Millennium Bug problems which might threaten ICI's computer equipment, and so our little enterprise had been thoroughly checked out, too. We weren't hoarding food like those who thought the end of the world was nigh, but we had accumulated quite a lot to cope with the fact that the children would be with us at various times and that the public holiday over Christmas and the New Year just seemed to go on and on. We let ourselves be carried along on the general wave of euphoria for what might just be the dawning of a new enlightened age – although, as calendars are so arbitrary, I couldn't really see what all the fuss was about. In non-Christian cultures, January 1, 2000 was just another day, even though places like China were happy to jump on the international celebratory bandwagon.

Jack decided to build me a new computer – from scratch – over the extended holiday period, as none of our customers was going to be working and requiring us to do any business computing. We went to Manchester and bought all the necessary bits.

Chris and Linda arrived on Christmas Eve to stay for a few days. On Christmas Day, Linda presented Chris with his special present: 18 James Bond films on video. It had taken her weeks to find them all. After lunch we made a family decision to screen the video of "Thunderball" but in the evening we all wallowed in nostalgia and watched "The Italian Job" on TV.

On Boxing Day, Geoffrey Morris rang to wish us a Happy Christmas and said that oil from a tanker which had sunk a few days before off the Atlantic coast of France had washed up on the nearby beaches but he didn't know if it would affect the local Charentais oyster and mussel beds.

Virginie also rang from St Paradis. She said the weather was very bad with high winds, but it looked as though our house was all right. We were delighted to speak to her and sad that we would not be there for the New Year, as in the past. We felt we couldn't leave Jack's mother on her own when the whole planet was going millennium-crazy, especially if the predicted power failures and food shortages did occur.

On December 27, news started to emerge about incredible storms and winds that were causing devastation in France. One of the main front page stories in *The Times* reported "the most violent winds ever recorded in Northern France ... in the storm of the century". Like the great English storm of October 1987, meteorologists had failed to predict its force. Poor Meteo France had warned the nation merely of "windy weather". What had materialised was 110mph winds – the strongest since records began. We looked at the maps and kept our fingers crossed for our friends and neighbours.

On December 28, we went to 'the Sales' in an orgy of Christmas-money spending. The weather news from France was bad. There had been a second terrible storm to the south of the first one, causing even more devastation. We hoped it might have missed the Limousin, but this sentiment was in vain. In the evening, we received an e-mail from Virginie, saying that in this storm the roofs of our barn and house had been damaged, as well as the chimney. She said that Georges had tried to telephone us unsuccessfully.

Georges rang again at 8pm, and I had a long talk with him. He was sounding almost shell-shocked by what he described as the *tempête,* which had raged for hours and caused tremendous damage to the local woods and countryside. He said we had lost the 'hat' from the chimney as well as tiles from the barn and slates from the house. Much of the area around St Paradis was without electricity. He needed access to the barn and asked if we could ring Paul and Elisabeth to give our permission for him to have the keys which they held for us.

I rang Elisabeth, who was equally shocked by the experience. The village electricity supplies had only just been restored, she said, and practically everyone had some sort of damage to their homes, although theirs was more or less all right. She agreed to give the keys to Georges and promised to ask her son-in-law Martin, the builder, to deal with the roof damage for us.

We followed the story closely in the media.

Official estimates put the number of trees felled or split in two at 270 million, from 18th century oaks in historic Paris gardens to entire plantations in the Vosges mountains. Almost no part of the country was undamaged and 87 people had been killed. The timber industry was said to be on the verge of ruin in the ensuing glut of wood, although much of it was so damaged it would only be good for pulp. Ecological opinions were divided over whether the phenomenon had been a disaster on a vast scale, or a blessing opening the way for a new reforestation programme. So many roads had been blocked by fallen trees from the beautiful avenues that had lined them since Napoleonic times, that safety campaigners argued these should not be replaced.

Electricité de France (EDF) said that many homes would still be cut off on New Year's Eve and appealed for equipment and workers to help with repairs. British electricity companies responded by providing emergency assistance. With much of his country resembling a battlefield, President Chirac said: "France has been wounded and many French people have been subjected to a cruel torment just as they were spending the end-of-year festivities with their families."

The Times reported that without France Telecom and SNCF, the railway network, the country had been propelled back in time. Hundreds of thousands of people were without phones and thousands were stranded when trains could not get through because of blocked lines. There was no drinking water along the western side of the country because the pumping stations had lost their power supply. Vast swathes of France were declared disaster areas.

Six thousand French troops were called in to clear up after the natural disaster, but there was so much for them to do that 100,000 citizens were still due to see in the New Year by candlelight. Emergency repair work on national monuments like Notre Dame and the Pantheon in Paris, and the abbey at Mont St Michel in Normandy, would be likely to cost 400 million francs. Insurance companies said total claims would come to more than ten billion francs. We took the hint and put in a provisional claim by fax to our own insurers.

The signs did not augur well for the new millennium.

On December 30 our 1790-vintage grandfather clock stopped and was very reluctant to start again. Jack wondered if the Millennium Bug had struck the old technology. In two days' time the handsome old clock would have seen the turn of three centuries – the 19th, 20th and 21st. Fortunately he was able to get it going again later.

While France struggled to recover from the *tempête,* the Brits were struck down by a virulent strain of the 'flu. Its sufferers included Alex and Michelle, who unwittingly infected Jack and me. We succumbed about a week later.

The two of us saw in the new millennium on our own. We set the video to record what was going on all over the world and walked down to the village centre at 11.20pm in a slight drizzle. There were many parties going on so the walk was accompanied by fireworks illuminating the sky all around. Some good friends were responsible for lighting a big gas-fired beacon on the playing field and setting off fireworks. The first occasion it had been lit was in 1992 when Jack and I had organised festivities on behalf of the twinning committee to mark Beacon Europe, to which we had invited a delegation from our twin town of Mornant. It was a great relief not to have had to organise things this time, but seeing the beacon structure – which we immediately associated with France, a speech by the French consul and an address by the Mornant mayor – made us think of our friends in the suffering country at this historic moment.

As the beacon burst into bright flame at midnight, people cheered, honked hooters, rang handbells and hugged one another while a cacophony of rockets and bangers was set off at private gatherings all the round the village. The sky flickered constantly, even when we couldn't see the individual fireworks. It was an emotional moment and we eventually walked back home hand-in-hand, mingling and chatting with lots of other friends, in an atmosphere of conviviality and simple celebration.

Jack's mother was watching our television and keeping the dogs company. I went in first so that I could open the front door again and greet Jack, who was carrying the little blue bag we keep for each New Year 'first footing', containing salt, coal and a coin. We hope the ritual will ensure that we have sufficient for our needs for the coming twelve months. It's worked pretty well, so far.

We opened a bottle of Gratien and Meyer sparkling wine from my mother's French home at Saumur and drank a toast to the new century. Then we watched the video recording of what had been happening while we were away, and switched over to the worldwide live television transmissions until we couldn't keep our eyes open any longer. We went to bed at 2.30am.

Although Granny said the dogs had been frightened by the fireworks while we were out, they did not appear to be too upset by the bangs which continued into the small hours, once they could cuddle down with us on the settee. They are usually utterly terrified by fireworks. Ziggy in particular becomes a quivering wreck and her fear is communicated to the others until all three are distraught. As we got ready for bed we were surprised to discover that as well as Goldie, our usual bedtime companion, Ziggy and Sally were wanting to be with us, too. Sally was quite a rare visitor because as she has got older she has found it very difficult to climb the stairs. We decided to give them a stress-free millennium celebration by allowing them to stay with us. Sally made herself comfortable on the floor, Goldie curled up at the bottom of the bed, and Ziggy wiggled her way into an almost human position stretched flat out between us with her head on the pillow.

When it came in February, Martin's bill for repairing the two roofs was about £800. He had replaced 23.5sq metres of second-hand tiles, six metres of ridge tiles and three sq metres of second-hand slates. We were enormously grateful to him, as we learned later that he had dealt with our house first, after replacing most of his own roof which had been blown away. There had been no internal damage at all to our property, thanks to his quick action. So many people in the vicinity had suffered roof damage that he was to be occupied for many months to come, just doing storm-related repairs.

On March 22, nearly a week in advance, we packed the trailer for our next visit to St Paradis. Although there hadn't appeared to be anything significant to go we soon filled it, with a white flat-packed wardrobe from Glenn and Carole next door, two new IKEA easy chairs, an old leather swivel chair from our sitting room, various boxes of goodies, some planters for the garden and carpet underlay for the small spare room where Bob had slept – not to mention the usual tools and boxes of bolts, screws and nuts.

After breakfast on Tuesday, March 28, we shoved the young dogs and their sack of food into my little car and took them round to our friends who care for them while we are away. Then I loaded up Sally with her food and bedding and delivered her to a nice couple we'd found who were professional 'dog-sitters'. She had been so miserable at the kennels the previous autumn that we thought it only fair for her to enjoy sympathetic human company in a house. In 1988 we'd rescued her from a dogs' home where she had spent most of the first two years of her life, and on the few occasions when we had been forced to put her in kennels she had thought we were abandoning her. We didn't feel we could burden our friends with three dogs, and Jack's mother was now too frail to cope with Sally, as she had volunteered to do before.

Things were complicated. Alex and Michelle had agreed to sell their house in Cheshire but couldn't find one they liked in Kent. They were about to move out and faced the prospect of putting their furniture in commercial storage. We said they could leave things in our house in our absence if necessary. Until they had bought somewhere else, Alex would continue to live in rented accommodation in Kent while Michelle moved in with her parents locally.

We had a good run to Portsmouth and whiled away a 30-minute delay before the ferry docked. When we'd deposited our stuff in our cabin we went along to the shop to see what sort of things were on offer and if they were any better than before, when we'd thought the ferry company buyers had got it very wrong. We were pleased to see that they appeared to have had a complete rethink on the merchandise. Instead of heaps of expensive junk, there was now a choice of good quality items at reasonable prices. I bought an attractive square-section glass candle holder, like a tall vase, in which a cube-shaped candle floated on water containing decorative pebbles. Jack treated himself to a set of computer speakers to use with the laptop at St Paradis.

The crossing was quite rough and we woke when a big wave hit the ship. Fortunately, neither of us is seasick provided that we are lying down.

It was a cold, wet, misty morning when we drove off the ferry at Le Havre just after 6am. We noticed immediately that diesel was now over 5FF a litre and as much as 5.99FF at petrol stations on the autoroute. It was the first time we had made the journey through France on a Wednesday and there was a lot of traffic.

We kept an eye out for storm damage, although most of it had been cleared up during the three months since the *tempête*. The worst case we saw in the northern part of the journey was a church just south of Rouen which had lost its spire and roof. Indeed, it looked as if the spire had fallen through the roof.

As we got into the Limousin the visible damage became greater. Many buildings had tiles missing from the end of their roofs, and in some cases whole sections of roof had been lifted off. For some structures in poor repair the storm had been the final straw and they had collapsed. Close inspection of the hedgerows showed newly-sawn stumps where damaged trees had been felled. In one short but exposed length of road, I counted eleven large vergeside trees that had been cut down. On our favourite 'back way' approach to St Paradis through the depths of the countryside it was apparent that the scenery was much more open than we remembered, even in winter. We could see farms in the distance that we didn't know existed.

As we passed through a tiny hamlet a couple of kilometres away from St Paradis we noticed white powder on the side of the road. We thought a tractor driver had lost a load of fertiliser from the back of his trailer and Jack slowed down for a second look. It was snow! As we went on, more and more became visible on the verges and in the fields.

Our first view of the house was from the back, across the meadow. We scanned it with some trepidation but were relieved to note that there was no immediately visible damage, though we thought we could see more of the Lebruns' property than previously. We were not sure exactly where the tiles and slates had been replaced on our roofs.

We arrived at the house at exactly 4pm, one of the earliest times ever. The shutters at the front had been opened and Paul or another friend had kindly lit a fire in the stove so that the kitchen temperature was 11°C – not bad, given that the place had been empty throughout the winter. We stoked the fire and had a quick look round inside. Everything appeared to be fine except for an insignificant but puzzling small wet patch which showed up on the wooden stairs. We opened all the shutters at the back of the house to let in the light and fastened the windows tight. We always left them fixed slightly ajar to let the building 'breathe' when we weren't there. Then we reconnected the electricity and switched on the electric blanket in our bed to do some preliminary warming before we made up the bed with its newly-laundered sheet, pillowcases and duvet cover.

Outside it was cold – only 4°C – so we unloaded the trailer via the door to the old salon to try to preserve the heat from the Godin. When we pushed the trailer into its usual place in the barn, there was no sign of damage or any problems that had been caused when bits of the roof were blown off, apart from some of Jack's woodworking wood which had fallen over and a quite lot of straw from the haylofts lying on the floor in the central section. We stood in the middle of the road and scrutinised the roofs of the barn and the house, which looked the same as always. Martin had obviously done very well in matching the second-hand slates and tiles he had used for the repairs. It would have looked very unsightly if he had used new ones. He also appeared to have put back the 'hat' which had blown off the *cantou* chimney.

While I unpacked, Jack ventured round the back of the house to look for signs of the storm. A door he had made from old oak planks for the loft of the chicken house had got bent hinges, and another smaller door at the end of the outbuilding had been wrenched off completely. At least one tree on the eastern border was broken at a drunken angle. Otherwise things were pretty much as normal. That was a relief!

I had bought Jack an old copper-plated kettle for Christmas and we put it on top of the Godin, mainly as an ornament but also as a small source of free hot water. It looked very attractive. However we discovered after a time that it wasn't a serious working kettle because there was no vent in the lid. As it heated up, water spurted out of the spout!

We heard a disturbance in the road and looked out of the window to see what was happening. Three scruffy black and white sheepdogs were outside, one with a chain hanging from its neck as though it had broken free from being tethered up. They were chasing each other and also, very dangerously, chasing any cars that passed. There was a risk that the swinging chain would get caught under the wheels of one of the vehicles. We thought the dogs belonged to a farmer who lived round the corner and were used for rounding up cattle, but we had never seen them at liberty before.

We ate the remaining sandwiches we had brought from England, made the bed properly and then went over to see Paul and Elisabeth. We'd bought Paul some bottles of his favourite "bon Bordeaux" at Orléans as a little present for looking after the house. Elisabeth wasn't there – she had gone to spend the afternoon with her daughter. Paul was being cared for by his son who was busying himself with the stove. Our dear old friend did not look at all well. We were sad to see that a single bed had been placed for him in a corner of the room, so that he no longer had to sleep upstairs.

We didn't want to tire him so we accepted a Ricard, then made our excuses and came home.

By the time we went to bed, the kitchen had reached an acceptable 17°C. It was such a relief to have the cheerful glowing Godin radiating so much heat so efficiently. The log fires we used to have in the vast *cantou* had always looked very homely but, as I said before, they had never raised the temperature of the room more than a fraction!

The fire had gone out by the time Jack got up in the morning and the kitchen temperature had fallen back to 11°C. It soon warmed up after he cleaned out the stove and relit it, starting with kindling and firelighters. After nearly six years at St Paradis, we were very used to the fact that living comfortably in the house meant wearing an ever-changing assortment of layers of clothing.

Two of the sheepdogs were still around, and we presumed that their *copain* with the dangling chain was safely tied up again. They were watching us slyly from around the corner of the stone plinth of the *calvary* outside Elisabeth's house and dashing back into cover when they saw us through the window. They were behaving just like naughty children.

We put the springy wooden-framed IKEA armchairs together. We had waited nearly two months for the cushions to be in stock at the Warrington store but when we unwrapped them one of the sets had been assembled in the wrong order so that the 'pillow' bit which should have hung over the front of the chair at neck-height actually dropped behind the back. This was irritating, but we found the chairs themselves to be blissfully comfortable. They rocked gently backwards and forwards as the sitter shifted position and supported the spine at just the right angle. We feared however they might be rather low for our elderly friends, who would probably need a *grue* to haul them out.

We popped across to see Elisabeth and Paul, and to ask if they needed any shopping. Paul seemed better than he had been the previous evening and we promised to return later for a longer chat. On the way back we were pleased to see some of the five kittens darting into the barn. It looked as if both white ones had survived the winter, in spite of the small one being in such a poor state in October. We were pleased – we hadn't liked to think of it suffering a lingering decline and starving to death.

We had a quick lunch of boiled eggs – we had almost no food in the house – and set off for the *départemental* capital via the back lanes. There were fallen trees along the way and it was clear from neat piles of logs in improbable places that many others had been cut up and left to season *in situ*. We stocked up on groceries and tried to compare the prices of French televisions, as we wanted to buy one eventually. But the big store selling them was being refurbished and the electrical department was in chaos. We started to investigate the choice of wire netting for the garden at an agricultural *bricolage* but it began to sleet and we gave up. Then we went to one of the builders' merchants on the industrial estate we'd discovered on our previous visit, but although we found some terrace tiles we liked, they did not have any in stock and couldn't get hold of any within the timescale of our stay. We felt the whole expedition was doomed and returned home the quick way, frustrated and ravenously hungry. The new road was coming along well and the skeletal new bridge looked spectacular.

At home we walked down the field to inspect any damage more closely. It appeared as if at least three trees in the hedge had been blown down, and one had fallen across the Route des Morts. This little lane was such a busy thoroughfare that the fact it had been blocked since December 27 did not appear to have inconvenienced anyone! We decided that priority should be given to clearing the offending tree out of the way.

The little oaks that had been marked with white polythene bags the previous autumn were growing well but it wasn't clear if the transplanted tree was thriving. There was quite a lot of moss on it and no sign of any significant shoots – although spring was running later in this part of the Limousin than at home in Cheshire. We always found it hard to accept that St Paradis was at the same altitude as Shap Fell. What we gained weatherwise by being south of Hartford we lost by being much higher.

Just after six we went to Paul and Elisabeth's for an *apéritif*. Elisabeth was pleased to see us for a longer social visit and Paul continued to be better than before.

After a curry supper, Jack sat down in one of the new chairs with the local free advertising newspaper and promptly went to sleep. I thought IKEA should use this in their publicity literature. Jack has something wrong with the circulation in his legs that makes them ache and prevents him sitting comfortably in any normal armchair for more than a few minutes. This is the main reason why he is always busy doing things, rather than resting on his laurels. I'm afraid I don't have the same problem. Give me a book and an armchair and I'm in heaven.

He woke up at 11.45pm and spent until well after 1am writing up the diary and dealing with e-mails. We finally got to bed at 1.20am, which would have shocked all our neighbours, had they known. Most people in St Paradis are in bed by 10pm or 10.30pm in order to make the most of the available daylight by getting up at crack of dawn. We try to follow this pattern ourselves but it doesn't tie in with our more urban biorhythms.

We got up slightly later than usual and Jack went outside to talk to the two lurking sheepdogs. Although they wagged their tails at him, they backed away as soon as they decided he was too close for comfort. He wondered if the dog which was chasing vehicles with the most determination might have been hit by a car at some time and was trying to get its own back.

After breakfast we got togged up in our chainsawing gear and went down to inspect the tree which was lying across the Route des Morts. We dragged it to one side so that it was not such a hazard. A nearby damaged tree had toppled so that it was hung up in the forked branches of another which was still relatively unharmed and we faced the problem of getting it down without it falling on us or taking the other tree with it. I cut away the encircling brambles and undergrowth with secateurs while Jack gradually lopped off branches to the point where he thought he could roll the remaining trunk out of the other tree, but this manoeuvre turned out not to be possible. He decided to use physics and gravity, and cut lengths off the trunk until it toppled out of the supporting fork under its own weight.

Then, having accomplished what Jack regarded as the challenging and interesting task, we did the more routine job of dismembering the tree which had blocked the road, until it was just a pile of spindly branches and a collection of logs.

At 1pm we stopped for lunch, both feeling the physical effects of a relatively inactive winter. Jack was damp with sweat and sat down in front of the stove to dry out. The IKEA chair worked its magic and he slept soundly for half an hour, although he vehemently denied it afterwards!

Then we made the Big Mistake. It was Jack's really, but I concurred, so I must take some blame too. We decided to run the trailer part of the way down the lane so that we could load it with the heavy cut wood. When the trailer was full, we reasoned, we could back the car up to it, hitch it on, tow it up to the road and – hey presto – we wouldn't have to trudge up the hill umpteen times wearing ourselves out by dragging awkward logs.

We did some more work on the tree, filled the trailer and then

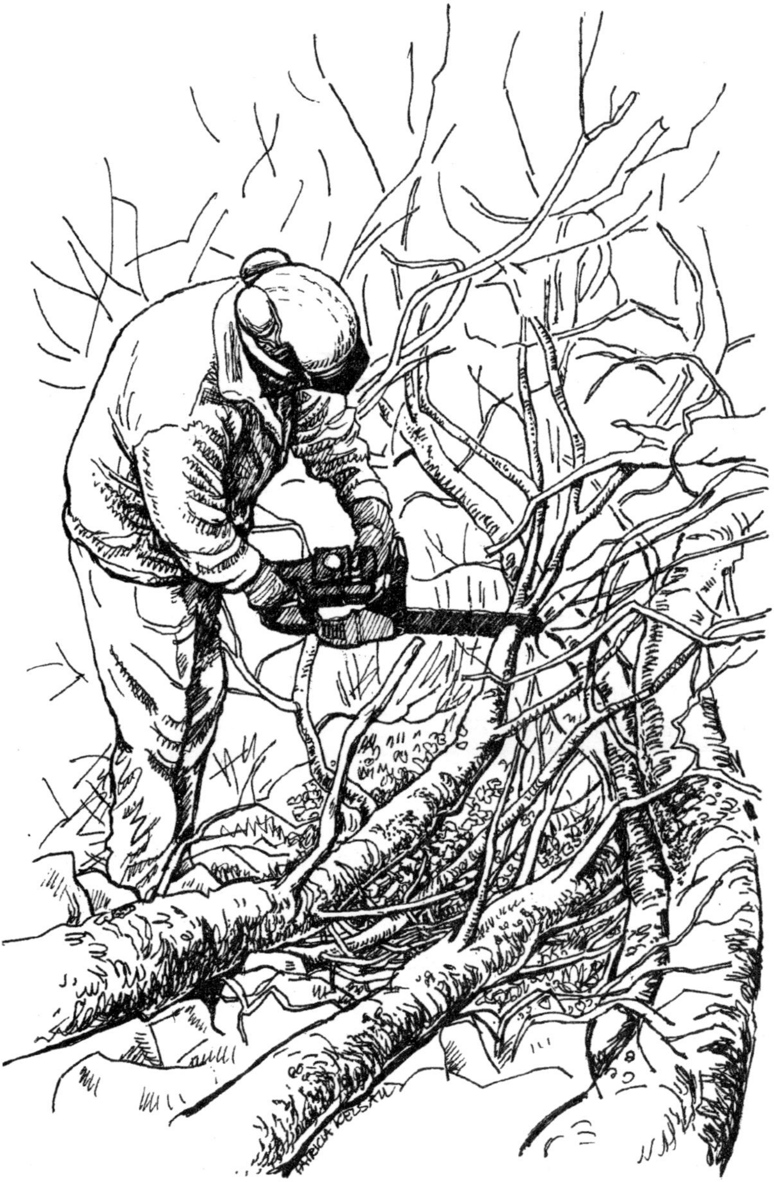

Jack did the more routine job of dismembering the tree which had blocked the Route des Morts, until it was just a pile of spindly branches and a collection of logs.

it started to rain. We put the chainsaw and tools in the boot of the car, before jumping in with the intention of driving away and going inside to get warm and dry. Things didn't work out like that.

Jack couldn't get any traction. The front wheels of the Peugeot just spun uselessly on the wet unsurfaced cart-track. We unhitched the trailer but that didn't make any difference. I lay on the bonnet to add my considerable weight above the driving wheels but that didn't help either. We tried cardboard under the wheels but it just got mashed up and soggy. Then I thought of straw, so we brought armfuls from the barn and pushed it under the wheels. Zilch. As a last resort, we took the blue tarpaulin off part of the sand heap, filled some buckets and laid down a trail of sand. I sat in the passenger seat, leaning well forward, and finally we got enough purchase to edge slowly ahead. Eventually after a lot of effort and false starts, we made it up to the metalled road at the end of the bread-oven building.

We couldn't pull the fully-laden trailer up the steep slope on our own, so we had to empty it and take each log up individually. This was exhausting but the final straw was hauling the empty trailer up the hill, Jack pulling on the towbar end while I pushed from the back. By this time we were both pooped so the trailer came up in short bursts with long rests in between while we sat on the front and puffed.

We were relieved that none of our *agriculteur* neighbours had seen the fiasco, although we wouldn't have been too proud to have accepted a helping hand from someone with a tractor.

Once the trailer was on firm tarmac, Jack reverted to Plan A. We refilled it with all the wood we'd so laboriously unloaded and moved, hitched it to the car and drove round to the barn – once again with difficulty, as the tyre treads were filled with sand and mud and there was very little grip. Then we put the saw-horse in the middle of the barn and Jack chainsawed the big logs into Godin-type lengths while I held them steady. We stacked the sawn lengths at the back of the barn on the wood pile and went into the house when it began to rain really hard.

It was 6pm and we'd been messing about for four hours. We sat down in front of the stove with a large *peu de rouge* as a reward.

An unknown car was parked outside Paul and Elisabeth's house, so we decided to leave them to their guests and stay put. Then there was a knock at the door. It was Georges, Angelique and their toddler, Eric. They had come to invite us to their wedding on April 29. The invitation was actually worded as though it were from Eric, asking us to "the wedding of his parents", and we wondered what the very religious previous owners of our house would have thought! We were extremely disappointed to have to decline, as we would have returned to England by then. It would have been a wonderful experience to celebrate such a happy event with all our friends from the village, but we were committed to holding book launches on April 21 and 25.

Eric was rather shy and tended to hide behind his parents, but a mini Mars bar broke the ice and we had lots of nice smiles. Jack took some photographs of him with our digital camera – my birthday present and our newest toy – and he was thrilled to see his image being played back. They also brought us a copy of the latest issue of the annual village *Bulletin* and we were very pleased that Patricia Kelsall's drawing of St Paradis church from "The Duck with a Dirty Laugh" was on the cover.

After supper we put our feet up, read the newsletter and listened to Dire Straits' "Money for Nothing" on the laptop's CD player. We hadn't the energy to do anything else!

We felt we needed to do some serious terrace research, so in the morning we went off to the city. Before we left we saw Michel who told us that Paul had been taken back to the clinic again – which was sad. On the other hand, we were sure that he would never have received such excellent, instantaneous treatment on the NHS.

At a big builders' merchants in the city we found some ideal multi-sized stone slabs on three weeks' delivery which would look wonderful, but at the equivalent of £30 a square metre we agonised over whether or not we could afford them. Buying them would make the cost of paving the terrace around £1,000 and now that we were living on a pension, that was a lot of money. There were also some nice 11cm square concrete setts in dull shades of dark grey, dark red and ochre at about £17 a square metre, which would also look attractive and bring a hint of colour to the bleak grey back of the house. The total cost of these would be less than £600. When we discovered that they were on only one week's delivery, we believed that the decision had probably been made for us.

Our favourite *bricolage* was closed and in the throes of being rebuilt. Some of the stock had been transferred to its other premises which usually housed only big items like plasterboard and wood. We thought they must be expanding but learned later that the main shop had been destroyed in a fire during the winter, which must have been a tremendous conflagration given all the paint, plastics and other inflammable materials that were displayed inside.

At a big hypermarket we found a *promo* on 200-litre waterbutts and bought one for 99FF. The price included a substantial stand and we were delighted. We had intended to bring one from England but it would have taken up a great deal of space in the trailer.

We also checked out microwave prices. When we first bought the house and needed to equip it as cheaply as possible, we had bought a second-hand microwave from one of my reporters for £35. It had belonged to his mother and was very old and very basic. Over the years it had become downright unreliable and I was frightened of it. I was determined to replace it during this visit with an ultra-modern digital microwave that would operate in precisely punched-in seconds rather than vaguely dialled minutes. I was the queen of molten butter and liquid 'thawed-out' gateaux, caused by my microwave policy of "surely it needs another ten seconds...?"

Then we drove to the *bricolage* down the hill and found that it had been doubled in size since our last visit. The new part, housing a massive garden centre, had opened only the day before and there were numerous introductory offers. All the stock was brand-new and in superb condition so we decided to buy some new geraniums for the kitchen windowsill, some fruit bushes – gooseberries, blackcurrants and redcurrants – for the back garden and a vine for seedless dessert grapes which we would plant at the front of the house as part of our campaign to systematically replace the ancient diseased vine growing across the barn and facade. We'd been searching for a vine for ages without success.

On the way home we remarked how uncannily quiet everywhere was. Then we realised the reason: an important France-Italy rugby match was taking place and the whole population was glued to its coverage. We switched on the car radio and were treated to the usual unintelligible frantic gabble from the French sports commentators. It amused us that all sports reporters, of whatever nationality, have an identical hysterical intonation regardless of which language they are speaking.

We had lunch at 4pm and afterwards Jack made up a strong solution of Roundup in a big watering can to clobber the *mauvais herbes*. He treated the front of the house while the sheepdogs peeped round the corner of Elisabeth's barn to watch, in between noisily pouncing on any passing wheeled vehicle. I went over for a long chat with her and to find out about Paul's health.

When the church clock struck at 6pm we noticed for the first time that Mme Echelle's turkey answered each 'bong' with a burst of gobbling. After this Jack and I made a special point of listening out for him, and he never failed us.

It was Sunday the next day, and we noted with pleasure that the kitchen was, as always, getting about one degree warmer each morning when we came downstairs and was now nearly 15°C. This was the standard rate at which the massive granite walls began to store heat during our occupancy and to lose the cold that they had retained over the winter.

A Radio Four early morning news item reported a protest march in Birmingham the previous day over the decision by BMW to sell off Rover with the loss of thousands of jobs. The journalist pointed out that one reason for the company's decline was the lack of support by British buyers. He added that French consumers supported their national car industry by overwhelmingly purchasing French cars. This led us to look up the private "Cars for sale" columns in the advertising free sheet for March 28, and our research entirely proved his point.

For sale were 278 Renaults, 175 Peugeots, 67 Citroens, 16 VW Audis, 10 Opels, 9 BMWs, 8 Fords, 7 Fiats, 5 Mercedes, 2 Seats, 2

Hondas and a Matra.

Jack busied himself re-potting geraniums, replanting gladioli bulbs, weeding and doing other gardening tasks while I prepared the lunch, with the radio on in the background. I was amused by a line in the literary quiz "Quote Unquote" defining retirement as "twice the husband for half the money" and went out to tell my pensioner spouse.

After lunch it was a lovely spring afternoon, with a strong breeze, and we walked down to the wood via the little lane past the restored *fontaine*. A tree had fallen into the duck pond during the New Year storm and was partly blocking the way. We noticed that the water level in the pond, now sadly bereft of ducks, looked lower than usual. The tiny stream from the pond was still running strongly along the little ditch at the bottom of our field but was no longer flowing into the field itself. The water carried on a short way and then seemed to vanish down what appeared to be a mole hole. We thought it would have come as quite a shock to the mole.

In the field opposite, on the other side of the narrow road, was a cream Charolais cow and a very small calf with the sweetest face and expression, plus two others of intermediate size who seemed to be teenage bovines in the throes of discovering the joys of sex. They came across to inspect us over the hedge and we had a little chat. As we walked back and turned towards the wood, they filed across the field in size order, which looked very organised, like a primary school 'crocodile'.

Our detailed inspection of the wood for storm damage was very satisfactory. There were only two significant trees which had been blown down and a small holly which had probably fallen because of an existing weakness at the base of its trunk. It looked as if its growth had been restricted by something tight, like a loop of wire. There were quite a lot of reasonably sized saplings coming along which would help to get the M-shaped half-acre wood going again. Many of the trees had been pollarded in years gone by to provide brushwood for the bread oven. It was nice to be able to move around easily in there, as later in the season the tangled brambles, low leafy branches and thick undergrowth became very constricting. Indeed, to my everlasting embarrassment, I had actually got lost in there at the height of a previous summer, as no two sides were parallel and I had completely missed my bearings for about half an hour!

When we got back to the house there were thousands of ants milling about by the front door, running up and down the door frame and along the front wall. A quick blast with an aerosol of ant killer soon sorted them out. Jack thought he must have disturbed a nest when he was gardening earlier in the day.

While I went over to see Elisabeth, he repaired the hinges of the oak door in the chicken house loft that had been damaged in the storm and fitted a new catch. When I returned, the wind had dropped and we sat outside enjoying the simple pleasure of a St Paradis late afternoon with its busy farm noises, lowing cattle, birdsong and peaceful atmosphere.

We decided to clear some more of the brambles while they were fairly dormant so that we could put up barbed wire along the short open boundary with the Route des Morts and block the bottom with pig wire, so that when we eventually brought the dogs with us they wouldn't be able to escape. Armed with very thick leather gloves, it was a satisfying job. After a short time Jack went off to do some more proper gardening while I did the destructive stuff more suited to my non-green fingers. He came back later and dug out the biggest bramble roots as I exposed them. It became quite addictive and we didn't stop until the whole lot was cleared and piled up on a blazing bonfire.

It was nice when we got up next day but bad weather was forecast. Jack managed to persuade the lawnmower to work with the aid of some WD40 on the flywheel and a blowlamp on the plug, then cut the grass in front of our house and Elisabeth's small area as well. Just as he was finishing, it started to rain. After lunch we went to the friendly builders' merchant with the English Setters, who had delivered the original materials for the terrace. We chatted to him in his office about what we were doing, and ordered five tonnes of gravel and two tonnes of sand so that we could finish levelling the surface ready for the paviors. He promised to deliver it during the afternoon in a couple of days' time.

On the way back along our favourite back roads we spotted a red squirrel for the first time in our lives. It was on the grass verge, quite unafraid, and stayed there long enough for us to see it in detail. It was much darker than I had expected from seeing specimens pictured in books.

At home we set up the saw bench and cut all the remaining small branches – from our ill-fated expedition with the trailer – into kindling-sized lengths, leaving them in heaps to dry out.

As the weather had brightened we decided to go down the meadow with the chainsaw and start dealing with the damaged trees further along the hedgerow that had fallen into a disused branch of the Route des Morts. This little *chemin,* which had once acted as an access to several other small fields to the right of our property, was shown on the village map but was rarely used, except by us. After a lot of rain, a little waterfall chuckled from a spring at the very end, and there was a fascinating granite rock half-way along which had probably been damaged by frost but looked like an elaborately-carved pagan sculpture. A few strands of rusty barbed wire hung across its entrance, presumably as a deterrent to wandering cattle. I thought I saw a cat sneaking through the long grass but when I approached more closely I could see that it was a big cock pheasant.

The land at the edge of our meadow sloped steeply down towards the *chemin*, levelled out across the pathway and then suddenly dropped another ten feet. A few trees on our actual boundary were down, but there was also a large one on the other side of the path that was completely uprooted, showing only the soil-covered crown of its roots at right angles to the ground where a three-feet deep hole had been gouged out. The tree itself had fallen into the bramble-filled field below and was resting on its branches. We didn't think it was our responsibility as the land on the far side of the *chemin* did not belong to us, but we didn't want to abandon it like that as a permanent scar on the landscape. We decided to leave it for the time being and deal with the easy tasks first.

We managed to cut several middling sized branches from our own damaged trees and I pulled them up into the meadow to start a primitive log stack. We thought we would follow the example of the other landowners with fallen trees and let the wood season where it stood for the recommended six years. The novelty of dragging logs up steep hills had worn off very quickly during the exhausting afternoon in the Route des Morts! Jack reasoned that he would have saved up enough to buy his coveted small tractor by the time it came for us to need them.

Black skies and rain led us to call off the session and we went back into the house. I prepared a simple supper which we shared with Elisabeth. Afterwards we enjoyed a pleasant evening together talking, watching videos of what we'd been doing and playing with the digital camera so that its photos were displayed on the computer screen.

She left at 10pm and we tidied up. Jack put some old French bread and some of his 'Panasonic wholemeal bread' in the blue plastic dish that we keep outside the front door for any passing hungry animals in need of a little snack. A minute or two later he found some spare dripping and gravy left over from a previous pot-roast and went out to recover the bowl so he could mix it in for some lucky canine or feline diners in the morning. He found that the wholemeal bread had already disappeared but that whoever had eaten it had rejected the rapidly-hardening remains of the *baguette*!

That night, in bed, we were aware of an odd metallic noise which seemed to come from the roof directly above us. When we investigated in the morning we discovered that the zinc 'hat' on the chimney which Martin had replaced for us, was damaged again. One corner had become detached and was flapping against the frame. We didn't know what to do for the best, because it was far too high for Jack to reach and we couldn't ask a busy builder like Martin to come back for something so trivial.

That afternoon we went to the city to order the multi-coloured pavoirs. We'd done our quantity surveying, worked out our sums and agonised over our choice, but we felt we should be sensible and buy the cheaper option. When we'd originally hung our noses over beautiful stone paving slabs we had not known that there would be a record-breaking storm or that we would be faced with part of an insurance bill for the roof repairs. There were also still plenty of other things we needed to do on the old house. Although it was structurally sound, 200-year-old farmhouses are, by definition, bottomless pits into which you pour your cash.

The transaction was complex: the price of 169FF per square metre was dropped to 152.76FF because we were buying so many of the concrete setts, but we had to have more than we wanted because they were sold by the pallet and we had to order three complete pallets. There was a 105FF deposit to be paid on each pallet and a 150FF delivery charge, so in English money the final total came to something like £580 less £30 when we returned the pallets (which in itself would require expenditure on another trip to the city).

That done, we went to a big electrical store and bought a Samsung microwave with a digital timer for 990FF. It was on a special offer and we had to take the model on display, as all the others had been sold.

Feeling rather pleased with ourselves, we returned home. En route we stopped off at a tiny hamlet of about five houses to photograph where a complete copse of trees had been levelled during the storm. They had stood by a stream, beside a stone bridge on fairly wet land, and it seemed that when the hurricane force wind had hit them, they had not been sufficiently well anchored to resist. The roots had been ripped up and the once majestic trees now lay in confused heaps on the ground.

As we were in an expansive mood, with nothing in particular to do, we decided to have a potter round some of the by-ways of the commune and its surrounds that we had not explored before. It was strange to discover that only a few miles from the wooded hills and tiny fields of St Paradis, which we knew so intimately, the landscape suddenly became flatter for a time with much larger fields. If someone had blindfolded us and dropped us there we would not have recognised it as home.

Back at the house we unpacked the microwave and got in the logs from the barn for the next 24 hours. Then Mme Echelle came for a chat. We were very pleased to see her and invited her in. She said she now had 13 grandchildren and told us about the recent wedding of one of her children in Paris when the family had hired a coach to transport them all from the Limousin. After the reception and meal in a local chateau they had all got back to their hotel at 6am. Unfortunately she didn't get much sleep as some of the grandchildren played a joke on her by knocking on her bedroom door not long afterwards saying that the coach was going and she was keeping everyone waiting – which wasn't true, as all the other revellers were still in bed! They eventually came home after lunch and arrived at Marcheville at 9pm. Shattered, we thought...

It was a cold grey day with steady rain when we got up. Jack was just putting his boots on to make a quick sortie outside to lay the plastic sheet in the entrance to the field ready for the delivery of sand and gravel – which was promised in the afternoon – when the lorry carrying them arrived.

The builders' merchant was much happier about reversing into the gateway this time and we noticed that he had fitted some new tyres on the back of his lorry. While I kept watch for traffic coming round the bend he dumped the sand at the rear of the sheet and the gravel at the front in two neat piles. He and Jack exchanged pleasantries and he said we ought to do our building work in the summer when it was dry enough for him to drive all the way round the back of the barn and put the materials where we needed them!

We saw Jan and Beatrice arrive for coffee with Elisabeth. I was invited too, so I went across and left Jack moving barrowloads of sand from the gateway to the heap beside the terrace. A few minutes later, Dirk and Pieter arrived. Pieter came to join the rest of us while Dirk and Jack stayed outside in the rain. Dirk wanted to ask if they could put the donkeys in our field for a few weeks because their hay was finished and they didn't have sufficient grass for the animals at home. They had suffered the same problem as all the local *agriculteurs* with stock that needed grazing – the weather had been so bad this spring that the grass had not got established. Jack explained that while we would be delighted in principle, the field wasn't completely fenced and we didn't know if Georges had got it earmarked for any of his stock. Dirk said the fencing wasn't a problem – they would just bring their own electric fence along. He didn't know Georges, so Jack said he would check with him if it would be OK. Georges had always managed our land for us very well and we didn't want to cause him any problems.

It started to rain really hard, so Jack and Dirk gave up their outdoor conversation and came over to Elisabeth's too, where we all crowded round the kitchen table.

We brought up the subject of the storm. It had had such serious consequences for everyone in France that it was a topic which recurred frequently in everyone's conversation. Beatrice told us their "hurricane story" in detail.

On the day of the storms they were due to go to La Souterraine station about 45km away to collect some friends who were coming to stay with them. The journey was awful and the car was battered around by the wind en route. When they arrived at the station they waited for ages but no one arrived. Then their friends rang on the mobile phone to say that the train couldn't get through and all the passengers had got to stay at Châteauroux. Jan and Beatrice tried to drive back home but were stuck for hours in a massive traffic jam, most of the time under a bridge where their mobile wouldn't work! Eventually they got hold of Pieter and Dirk to ask them to look after the young dog who had been left on her own. (We discovered later that the older one had died since we had last seen them.) The police came along and took the cars from the queue in convoy back to La Souterraine. Jan and Beatrice were not given the option of going in their preferred direction, the opposite way. The hotel in the town had closed for Christmas and they drove round looking for a public hall where they had been told that people were being accommodated. They couldn't find it. Everywhere was closed. They tried the station again, to no avail. So they drove round slowly for four hours with nothing to eat, with the heater on in the car to keep warm. Eventually they slept in the car. They listened to the radio and finally heard that the road was open again. They set off and found a white-out of snow. After a nightmare journey they arrived home. There was no electricity. Later they had another phone call from their friends saying that they had now arrived at La Souterraine, so Jan and Dirk got back in the car and returned to collect them. Pieter and Dirk were without power for two days, and Jan and Beatrice for three. Because their central heating and hot water systems needed electrical timers and switches to operate, both households were also without heat (except in the one room where each had a fireplace) and hot water until the electricity supply was restored. Non-electric heating appliances were almost impossible to buy because the demand was so great, and there were dark hints about various traders who had tried to profiteer. One local shop was said to have got in a stock of candles and portable fires and charged three times the going rate for them. Everyone had been frozen – and the more unusable modern appliances they had, the more they had suffered. We were so sorry that we hadn't known about their plight. We had spent years without modern appliances in our old house and were geared for survival. We had five portable gas heaters which we would gladly have given our friends to use as long as they wished, and enough gas bottles to keep them going for a few days. We also had a 15-tog duvet, hot water bottles and a big stock of candles. We made everyone promise that if ever an emergency like this happened again when we were away, they would raid our house for whatever might be needed.

As Elisabeth's lunchtime approached, Pieter and Dirk invited everyone present to dinner in a few days' time. We all embraced and split up. Jack returned to sand shovelling as the rain had decreased to a slight drizzle, and I joined him after accepting Elisabeth's kind offer of the loan of her wheelbarrow. It was a different design from ours, with an A-shaped frame with the point sticking out at the front. This was very good for tipping as once you had dug it into the earth the barrow stayed put whereas ours was still on its front wheel and tended to wobble off line, but it had the disadvantage that unless you had very short arms or made sure to keep the handles low and push it very flat, the front would suddenly embed itself in the ground and bring you to a sudden and unexpected halt with your nose in the sandy contents.

We developed a time-and-motion scheme whereby Jack pushed and I shovelled. With two barrows on the go there was always one spare for me to fill. It was easier for me to do this than try to steer them up the gang-plank into the terrace 'box' and then empty them. After a few tries I found I hadn't got the strength to manhandle the barrow with any expertise.

We soon had the two tonnes of sand shifted and started on the gravel, continuing until we felt hungry and stopped for our own meal.

Afterwards Jack drew a map of St Paradis to send to the merchants who were due to deliver the coloured setts later in the week. We weren't really in their area, as the city was actually in the next *département*, so their office staff had never heard of our tiny hamlet and we feared that our delivery might end up somewhere completely different which had an approximately rhyming name. We hadn't got any stamps so we drove down to the town to buy some at the post office. At the main crossroads on the edge of the medieval centre a large *convoi exceptionelle* was trying to negotiate the narrow right-angle bend, and failing miserably. We nipped round a short cut to avoid the jam that was building up. Marcheville had certainly been at an important crossroads since the Middle Ages, but apart from the wide market square, the rest of its streets were not suited to modern commercial traffic. However, since a by-pass might come uncomfortably close to St Paradis, we selfishly hoped the townspeople would continue to put up with their daily onslaught of juggernauts.

We moved some more gravel, cut up some wood when it rained and then baulked at gravel barrowing when the rain stopped. It was an incredibly boring pastime. Instead we inspected the transplanted tree at the bottom of the field. It was still not showing any signs of life although most of our other trees were in bud. We walked round the perimeter looking at the state of the hedging – with a view to seeing how donkey-proof it was – and then climbed down into the disused lane to get a better look at the tree that had fallen into the field. It was easier to explore when Jack wasn't encumbered by heavy chainsawing trousers, a safety helmet and a big gauze mask. Clambering partly down the initial three-foot vertical drop, supported on the most robust branches, he was able to see that the bank had once been neatly faced with stone from the edge of the path down to the overgrown field. The land then fell away very steeply from this point. He could also see, from that angle, that the entire field was filled with brambles that were taller than a man. They stopped neatly at each barbed wire boundary. From this we concluded that the field had been unused for many, many years, although the ones surrounding it were grazed regularly by animals in a rotation system. We wondered if it had once belonged to Marguerite and was still in the ownership of her nephew. We knew that the Xaviers had been conscientious farmers who kept their land well maintained and it seemed a shame that the trouble they had once taken to wall the bank so neatly had been wasted.

I wasn't in the mood for being outside in the cold and intermittent rain, so Jack said he could manage without me. While I read a book in the warm kitchen, he cut off all the branches of the broken trees that he could reach safely on his own. He learned to be observant and nimble on his feet when large bits of tree failed to fall in the direction he had predicted.

I tried to make him a nice supper to compensate for his chilly afternoon's work. Setting the table nicely, I thought I would add a romantic touch by lighting the square-section candle holder I'd bought on the ferry. It looked really pretty to start with, as the square candle floated on its water above multi-coloured pebbles. Unfortunately we soon discovered its basic design drawback. The candle burned very deep so that the wick was soon surrounded by wax and there was not enough room to get any oxygen to it. Only the tip of the flame showed when it was alight, but more often than not it went out. It had also burned more on one side than the other so that the candle was not balanced symmetrically and floated with one edge under the water! It was a great disappointment and we were surprised that the manufacturers had not discovered the problems early in their product research. Perhaps they didn't care.

It was miserable and damp the next day, too, but the temperatures had soared to a Mediterranean 3.5°C. In spite of continuing drizzle we decided we really must move the rest of the gravel, so Jack took another dozen or so barrowloads from the heap in the gateway. I was excused shovelling, so I went in search of little horse chestnut shoots, dug them up and transplanted them around the edge of the field in the hope that one or two might grow into big trees for the benefit of future generations. I marked each one with a bamboo cane

While Jack was having a rest, he was surprised to see a tractor and trailer stop by the little junction at the end of the field and dump a load of rubbish, apparently in the pond. Indignant, he fetched the camera from the kitchen and took a photograph of the culprit as he came up the road. It wasn't possible to see who was in the cab, and we didn't recognise the tractor.

We decided to walk down to have a look at what this vandal had done. En route we bumped into Mme Echelle's son, who was cutting firewood and we passed the time of day. When we got to the heap we discovered that it was on the grass verge and not in the pond as had appeared from Jack's original vantage point. It was all scrap metal. As we were turning back, the tractor and trailer returned and dumped some more scrap in the same place. We suddenly realised that it was the day for the yearly scrap metal collection, organised by the commune but advertised in the annual newsletter as on "a date to be arranged". It was all picked up by the local scrap metal dealer (who had the wonderfully incongruous name of "Monsieur Ferrari"), and the money raised went into the commune's funds. It was an accepted thing that if you fancied an item that someone else had thrown away, you could take it in return for a small donation. Dirk and Pieter had acquired a fine old-fashioned plough in this way, which now stood as an ornament in front of their barn.

When we checked the e-mails, we found one from Chris and Linda, who were coming to France later in April and were due to spend a couple of days with us after a wine-buying holiday in Champagne with Linda's parents and before going south to the Dordogne. They said it was cold and miserable in England too, with snow earlier in the week.

We moved some more gravel and then Jack dug a hole in the corner of the terrace to take a large plastic box which would act as a sump for our planned water feature. We had a slight difference of opinion on what we wanted: I fancied an amphora on its side from which the water poured with a pleasing sound; Jack concurred with the pleasing sound but wanted to build a rocky waterfall instead. I decided that the thing was so far in the future that it wasn't worth discussing in detail for at least another year. First pave your terrace...

At lunchtime Jack had a shock when he was about to eat his 'pudding' - an ice cream cornet – seated at the computer, writing up the diary. He's an ice-creamaholic, you understand. He uncoiled the thin cardboard wrapper without paying any attention and discovered that he had a cold, wet handful of ice cream. There was no cornet at all! Obviously the machine at the factory had failed the put the cornet in the wrapper and had just filled it with ice cream!

I went over to Elisabeth to see if she needed anything from Marcheville. We were going to buy some bread and food, as Georges and his family were coming to have an evening meal with us. She asked us to pay her insurance at the local office.

We parked in the market square and were interested to see a rash of posters pasted all over the big noticeboard there which usually advertises forthcoming events. They were all protesting about a Government proposal to investigate dumping nuclear waste in the region. We'd heard from Dirk that the idea had caused a drop in demand for local houses as second homes. One neighbour told us that nothing would come of it because President Chirac came from the Limousin and his friends in high places would never allow it, while another neighbour said that the Creuse was being picked on because it was so depopulated that there were not enough voters to oppose it. Conspiracy theories abounded. I memorised a few of the slogans:

"La Creuse n'est pas le trou de cul du Paris" (The Creuse isn't the arsehole of Paris)

"Les maçons de la Creuse ont construit Paris, maintenant Paris veut détruire la Creuse" (The masons of the Creuse built Paris, now Paris wants to destroy the Creuse)

"Après les vaches folles, les vaches irradiées..." (After mad cows, radioactive cows...)

The insurance office was so unused to having its bills settled in real money that the manager had to raid his petty cash box for some change. He was very charming and gave me a souvenir thermometer and a pen, which I passed on to Elisabeth later.

When I bought the bread the shop was empty and I had a long chat to the baker's wife about the storm. Because Jack now made the wholemeal bread which we ate ourselves, I hadn't needed to use the regular *boulanger*'s van which served St Paradis and I hadn't seen her during this visit. She said that the town campsite had suffered severely because it was surrounded by conifers, which had been more susceptible to damage because of their wind-resistance.

We went to have a look and were very sad to see the destruction everywhere. There were large heaps of pine trees stacked on the side of the road and great swathes cut through the pine woodland that fringed the campsite and provided welcome shade in the summer. We thought it would take a lot of work to clear up before the holidaymakers arrived.

Jack continued to move the gravel and I helped him from time to time. I was busy preparing the evening meal. When he couldn't face barrowing any more, he marked the precise levels for the terrace with pieces of wood, using a long piece of I-section aluminium with a spirit level taped to it.

We had a very enjoyable time with Georges, Angelique and Eric, who soon lost his shyness when I presented him with some stuffed toy friends and we all played "boo" round the edge of the sofa. When he discovered the joys of the computer keyboard after we'd had our meal, he was in seventh heaven. They brought us a bottle of wine and some attractive ornaments depicting the local chateau and scenes of Marcheville, which we immediately displayed on the new dresser.

During the course of the evening we asked Georges if he would mind Dirk and Pieter grazing their donkeys on the field, and he said it would be fine.

Bearing in mind the fact that it was April 7, we were surprised to find the field white with frost in the morning and the thermometer registering 0.7°C outside. We hadn't been given a firm date for the delivery of the setts but were beginning to wonder if they might come in the next day or two.

We were just starting breakfast when we heard a lorry arrive. It was them! The vehicle was too big to reverse through the gateway, so we agreed that the driver would use the hoist on his lorry to unload the three pallets into the field entrance. The coloured setts were randomly mixed and actually contained in enormous white plastic fabric bags which were resting on the pallets – so we ascertained that the merchant didn't want those back too. We were pleased when we were told that they weren't required, as we thought they would come in handy for us to use some time.

I kept my usual watch for any traffic which might crash into the lorry as it took up the entire road, and chatted to Michel who was passing en route to his vegetable garden. He asked us round for an *apéritif* at noon.

We decided to make a quick dash to a nearby town to get some nice plants for us and Elisabeth to take as gifts to the two Dutchmen when we went round for our meal that evening. There was very little choice in Marcheville except on market days. We bought some lovely pot plants in a garden centre and then, whilst looking for some glue for the water feature sump in the *bricolage* opposite, I found a pair of patio lights of the exact design we wanted, at half price. There were lots of other bargains but we didn't have time to investigate them. We were pleased with our flying visit.

We just managed to make it back home by 11.58am, in time to be politely late at Michel's at 12.02pm. We had a good chat and then were delighted to be shown round the house which one of his sons had bought as a holiday cottage. It had belonged to Monsieur Lebrun and stood a few feet from Michel's front door on what appeared to be the same plot of land although, by the complications of French inheritance law, it wasn't. The property consisted of an unoccupied double fronted little house, a miniature version of ours, with a bread oven building opposite constructed over a *cave*. It had been on the market unofficially for some time, and Hugo and Harriet had looked at it, but since it had no land whatsoever, it wasn't an attractive buy. However, if your father owned most of the land around it, it was an ideal buy. In the past, we had managed to peep through the dirty downstairs windows when we walked past, but we had never been inside. First, though, Michel showed us the neighbouring barn, which had a chimney. It turned out to have been the very primitive building where Georges' grandmother had been born in the second half of the 19th century. One would never have thought it to have been habitable. It had a stone sink arrangement on one of the walls and a hole for a bread oven in another. It must have been absolutely freezing. There was no first floor in it now, but it was high and presumably at one time it would have had a *grenier*.

The building work on the little house was being completed by the youngest of Mme Echelle's sons, who worked for a firm in Marcheville. He was doing a very nice job – and had only a five-minute walk to get to work and nip back home for lunch. The house was basically three up, two down, with a staircase in the centre, and we reckoned it was more or less contemporaneous with Virginie's which had been rebuilt in 1905. The builders had enlarged the windows so that they were now double-glazed and about the same size as ours but still in proportion (originally they had been considerably smaller). They had moved the front door, which used to be in the centre, to take the place of one of the windows so that it now led straight into the kitchen. The old front door 'hole' was now a window into the main room, making it surprisingly sunny and light. The floor downstairs was concrete and there was a *cantou* in the kitchen of a much more 'modern' design than ours, as were the stairs. Our steep staircase was very crude and had obviously been hand-made as he went along by a carpenter from a supply of thick-sawn oak planks.

Upstairs, was a large bedroom running from front to back, and two others separated by a thin partition wall. They had all been covered with violently bright blue and black wallpaper, topped by a pretty border with deep curves in it. More stairs led to an attic with pristine roof timbers, like ours. The house felt much bigger inside than it looked from the outside.

The bread oven building opposite had proper hinged iron doors on its oven (ours had a loose metal cover with a handle, that was pushed roughly into place), which was shallower than our two-metre deep *four à pain*. Michel's son was going to turn this into a workshop. Below was a *cave* with a vaulted ceiling like ours, built into the side of the hill so that it was at ground level on one side and well below ground on the other. It was reached by a door at road level. Michel said they had bought the field next door – which we had never realised was not his – and were going to put in a curved drive leading to the little house. They had also bought other little parcels of land to give undisputed access.

As usual, we probably stayed too long, in that whenever Michel and his wife come round to us for an *apéritif* they stay exactly 60 minutes and then make their excuses. However, it had been a fascinating tour round the property, showing what could be done with ostensibly unpromising material. The house, like so many other Creuse properties, was very soundly constructed and its smart new wooden windows and repointed masonry had completely transformed its appearance. It was now one of the prettiest in the village rather than a sorry, cobwebby shell.

After lunch we continued to work on the terrace until 6pm when we smartened ourselves ready to go to dinner with Pieter and Dirk. Jack made an experimental nine-inch flat strip of sand on top of the levelled terrace to see how the next phase would go. We picked Elisabeth up in the car and arrived at 6.30pm to find Jan and Beatrice already there.

We admired the new terrace which they'd had installed by their builder since our last visit. They had used terracotta tiles – which we had once wanted for our own terrace until we were persuaded that the red would be out of place against the granite walls of the house – and these looked superb. We wondered if we would regret buying the much-darker setts which were currently taking up so much room in the field entrance.

The view over the lake was idyllic and the sound of the burbling stream along the border just added to the magic. Dirk said that the major landowner in the village, who had the big walled *maison de maître* nearby as his holiday home, had drained the lake the previous autumn and it had only just refilled itself. The villagers were annoyed because they had helped him with the harvest but had received no free fish for their pains, as was the custom since time immemorial. We were sorry we hadn't seen it in this state, because we couldn't imagine how it would look when it was empty. The wide shimmering lake was such a dominant feature of the landscape that it was hard to think of it as an expanse of brown mud.

Dirk served a wonderful Indonesian meal. Jack and I had never eaten Indonesian food before but it is as common in Holland as Indian fare is in Britain and all the Dutch present were very familiar with it. Both countries had developed a taste for the delicacies of their former colonies. We started with delicious rice-based puffs that Jack and I would normally buy in packets in England – well, Dirk had made them from their basic ingredients and fried them in boiling oil while we waited. They were mouthwateringly gorgeous, as was everything that followed. I wished I had a quarter of Dirk's skill as a cook.

Jan and Beatrice asked if we were going to the annual *choucroute* supper to be held on Saturday, April 14. We hadn't heard about it and Beatrice explained that it was the spring event organised by the commune and held at the *Salle des Fêtes*. It traditionally marked the end of the winter when just about the only preserved food the *paysans* had left was their bottled sauerkraut. I can't stand sauerkraut, whose smell reminds me of old dishcloths, but we were keen to take part in a communal party and asked Beatrice to get some tickets for us. Elisabeth said she'd like to come, too, if Paul was still in the clinic.

At the end of the evening, Jan encouraged the tabby cat to do her party trick of supping milk from her paw as if she were on a TV advertisement. I took some photos of her – and everyone else – with the digital camera, which was still a novelty for us.

We woke to a bright sunny morning but the north-facing field was covered with white frost and it was only 3.3°C. Luckily, as the day went on it became typically springlike with warm sunshine and hardly any wind. When we stood at the top of the granite back steps arm-in-arm, surveying the countryside, we were very amused to see that a cat had walked exactly along the very centre of the sandy strip on the terrace and left a neat trail of footprints. We wondered what had been going on in its mind at the time.

After breakfast I helped Jack to run cable ducting along the edge of the terrace wall, to take cables that would power the patio lights and the water feature pump at a very much later date. We experimented with breeze blocks to see how high we might be able to build up the rocky waterfall that Jack had in mind. We had no shortage of big rocks to use as raw material when the time came.

In the afternoon we went back to the *bricolage* where we'd bought the half-price patio lights, to get some bits for the wiring and an exterior tap so that we could have an easily-accessible water supply for the garden. I also bought some adhesive lace shelf-edging to soften the three white melamine shelves in the back kitchen which I had always regarded as being a bit too modern for their surroundings. We investigated the prices and specifications of pond pumps in the garden centre, but they were all too big and powerful for what we had in mind.

When we returned I went over to see Elisabeth. She told me she was hoping that an electrician would come soon to rewire the house for her. The existing wiring was very old and potentially dangerous. Paul was still being treated in the clinic but was due home the following week if he was well enough.

Jack fetched me back to say that Pieter and Dirk had arrived with their dogs to put up the electric fence for the donkeys. They bisected the field with yellow metal stakes and then ran them round in an oblong, threading the potentially electrically-charged ribbon of wire through them and making a safe enclosure. We talked outside for a time and then invited them in. We all sat by the fire and chatted for another hour or two. Pieter admired the Edinburgh Woollen Mill chequered shirt Jack was wearing and mentioned that he'd paid the equivalent of £75 for a shirt in Holland and found it later for only £25 in the United States. We said that Jack's shirt had cost about £6 in a special offer in Northwich! I promised to buy him a similar one in England but forgot to ask what size he was.

When they'd gone I cooked spaghetti bolognese in the new microwave and it turned out very well. We'd been using it to thaw out butter from the fridge to perfection (ten seconds at the lowest setting) but this was the first time I'd attempted to make a meal in it and I was pleased with the result. The dish could perhaps have done with a bit longer, but we were very hungry.

Next day we started to do more things in the bathroom, to the strains of classical music on the CD player which filtered up the stairs. As we were working in there, a most horrible smell arose. When we couldn't stand it any more and had ruled out any source in the bathroom, I went downstairs to check. Mme Echelle's little black and white bitch had let herself in, got trapped and pooped on the back kitchen floor. When I found her, she looked guilty and scuttled off home as fast as her legs would carry her. I got out a bucket and some disinfectant. *C'est la vie...*

As the *lambris* crept round the bathroom walls it began to look more and more civilised. Jack wired up the main convector heater under the window and a smaller one we had bought to keep towels dry (when we'd rigged it up with a safety cover). We connected the cable into the fusebox downstairs and turned both fires on. Lots of grey smoke and fumes came out of the larger heater and after making sure there was nothing seriously wrong we decided that the cause was accumulated rubbish on the elements and let it burn itself out.

We were disappointed to find that some of the packs of *lambris* were not properly seasoned. We hadn't expected them to have been dried out for six years, like our best oak firewood, but we had hoped that they wouldn't smell of damp pine when the wrapping was opened and reveal planks which were warped. Jack left them leaning individually against the landing wall to sort themselves out for a day or two.

After supper, with nothing he could do in the bathroom, he settled down on the settee to read "At Dawn We Slept", the vast scholarly story of Pearl Harbour and the events leading up to it, which I'd bought in a book sale at Northwich Library. He had been studying it on and off in the downstairs loo for three years and at last the action had moved to within hours of the Japanese attack... I curled up beside him with a less demanding book of my own.

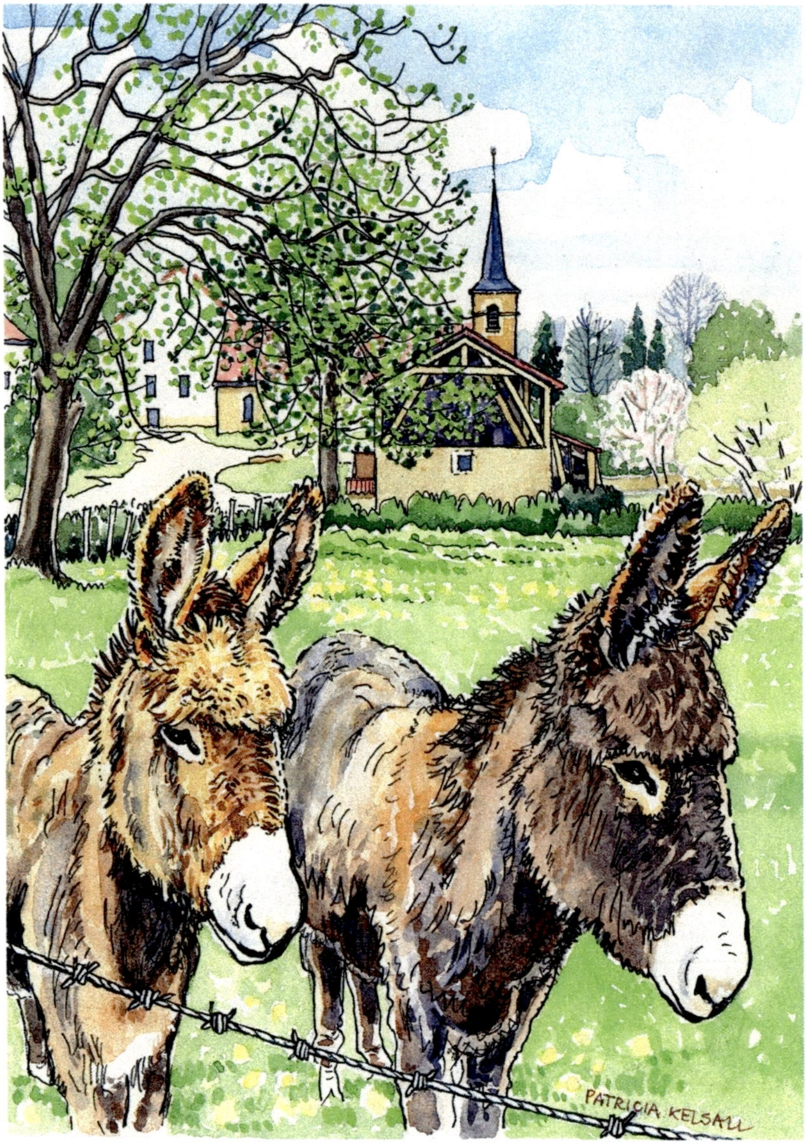

Dirk and Pieter's two young donkeys came to stay for a while in our field, and provided a delightful focal point for us. I couldn't remember their names, and called them collectively "The Donks".

Chapter Twelve – April 2000
Donkey delights

When Jack got up in the morning, he turned on the big convector heater in the bathroom so that it would be warm for me, pulling the heavy curtain across the doorway to keep in the heat. I was fast asleep and didn't know of his kind gesture until I ventured into the bathroom half an hour later wrapped in my thick towelling dressing gown, anticipating the usual goosepimples when I took it off. It was a novel experience to be able to go to the loo and get washed in comfort for the first time – apart from a summer heatwave.

Downstairs, I looked at the diary date on the computer and realised with mixed feelings that it was the first anniversary of my mother's death. A lot of water seemed to have flowed under the bridge since then.

I watched the sheepdogs through the kitchen window with my heart in my mouth. They still insisted on snapping at the wheels of every vehicle which came along, including a massive lorry filled with crushed stone that could have squashed them flat in a fraction of a second. When the postman arrived at Elisabeth's to deliver her mail and enjoy his daily cup of coffee, they stood guard by his bright yellow van and chased him when he left. Then they waited for him very seriously all the time he was at Michel's and conscientiously chased him a short way down the lane when he drove on from there. Afterwards they resumed their station in the middle of the road near the *calvary*. They surveyed all that was going on until the mobile hairdresser approached Elisabeth's in her new green car and was duly harassed and pursued to a standstill. One of the dogs had a decided limp: presumably he had shepherded one vehicle too many.

Seeing La Poste reminded me to write some postcards to friends and relations in England. Since I felt completely at home at St Paradis and never had the impression of being 'on holiday',

I rarely remembered to send that sort of correspondence until the last day or so of a visit – by which time it was too late. I walked down to put the cards in the little postbox in the wall near the old auberge. There were actually two postboxes, one rusty and abandoned but not sealed up, the other painted yellow and bearing a list of the times when it would be emptied. It always seemed quite inconceivable that one could post a letter in this tiny hamlet which would find its way safely to the other side of the Channel and be delivered at its foreign destination in a couple of days. And though the rural postal system seemed delightfully old-fashioned, with the postman's regular coffee breaks and friendly chats, it actually worked very efficiently and the postbox was always emptied exactly on time.

We decided to do some work on the Triffid Plantation. Jack dug up the roots of the plants while I picked up the inevitable broken glass, ancient light bulbs, cow ampoules and pottery. I found an interesting brown glazed and decorated 'brick' on which was written *'-hauffeuse'*. We wondered if it was a bed-warming device.

I cut back the brambles on the edge of the garden boundary to neaten up the appearance of the lane. The land dropped into the Route des Morts from the house in the same way as it did into the disused field, and as I cleared the tangled prickly branches with big secateurs I uncovered another handsome retaining wall. Stones had fallen out of it over the years but Jack said it would be recoverable with the aid of a bit of modern technology such as reinforcing rods and concrete.

Jack lit a fire and by the evening most of the Triffid roots, brambles and other junk had been consumed.

After a salad lunch we continued working in the lane and the back garden, where we planted the gooseberries, blackberries and redcurrants that we had bought in the new garden centre. I also dug up two elder whips growing in the middle of the Route des Morts and transplanted them under the barbed wire fence to make the beginnings of a hedge. While we were doing this we came across a dead mole. It looked quite healthy and didn't seem to have been injured in any way but was flat out on its back with its feet in the air. We gave it a ceremonial burial.

We also moved the green plastic compost bin that we had

bought from the local borough council in England, so that it was no longer right next to the terrace. When we examined the compost inside it was a mass of slime without any worms, unlike the fertile brown soil that Jack produces on our big compost heaps in Hartford. This was a disappointment as we had been religiously composting all our waste vegetable matter. Jack had been loath to construct similar walled heaps in France in case they encouraged snakes. We'd already discovered one viper in the garden a few years previously, which had caused great interest among the neighbours.

Jack managed to cut the grass without the mower stalling and had just finished when Georges and Eric came round to bring us some leeks freshly picked from their garden. We showed Georges the concrete setts, which we knew we were going to have to move away from the gateway so that they were out of sight and the field could be used by animals in our absence. He offered to lift the bags with his tractor but said that it could only take 600-700kg at a time on the front-loading prongs which were really designed for bales of hay or straw. There were labels on the bags stating that the maximum load they would hold was 1500kg, and Jack worked out from first principles that we had 2975 blocks measuring 11cm x 11cm x 5cm and weighing a total of 3.57 tonnes. By his calculations each bag was 1200kg, so if we emptied half of each one manually, Georges could do the rest. Our friend said he would come round after lunch the next day.

This concentrated our minds: we would have to get cracking. We discovered that we could get 50 setts into a wheelbarrow at a time, in three layers of 16 blocks with two spare ones on top. This represented about thirty barrowloads, which if you said it quickly enough, didn't sound too many.

We employed the same system as before, with me loading and Jack barrowing. I started by using one hand and cramming the setts on top of one another under my bosom but eventually I decided to be a robot: swing to the side, pick up a sett in each hand, swing back and put them in the barrow; swing, pick, drop; swing, pick, drop... I should have made a celebrity exercise video out of it.

We'd done lots of barrowloads when Mme Echelle's son

stopped for a chat, surrounded by a fluster of dogs. I talked to him while I filled and Jack pushed. We did two more barrows after he left and then I went inside to make some curry for supper. Jack tidied up and got in the firewood for tomorrow.

After all the day's exercise we were tired and went to bed early at 11pm.

Immediately after breakfast Jack went on the Triffid Plantation and dug up more roots, as well as some pre-war shoe soles and other rubbish. Everything went on the bonfire. He then dug a hole in front of the barn near the right-hand big door, to take the new vine. He had to tackle the underlying granite with a cold chisel and increasingly heavier hammers. He poured some water in and it didn't drain away very quickly at all. Eventually he attacked the granite with a long masonry drill, filled the hole with earth, planted the vine, inserted a cut-off Orangina bottle down beside it for watering purposes and built a little stone wall round it to contain the soil.

Then we went back to block-barrowing, had a quick lunch, and continued. I began to feel sick, probably from all the bending on a full stomach, as we were well down the bags now and the setts were getting harder to pick out. They had settled into the bags and were tending to wedge one another in place. Anyway, we managed our goal of half-emptying the three big sacks before Georges arrived with his big green tractor at 2pm.

It only took him ten minutes of very skilful manoeuvring to hook up the bag handles and move the bags round to the back of the barn, near the terrace. He wouldn't stop for a beer, saying that he was busy with fallen trees. He must have thought I was mad, but I took a photo for the family album. It had taken us hours to move the equivalent number of setts by hand and to watch them being carried so easily was a wonderful relief.

I walked over to see Elisabeth, as usual. She said that Paul wouldn't be coming home from the clinic for another eight days or so.

We went into the barn to fetch the longest ladder and were amused to see that there were now muddy pussycat paw prints not only all over the bonnet of the Peugeot but straight up the driver's windscreen too. Earlier Jack had seen one of Mme Echelle's dogs chasing a cat with such vigour that the cat shot straight out of the barn like a cartoon character without taking the slightest notice of him.

While I attacked the brambles around the well and the dry stone wall near the field entrance, Jack took advantage of the lack of wind to climb the ladder and tidy bits of the vine growing across the front of the house which had become detached during the winter storm. Then he took it round the back to mend the air vent for the *fosse septique* which ascends almost to gutter level. The tall narrow plastic pipe had come loose and was swinging about.

Then the weather changed abruptly, becoming cold, grey and very windy. I tried to do some planting of baby chestnut seedlings in the field but it began to rain so hard that we brought in the tools and retreated to the kitchen, where there was a mystery buzzing noise like a didgeridoo. We didn't know if it was an enraged captive hornet somewhere or perhaps the 'hat' on the chimney making music in its new distorted shape.

The donkeys arrived at 5.30pm in the pouring rain, but we didn't notice until they had been safely turned out. Poor Dirk and his two companions who had walked them from the next village were soaked to the skin (Pieter had gone to Holland for a few days and wasn't available to help). Rather than ask them in, to sit around politely in wet clothes, Jack drove them straight back home so they could get dry and change. Dirk said they had led the donkeys over the sand and gravel left on the sheet of plastic in the gateway and the young animals had been afraid of the strange slippery surface. We couldn't spot a battery connected to the electric fence, and guessed it was a purely psychological barrier. But the donkeys were so pleased to see all the tasty new grass in the field that they had little incentive to stray elsewhere – at least for the time being. They started to eat immediately.

Later, when the rain had stopped, Jack finished installing the exterior water tap and then began to clear up the last of the sand and gravel that had spooked the donkeys, while I prepared some food. Mme Echelle's youngest son – who was doing the building work on Michel's house – stopped to talk and then came back with a wheelbarrow of his own to help out, which Jack thought was really kind after he'd had a busy day filled with his own hard physical work. His brother, who had been visiting Elisabeth, joined in.

When he returned to the house Jack's ears were suffering from wind burn and felt really sore. It was certainly not balmy spring weather. Gitane scratched at the door and was rewarded with some gone-off goats' cheese and discarded pizza crust. She stayed with us, curled up on the mat in the warm glow of the wood-burning stove, until 10pm.

During the night it poured with rain and there was a high wind. Once again we could hear banging and at first we thought it was the spare room shutters, which we had left open. When we checked in the morning we could see that the zinc 'hat' on the chimney had become even more detached in the gale and was now only held tenuously by one corner while it bashed itself against the three supports. It looked small from the ground but it actually measured 1m x 60cm. We were very afraid that a gust of wind would make it fly off and decapitate someone on the ground below, and wondered if we could find a tradesman somewhere to take it down for us.

The donkeys were still happily in the field and came shyly when I leant over the barbed wire fence and called to them. I couldn't remember their names, and called them collectively "The Donks". They could see where Pieter and Dirk had threaded the yellow electric fence ribbon through special bolts on the fence posts which Georges had installed the previous summer, so they were reluctant to come too close. I was thrilled to have some equine animals in our field while we were there. I knew that Georges grazed horses in it once a year, so they could eat what the cattle had rejected, but we had never been staying at the house at the same time.

We drove to the *départementental* capital and bought all sorts of things from mirror glue to our favourite Pinot Noir wine from Alsace. In the big hypermarket car park we were thwarted by a battered car whose driver came the wrong way down the road, tried to get into a space that was too small, panicked and generally caused havoc. As a result of packing our purchases too quickly in order to get out of his way, a strawberry flan that we had bought as a tea-time treat fell off the freezer box where it had been placed temporarily and disintegrated into incredibly sticky red chunks.

Back home we moved the bed in the room where Bob had slept, and started to assemble the second-hand white wardrobe that our neighbours in England had given us. Then we started to work out how to glue four large IKEA mirror tiles to the bathroom wall above the tub, to reflect the light from the window and give the impression that the room was more spacious. While we were doing this, we saw that Hugo and Harriet had arrived at Elisabeth's so I went across to invite them for a drink later in the week.

I came in at the end of a conversation in which Elisabeth was relating that a small black and white dog had been run over and killed that morning as a result of chasing a vehicle, and that its owner was devastated. I couldn't work out from what she said whether it was one of the sheepdogs or Mme Echelle's fox terrier Milord, a good friend of ours in spite of the fact that he widdled in the kitchen if he ever got the chance to venture inside. We had seen the little black and white terrier bitch recently, so we knew it couldn't have been her. We weren't aware what relationship the collies' owner had with her dogs, but we did know that Mme Echelle adored hers even if she did scold them all the time.

When I returned home, Gitane came to see us and we told her to tell her friends and relations that chasing vehicles was not a good idea.

The weather continued to be miserably cold and we felt sorry for the donkeys. They didn't have a building to shelter in, although there were lots of trees to temper the worst excesses of the wind and rain. Hugo had said that it had snowed in the capital, which they had left a few minutes after us.

I love whisky and had bought some 'Breton whisky' in the supermarket as an experiment. It was only 59FF for 70cl and I thought that if I developed a taste for it, it would save us some money. Unfortunately it wasn't a patch on my favourite Islay single malt, with its distinctive peaty tang. In fact, it didn't taste of anything except fiery alcohol and gave the impression that it had been made with Breton tap water! A year later, it is still at the back of the drinks cupboard, untouched, which must be a record.

We stuck two mirror tiles on the bathroom wall and held them in place with *lambris* while the glue set. Then we ate some bread and cheese, and tucked into the sorry broken remains of the strawberry tart.

It was sunny when we got up but soon reverted to being a cold, grey windy morning. From the bathroom window I watched the donkeys having a lovely time chasing round the field. I could see them communicating with one another and deciding where to gallop and when. They were just like Ziggy and Goldie, the pups, especially as their game started with the little donkey grabbing the big one round the neck and biting it!

Milord scratched at the door for a biscuit, so we knew he was all right. It must have been the smaller of the two sheepdogs that had been run over, we decided. We had not seen either of them this morning and thought that the survivor must be tied up at home like the third one we'd seen trailing its chain on the first day we were here.

We looked up the telephone number of the roofing specialist who had fixed the 'hat' for us but couldn't track him down in the telephone directory. Eventually we found his original bill and rang the number on it – which was unobtainable.

We worked in the bathroom all day, doing *lambris*, decorative edging, mirror tiles and ordinary wall tiles. We had decided to be lazy and just put up complete wall tiles which did not need any intricate cutting. There was so much wall to tackle that we didn't need to get bogged down with fiddly bits at this point. We just wanted instant coverage! We had our usual tiling 'system' going whereby I soaked each tile, put blobs of adhesive on the back and then handed it to Jack to stick to the wall. He had a better eye for these things than I did – my tiles had a tendency to wander and weren't so uniform as his.

We were dealing with the tiles on a workbench in front of the bathroom window, with a birds-eye view of The Donks. It was such fun to have them in the field that our work rhythm soon became: put up one tile, watch the donkeys, put up another tile, watch the donkeys, and so on. It reminded me of the time in about 1980 when the boys had won some goldfish at the fair. Before the novelty wore off we would sit at the dinner table watching them in their tank as if they were a fishy television set. The remaining one doesn't get so much attention now. Does anyone know of a home for geriatric goldfish?

Around 6pm we stopped to get ready for a visit from Hugo, Harriet and Elisabeth. Just after they arrived Monsieur Lebrun's daughter and her husband popped in for a chat, but refused to stay when they saw we had visitors. They commented on the loose 'hat' and we were afraid that its banging had kept them awake the previous night. We gathered that they, too, had failed to get hold of the roofer when they wanted him, but they gave us his mobile number just in case we were lucky. We gathered that he drank too much – which is not really a useful habit in someone who takes his life in his hands in dangerously high places every day.

After they'd gone, Jack asked Elisabeth about the dog that had been killed and she confirmed that the smaller sheepdog had been crushed under the wheels of the postman's van as it tried to bite the tyres. The poor *facteur* was upset but he couldn't have avoided the accident. From his position behind the steering wheel, he couldn't even see the dog as it hurled itself at the wheels. Everyone was sad, but not surprised.

Next day our thoughts were with Alex and Michelle who were going to sign the final documents for the sale of their house in Cheshire. They still hadn't found anywhere they wanted to buy in Kent.

After breakfast we took some of the stale bread and went to feed the donkeys. They didn't speak English but we'd found that if I stood by the fence and shouted "Donk, donk, donk! Come on, come on, come on!" they would stop munching the grass or chasing one another and wander along for a spot of socialising. After a lot of sweet talk from me and the offer of chunks of Jack's Best Bread, they overcame their shyness and scoffed it all. We remarked that they had wonderfully soft noses.

It amused us that the two animals were so used to being

constrained by a working electric fence that they respected the one which was confining them to half of the meadow, even though it wasn't attached to anything.

Jack levelled out the gravel that he and the young builder had barrowed from the pile at the gateway. There was more than enough to fill the terrace 'box' to the required depth, so he was pleased with his quantity surveying.

We had a council of war about the bathroom and measured the door and the frame. The nicely-carved old door no longer fitted because we had raised the floor level with the tiles and their underlay of chipboard and polystyrene. It had also changed shape when we had had the filthy old paint professionally stripped off in a tank of non-caustic chemicals four years before. The contractor had told us to let it dry out well before refitting it, and we had certainly taken him at his word!

We agreed that although it would be simpler to cut the shape we required out of the door frame, it was just too awkward to do because Jack couldn't get the saw into the right position. So we decided to put the special 'door manipulating' attachment for his new Triton 2000 woodworking machine together and use it to cut bits off the door.

The large, beautifully-engineered tool took nearly all morning to assemble and was a focus of interest for any of our male friends who happened to be wandering past. We worked half the time on the bench in the dark cowshed part of the barn under a fluorescent light strip, and the rest in the airy and sunny central section where we did the final assembly. The psychological contrast was amazing. I told Jack that anyone who spent any length of time in the cowshed would suffer from SAD (Seasonally Affected Disorder). I found it an incredibly claustrophobic and depressing place.

As we were coming in for lunch we saw M Lebrun's daughter and her husband in their garden. They said they had checked with the Mairie and learned that the roofer had suddenly left the district and gone to live in Provence. We were back to square one.

Between the courses of our meal we went out for a donkey chat which is what you do if you have Donks in your back garden and are quite potty. The 'hat' on the chimney was flapping about a lot in the breeze and we expected it to break or tear off very soon.

We spent the afternoon with the woodworking machine, shaving or sawing slivers off doors. We started with the bathroom door and found it so easy and satisfying that we decided to do all the paint-stripped upstairs doors that no longer fitted their frames. They all grated or stuck to the floorboards because they had distorted themselves out of shape over 120 years. The new equipment worked so beautifully that we could cut a fraction of a millimetre from them, and the old pear and poplar wood was a pleasure to cut. It became quite addictive and we seemed to spend ages charging around carrying doors up and down our awkward staircase as we tried to get them to fit exactly. When we had finished, the luxury of having custom-fitted doors, that opened and closed at the push of a fingertip, was marvellous.

I went round to see Elisabeth at 7pm for a chat and to confirm that we would take her to the *choucroute* supper the following night. She gave me a rock-hard *baguette* that she had bought some days previously but not eaten, as a present for the donkeys. I broke off two pieces and the Donks were very pleased to sample them. They came to us more easily each time we called them over, and were getting used to us being their only human contact. They were now allowing me to stroke their noses and necks before they backed away and were happy to be talked to in friendly foreign baby language.

There was a lot of rain and strong winds during the night and the 'hat' became even more dangerous as a potential flying guillotine. We were really worried about it. What Jack's mother would call its "biffing and banging about" was keeping us awake and we were sure it was annoying everyone else in our little cluster of houses. We didn't know what to do for the best, as it was very high up and no-one in the village had a ladder long enough to reach it.

Gitane came for her morning treat and while Jack was in the Library she sat on my knee in the new chair beside the fire, at first sitting bolt upright and looking out of the window, then snuggling down with difficulty across my lap and having a snooze. When she became too uncomfortable, she clambered off and basked in front of the fire, making herself entirely at home. It was so comforting to have a resident dog that we were glad we had gone through the initial procedure of getting pet passports for our three, in order to bring them to St Paradis in the future.

We went to the city to return the pallets and do some shopping. En route we saw a new road sign counselling "prudence" and saying that six people had been killed in six months over one kilometre. Then there was another identical sign about a kilometre further along. We didn't know what to make of them. Twelve people dead over two kilometres? Who knows? The road was so dangerous that we quite believed the worst prognosis. It was rumoured to be the most lethal in Europe, especially in our part of the Limousin where the single carriageway ran dead straight up and down hills which would hide an oncoming intercontinental juggernaut in a dip until the moment an impatient French driver decided to overtake into its path. We'd witnessed numerous buttock-clenchingly narrow escapes and seen photos of gruesome accidents in the local newspaper.

When we neared home we could see from the back road that the 'hat' had finally gone. We prayed that it hadn't damaged any buildings or hurt any of our neighbours. When we found it, the big battered sheet of zinc was lying innocently in the Route des Morts against the Lebruns' stone wall without having done any harm at all. We were very, very relieved. It hadn't caused any damage on the way down and if we'd had a choice of where it should ideally fall this would have been the spot. Marguerite was looking after us again.

We pottered about in the afternoon, given that there wasn't time to get seriously dirty or into a major job before we needed to be ready for the *choucroute*.

Jack installed the bargain water-butt. We realised why it was so cheap when we discovered some of its drawbacks. Jack had to cut his own hole for the plastic tap at the bottom and then almost had to climb inside to fit it. The washer didn't go in place properly and became damaged as he screwed the tap into place, so he had to make another one. We put some water in from the hosepipe to stabilise the butt and then turned the tap on to see how well the water would flow. It didn't flow at all. Eventually we discovered that the tap was full of mud from when the butt had been lying on its side and the water pressure was not enough to wash it out. After a lot more messing about than we would have expected, the butt at last deigned to hold water and release it.

Then we wandered down to Charles' house to ask him and his wife for an *apéritif* the following lunchtime. They said they weren't going to the *choucroute* because they didn't like it and thought it would lie heavily on the stomach at night. We suspected they were right. Michel had already expressed the same sentiments.

We collected Elisabeth at 7.25pm and were among the first at the *Salle des Fêtes,* which had been converted from the original *mairie* and the old school and served the six small hamlets in the commune. We gathered that about 80 people were coming. As we went in, a large container was being piled up with *choucroute* and thick slices of meat. The meeting room had changed since the last time we had been inside and had been modernised, with cream-painted acoustic tiles all over the walls, a suspended ceiling, new windows and a new speaker system. The progress of the work had been reported faithfully in the *Bulletin* and the commune was very proud of its improved facilities. We bagged seats at one of the long tables and waited for Jan and Beatrice, who arrived half an hour later. I was right at the end of the table, opposite Elisabeth and, being slightly deaf, couldn't really hear much of the talk going on. I gathered that the people seated near Jan and Beatrice were a former Mayor and his party, who were nice and made occasional conversation with us. A lot of people we knew were not there, either because they didn't fancy *choucroute* or because they had other engagements like Pieter and Dirk. Only Jack, Elisabeth and I were representing St Paradis.

The event had been organised by the current Mayor and her team of farmers' wives and councillors. As always, we admired her energy and dedication to her job. She introduced us to her husband, and we introduced ourselves to various other folk in the spirit of trying to be neighbourly. It was so funny – we didn't know people but they knew us. As soon as we said: *"Nous sommes les anglais de St Paradis"* they replied "Yes, we know – and you've got Pieter and Dirk's donkeys in your field..." We decided that it would be quite impossible for either of us to have a secret affair because the whole commune of 200-plus souls would know within 24 hours.

After an interlude of noisy chat, people brought round nibbles, then *kir*, then bottles of Nantais or Alsace wine, then 1664 beer and then a *tarte flambée* starter, which was new to us and like a very thin and tasty *quiche lorraine*.

This was followed by bread and the *choucroute* itself which was piled high on the plates with two types of sausages and a wedge of ham or pork. It was incredibly filling. I didn't see anyone eat an entire mountainous helping and most people left quite a lot of their cabbage. Afterwards we were served a thin slice of cheese each and a big portion of Black Forest gâteau made by one of the Marcheville *boulangers*. The last offering was coffee, which we declined on the grounds that it would keep us awake. I retained our paper napkins and smuggled out the left-over meat from our part of the table, to give to Mme Echelle's dogs for breakfast.

Part of the way through the meal, in a space on the other side of the hall, an impromptu band made up of local amateur musicians on trumpets and accordions started to perform traditional tunes. Then, without getting up from his place at the table in the middle of the room, a young chap in a green jumper began to play the spoons, extremely well, as if he were Ginger Baker providing the percussion accompaniment to the other instruments. Someone whispered to us that he was a bit simple, but nobody stopped him and he played like a virtuoso.

As always at a French social event, there were lots of children, who behaved impeccably if boisterously and held their own parallel party, charging round through all the different doors of the *Salle des Fêtes*, hiding under the coat-racks, playing football, fighting, falling over and generally having a good time. They kept going until nearly midnight, by which time we were wilting ourselves. Jan and Beatrice looked at the clock and said they must go because they were looking after Pieter and Dirk's dogs, so we followed their example and we all went home.

Jack and I slept well with no ill-effects from the *choucroute* and all the 1664 liquid refreshment that we'd used to wash it down.

Mme Echelle's dogs thought it was Christmas and New Year rolled into one when they saw the big pieces of ham and pork that we'd brought back from the feast for them.

We worked on the bathroom in the hope of having it in a reasonably nice state when Chris and Linda arrived to stay the following day. I grouted the tiles we'd put up while Jack installed a skirting board and added some final pieces of *lambris*. Then he fitted civilising accessories like a pine-framed mirror, a toothbrush holder, a soap dish and a towel ring.

We enjoyed a happy hour with Charles and his wife, and had a quick salad lunch. In the afternoon Pieter came round to talk to the Donks and give them a bag of old bread. After he left there was a tremendous rain storm which quickly filled the new water butt to overflowing. We had positioned it under the downspout which takes all the water from the roof at the back of the house. The storm was coming from the north and lashed our exposed buildings with furious grey sheets of rain. In bad weather, when we looked out of the little bedroom window, it always felt as if we bore the brunt of any wind, snow or rain that had travelled unobstructed from the shadowy hills on the horizon, gathering strength as it sped along. While we were upstairs working, we could hear plopping sounds and discovered a leak in the roof. We put a bucket under it to catch the drips. The leaks between the slates were never constant – they depended upon the angle of the rain and the direction of the wind. A bucket part-filled during one torrential rain storm would be in the wrong place for the next.

When the rain abated a little, I grabbed an umbrella and dashed across to see Elisabeth. She said Paul was expected to come home shortly, though he was still very unwell and had lost weight. He was looking forward to seeing us before we left.

I was doing something in our bedroom at about 5pm when I chanced to glance out of the window towards Michel's farm. The aftermath of the storm had created an extraordinary effect. The trees on the hill behind the farm and beyond the Lebruns' garden were bathed in bright orange light as if they were in full russet autumn leaf instead of spring green. Their branches were a ghostly white and they appeared to be on fire. The sky behind the hills was purple and a double rainbow made two hazy arcs over the village. I called Jack and we ran outside with the digital camera and our video camera, trying to freeze the moment for ever.

Behind us, the scene was quite different. We went through the house and stood on the back steps looking north. The little woodland was in stark silhouette against a vivid yellow backdrop and as we watched, the sky changed colour, shading to orange after a few minutes.

While I was buying bread from the *boulanger*'s van next morning, I spoke to Michel and his wife about it. He suggested that it could have been an aurora. There was a general feeling that it might be a 'sign', what with the Millennium and all that.

When we returned to England we spoke to some friends about the phenomenon and they said they had been in the north of Scotland at the same time, where the sky had turned green. Some months later, Jack spotted an article in an astronomy magazine illustrated with photographs taken in several different countries, all showing bizarrely-coloured skies pictured on the same day. Michel had been right – the effect seemed to be connected with the aurora borealis.

One of the last things we did to prepare for Chris and Linda was to fit the original 19th century porcelain-handled lock on the bathroom door, and screw on a small brass bolt that Jack had found in one of our hundreds of boxes of useful objects. The *"Vacant-Occupé"* sign could now be banished for ever. Then Jack made a doorstep to cover the edge of the newly-tiled floor. We felt that things were now so posh that we could quite happily invite the Queen to stay.

In the morning we carried all the spare wood and chipboard down from where it was usually stacked on the landing (where it might come in useful for jobs upstairs), and piled it in the barn. Next Jack packed up his tools in their boxes ready to be taken home to England. This made the landing into an unremarkable neat area at the top of the stairs – like everyone else's – rather than an assault course where we had to thread our way between materials and equipment, and risk being skewered by an electric drill. The focus on the landing now returned to our glass-fronted china cabinet which housed many of the treasures we had found in the house. Up here they could be a talking-point for passing guests but they were out of direct sunlight and would not deteriorate or gather dust.

We were really excited about Chris and Linda's visit because although they had been to the house several times on their own – and Chris had been an invaluable help when we'd stayed immediately after the purchase went through – it would be the first time we had all four been under the same roof at St Paradis since we decided to buy the property in June 1994. Linda and I had both fallen hopelessly in love with the old place when we'd had our initial viewing with the estate agent, and our enthusiasm had soon rubbed off on the men.

Just after lunch the couple rang on their mobile phone to say that they had made good time on their journey from Champagne and were about an hour away. They arrived very promptly. It was great to see them and to have the pleasure of showing them round the house. We had made a lot of improvements since their last visit, two years before. They brought us a souvenir bottle of Millennium champagne as a special present. We introduced them to the Donks but they declined the offer of carrots to hand out – Chris said he was frightened of donkeys, having been bitten by one some years previously. Obviously he hadn't inherited the family equine-loving genes. (It's surprising what you find out about your grown-up children, isn't it?)

We had invited Dirk and Pieter for supper, and needed to go and buy some *pâté*. While Chris and Linda had a rest at St Paradis, Jack and I went to Stoc where I attempted to buy a swede but did not know what it was called in French and couldn't find a picture of it on the weigh-it-yourself machine. It turned out to be a *chou-rave*. The fellow customer who enlightened me with this basic information clearly thought she was dealing with someone slightly mentally subnormal. On the way home we stopped at the big agricultural merchants to buy four fence posts and Jack fell in love with a small tractor on the forecourt. Unfortunately – or, maybe, fortunately – it didn't have a price tag on it.

Chris warned us privately that Linda had a tummy-ache from a muscle problem and probably wouldn't eat a great deal, although she didn't want to draw attention to the malady herself. As someone who regularly used to strain my stomach muscles, I sympathised silently with her. It wasn't until the following day that I realised from the context of another conversation that she had actually eaten a bad mussel in a platter of *moules marinières*!

Pieter and Dirk arrived at 7pm, with a bottle of champagne and a jar of home-made chestnut jam. They brought the dogs with them and Chris and Linda were very smitten with the little white Jack Russell. She hid a biscuit in a corner of the kitchen and then proceeded to sit and stare at it for a long time. She looked enchanting. Her owners invited us all round for a coffee in the morning so that Chris and Linda could see the house by the lake that we had been raving about for so long.

In the morning, Chris and Linda reacted to the peace and calm of St Paradis by oversleeping. Linda felt better but now Chris wasn't very well, which was a shame. While they got up, Jack and I investigated in the cellar and found that the temperatures marked on the maximum-minimum thermometer that we had put down there the previous autumn varied between 3°C and 13°C. It was currently showing 8°C. We were surprised that a *cave* which had been used long ago as a cheese store for the next-door dairy should vary so much – we thought the whole idea of a purpose-built *cave* was that it maintained approximately the same temperature regardless of the seasons.

After breakfast, Chris drove us down to Dirk and Pieter's house. It was a beautiful sunny day and after a walk round the land, admiring the view and the setting, we all sat out on the terrace where we enjoyed a cup of coffee and a slice of fruit tart that Dirk had made earlier. The panorama across the lake was spectacular and we watched some coots swimming around. A pair of herons appeared and flapped about in the trees bordering the stream that runs through the garden. The surface of the water was twinkling in the sunshine and its steady chuckling sound made hypnotising background music. Chris and Linda agreed that it was a wonderful spot.

On the way home we called in at the cemetery to check that Marguerite's family grave had survived the big storm. The tomb is sheltered by a typically Creusoise greenhouse arrangement and was unscathed, but the flowers left in memory of some other 'occupants' of the graveyard had ended up being blown down the steep hill and straight into the neighbouring trees where they were trapped bizarrely among the branches. The light was so good – almost Mediterranean – that we could see clearly for miles, right to the mountains on the horizon. I've often fantasised that when I die my remains might be buried here, near Marguerite's, so that we can both look down on the house we love so much. However, I fear the bureaucratic ramifications of an international EC interment might be too much for the family to tackle. Perhaps they could smuggle my ashes over in a supermarket carrier bag and pop them down the nearest rabbit-hole.

At noon we went to have an *apéritif* with Charles and his wife. Their house had originally been part of the old *auberge* and had been partitioned off from it. We sat in the kitchen for an hour, chatting about life in St Paradis now and in the 'old days'.

We had salad for lunch because we had been entertained so well during the morning that none of us was hungry. As we were finishing we saw Elisabeth out by the communal wheelie bins. I went to see how she was, and she said that Paul had just come home from hospital. Jack and I walked over to greet him. We were very pleased to see him sitting under the parasol in the balmy sunshine. We told him not to get up and I kissed him tenderly on the cheeks when he offered them in greeting. He had lost a great deal of weight and was now very thin – but he was chirpy, delighted to be home and seemed to understand us better than usual. We had a good talk.

After our meal, Chris, Linda and I went down to Marcheville to get a bank statement and buy some petrol for the lawnmower, so that Jack would have enough fuel to cut all the grass before we left for England the following day. Then we three sat in the kitchen reminiscing about how the house had been when we had first seen it six years before. Linda was sitting in an armchair doing her cross-stitch, and Chris was snoozing on and off, on the sofa in front of the *cantou*.

In the early evening, we opened and drank the bottle of Millennium champagne as a celebration of the fact that we were all together in the house again. Apparently the test of a good champagne is that it has very small bubbles – and this one did. We took souvenir photographs using the self-timers on our digital cameras, shuffling people about to get them fitted properly into the viewfinders and taking repeat pictures when we discovered that someone's head had been cut off.

There was an e-mail from Alex. He and Michelle had moved out of the bungalow, put some of their stuff in our house and the rest in storage, and were heartily sick of looking at prospective new homes in Kent, which turned out either to be ideally placed but too expensive or affordable but not ready for months to come. "I need a rest from bloody houses..." was his heartfelt conclusion.

We had a curry and *tarte tatin* for supper and went to bed early.

After breakfast, Chris and Linda loaded up their car and set off for the Dordogne and the second part of their holiday. We packed our car and trailer, cleaned out the Godin and tried to eat up as much of the left-over food in the fridge as possible. I'd bought far too much bread, as usual, so the donkeys did remarkably well for snacks.

When everything was ready, we drove the few yards up to Elisabeth's gate and went to say our farewells. Paul was fast asleep in a chair in the kitchen, looking very frail and vulnerable. Elisabeth said he had especially wanted to see us but as we looked down on his peaceful face we didn't have the heart to wake our dear old friend from his slumbers. We knew, deep down, as he probably did, that we would never see one another again. It was a very sad and emotional moment for us. Paul had been with us at St Paradis from the very first day in September 1994. The little man with the big heart and the huge personality had liked and accepted his eccentric English neighbours, had single-handedly taken on the care of our house and garden as a labour of love, and had gladly become our mentor. It didn't matter that we often did not understand one another – the communication was at a level beyond language. It had been a privilege to be his friends and to be able to call him "our French father". If he had been awake, I would have held his hand and told him how much we loved him and how grateful we were for everything he had done. But it was not the right moment. He was too ill. If we had woken him, he would have been confused. It was kinder, and so much harder, to ask Elisabeth to kiss him for us, to embrace her with love, knowing the sadness she would soon be facing, and to leave.

In the car, Jack and I were silent, engulfed in our own thoughts and memories.

Paul died the following month.

His real name was Julien Pauly.

Life at St Paradis goes on, because life must go on, but it is not the same without him. Everyone says so.

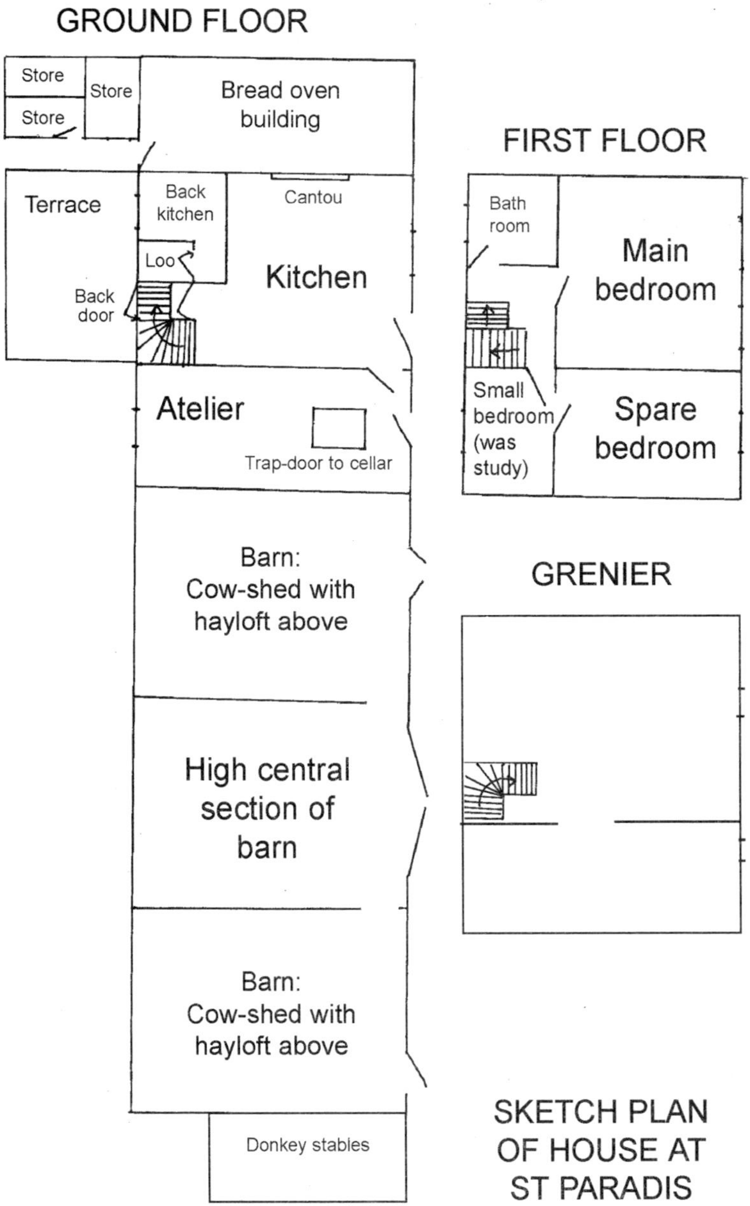

SKETCH PLAN OF HOUSE AT ST PARADIS

From Léonie Press, 13 Vale Rd, Hartford, Northwich, Cheshire CW8 1PL (01606 75660) or order through your bookshop quoting the ISBN

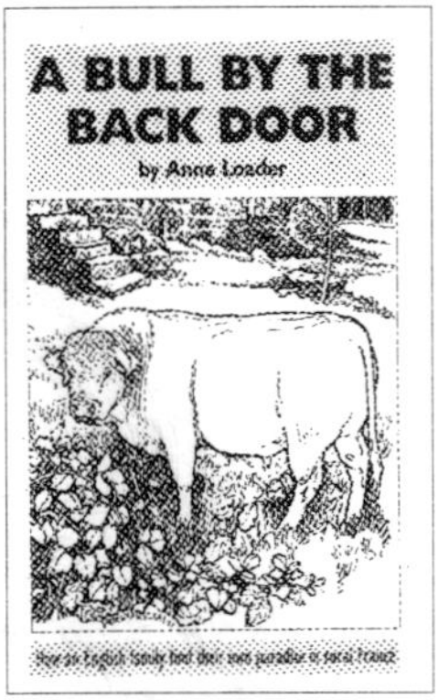

A BULL BY THE BACK DOOR
by ANNE LOADER

An unexpected legacy enables the Loader family to buy an old stone farmhouse in the depths of the French countryside. It has been unoccupied for years but they are drawn to the charm and dignity lying under the grime and cobwebs.

Even before the purchase goes through 'Les Anglais' are welcomed with genuine affection by their new neighbours. From their very first day at St Paradis they begin to make close and lasting friendships in spite of the language barriers. But it is not only their neighbours who welcome them. Soon they are aware that the spirit of the former owner seems delighted to see her family home being restored to life. Indeed, it appears uncannily almost as if she has chosen the Loaders for this task as she gives them daily 'messages' about sentimental treasures hidden in the house.

ISBN 1 901253 06 6 Price: £8.99 plus £1.30p+p

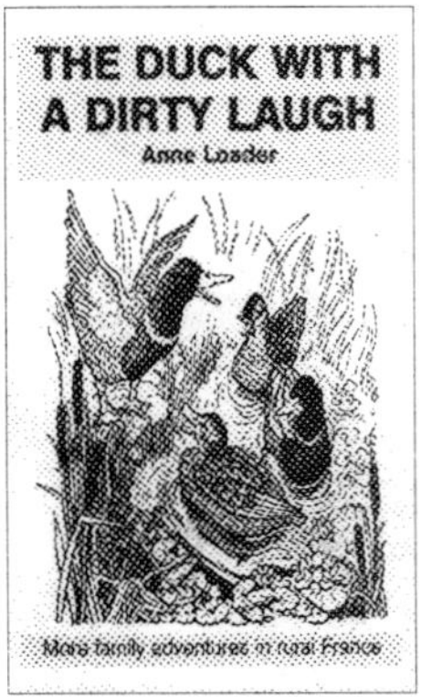

THE DUCK WITH A DIRTYLAUGH
by ANNE LOADER

This much-requested sequel to "A Bull by the Back Door" continues the Loader family's story. Renovations to their old house are going well but slowly, as they tackle every aspect of the work themselves. They have promised the spirit of the former owner that they will bring the place back to life but not change its character. She still seems to be with them as they get busy installing electricity, plumbing and drains – and doing the decorating. Old friendships prosper and new ones are made. Just when it seems everything is perfect, tragedy strikes at home in England and they face a period when just 'hanging on and surviving' is the simple goal. Their first test at St Paradis is coping with the coldest weather in Europe for a century: it's –12°C outside and 1.6°C in the kitchen, the water is frozen, it's snowing hard and everyone in the hamlet is ill...

ISBN 1 901253 09 0 Price: £8.99 plus £1.40p+p

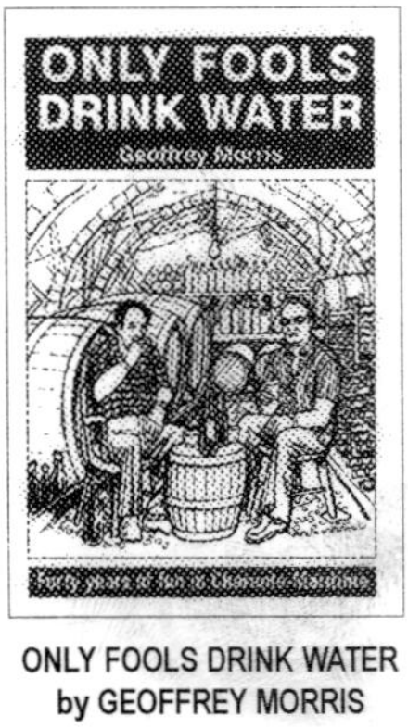

ONLY FOOLS DRINK WATER
by GEOFFREY MORRIS

Geoffrey Morris and his wife – jokingly dubbed 'senile delinquents' by their son – have been enjoying hilarious escapades in the Charente-Maritime region of France for more than 40 years. They have lived there for 20 years and are now naturalised French.

This witty book chronicles the author's experiences among the Charentais farmers, fishermen, gendarmes and bureaucrats, and gives a very good introduction to earthy French slang. He says: "Be warned. One needs to be slightly crazy to change country and nationality to find a very happy refuge on the coast of Biscay."

Review: *"This is another of Anne Loader's inspired productions for the Francophile with a sense of humour, for whom it is an absolute 'must'"* - Living France

ISBN 1 901253 10 4 Price £8.99 plus £1.40p+p

Any excess postage received for multiple orders will be returned